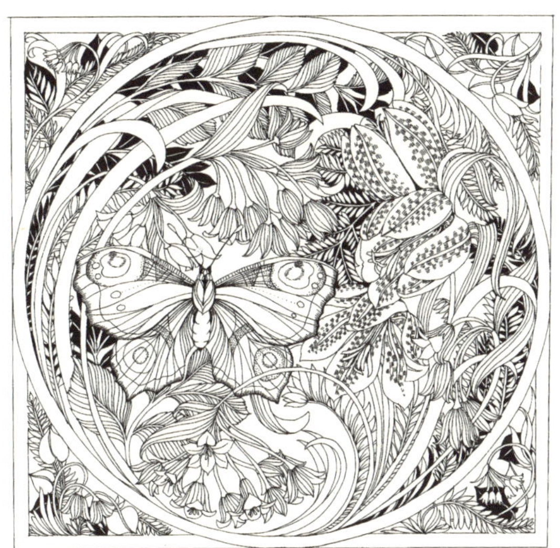

THIS BOOK BELONGS TO:

....

Leila Duly

FLORIBUNDA YEAR

A Flower Coloring Companion

LAURENCE KING PUBLISHING

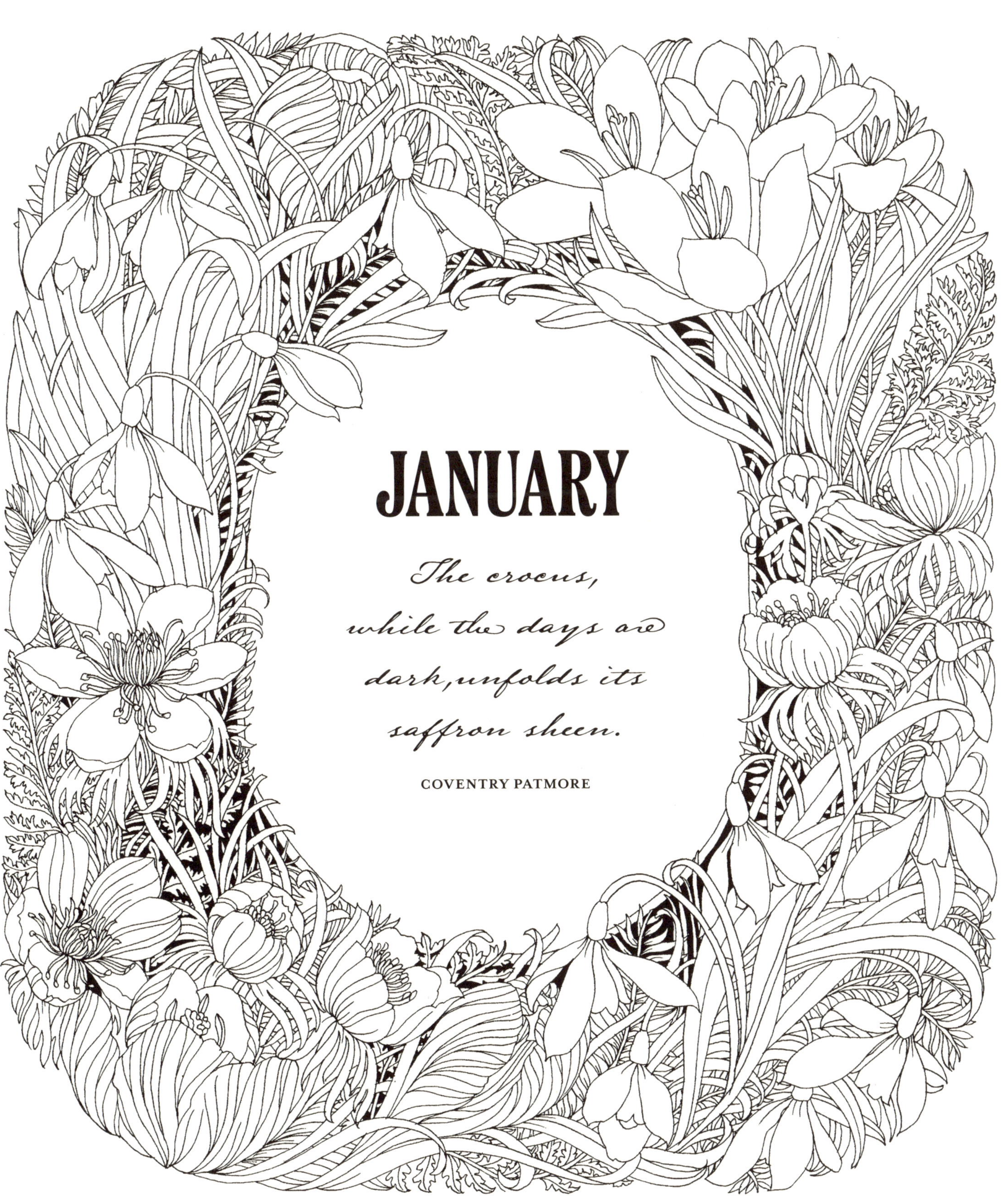

JANUARY

The crocus,
while the days are
dark, unfolds its
saffron sheen.

COVENTRY PATMORE

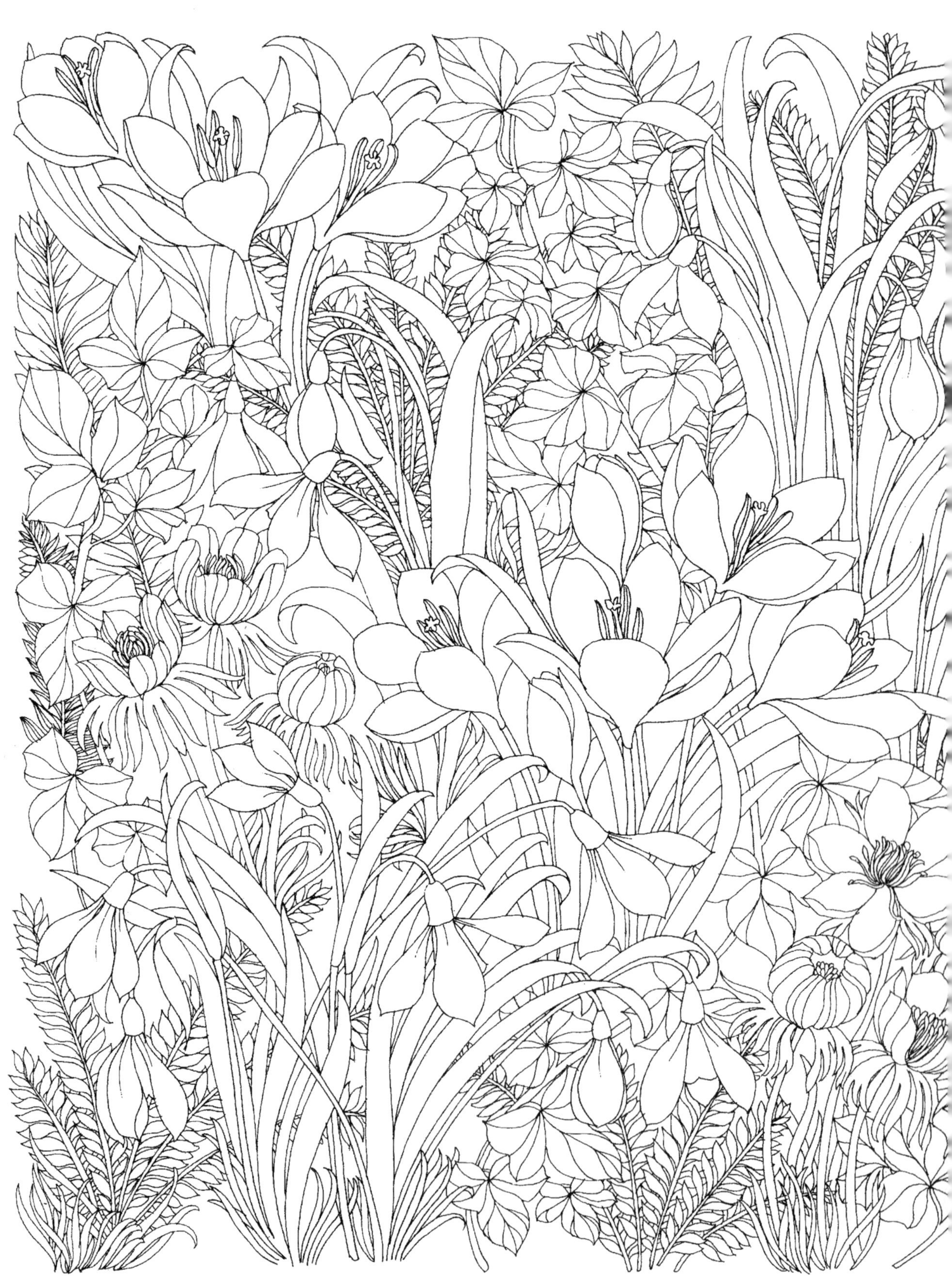

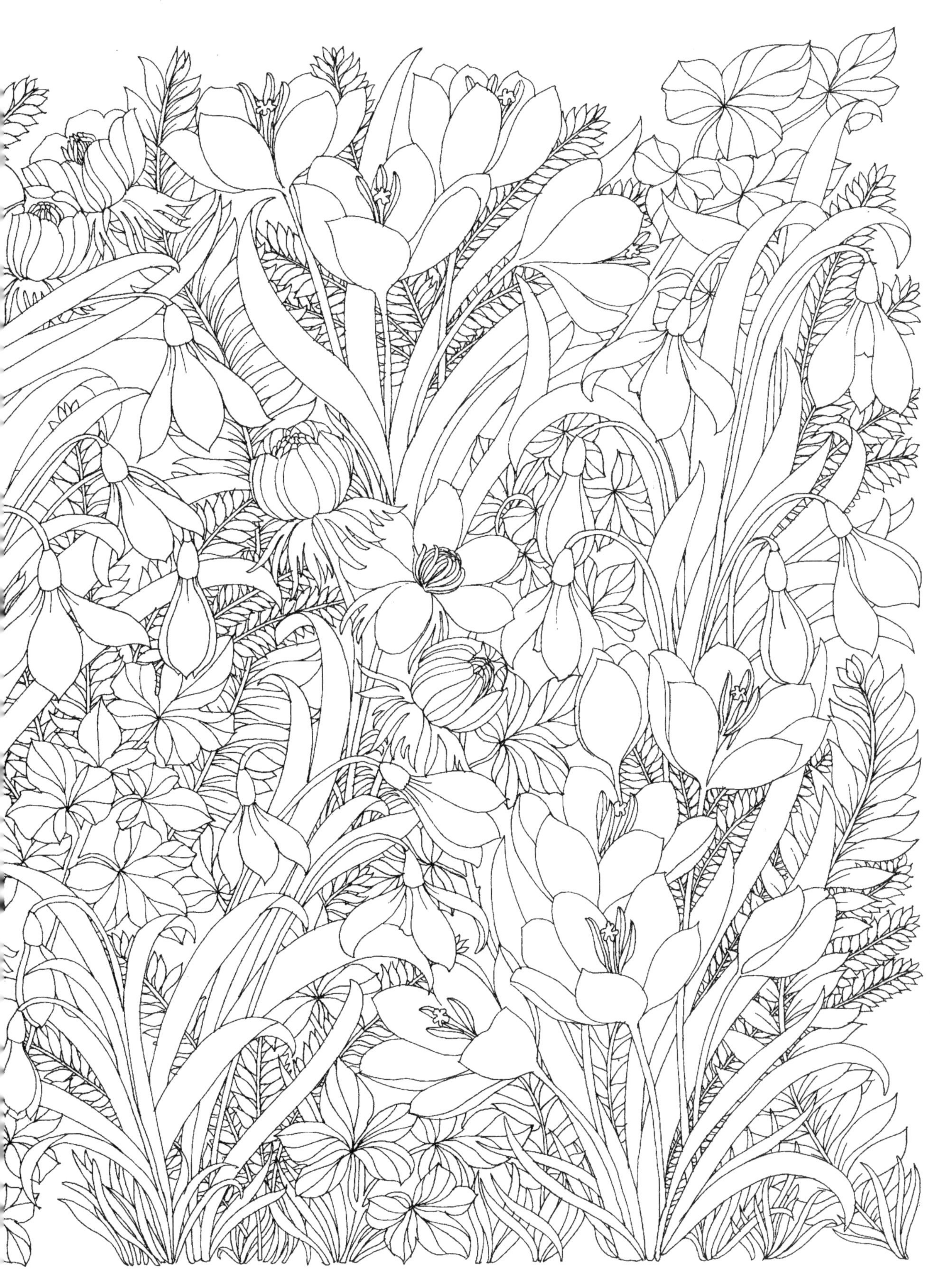

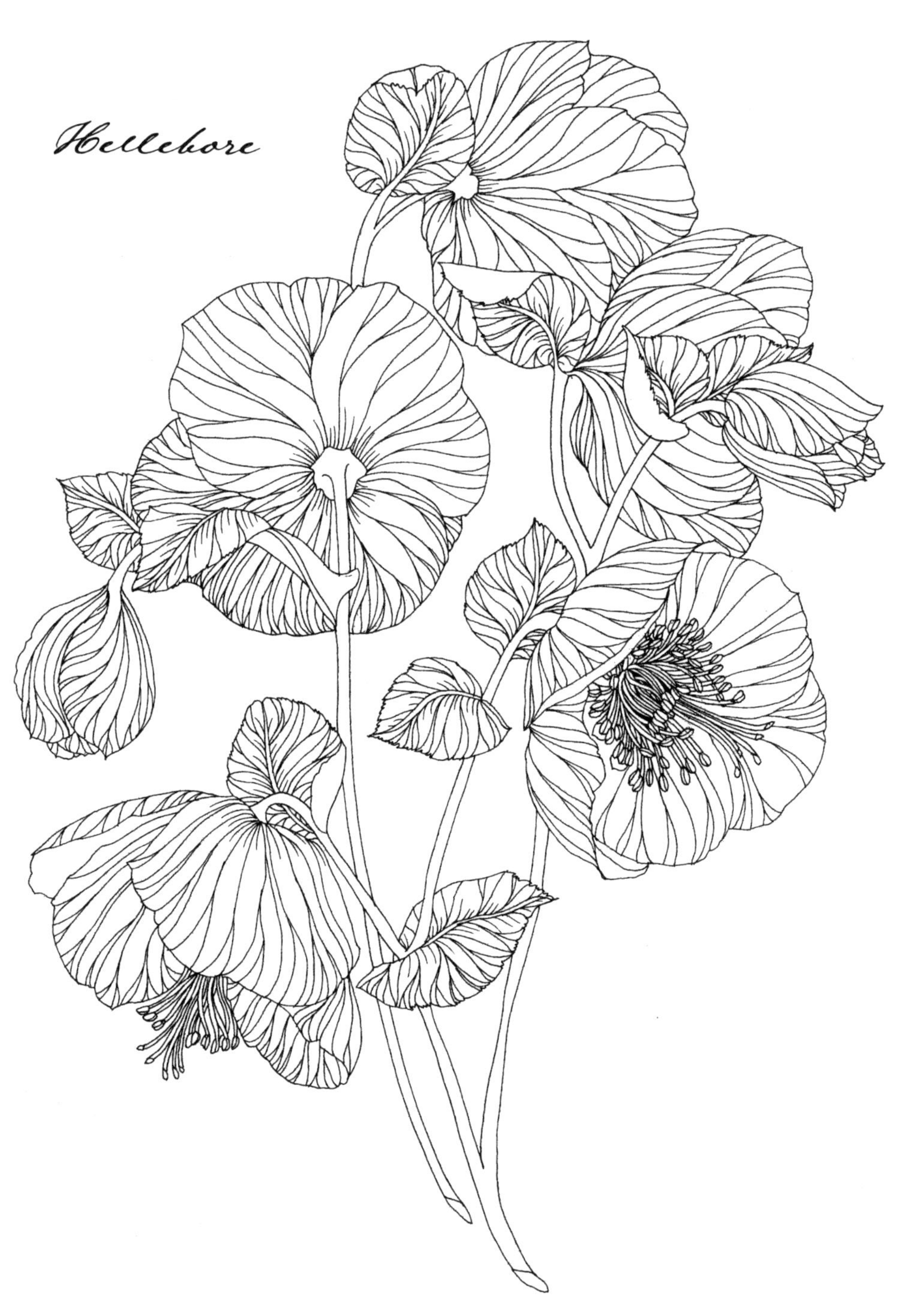
Hellebore

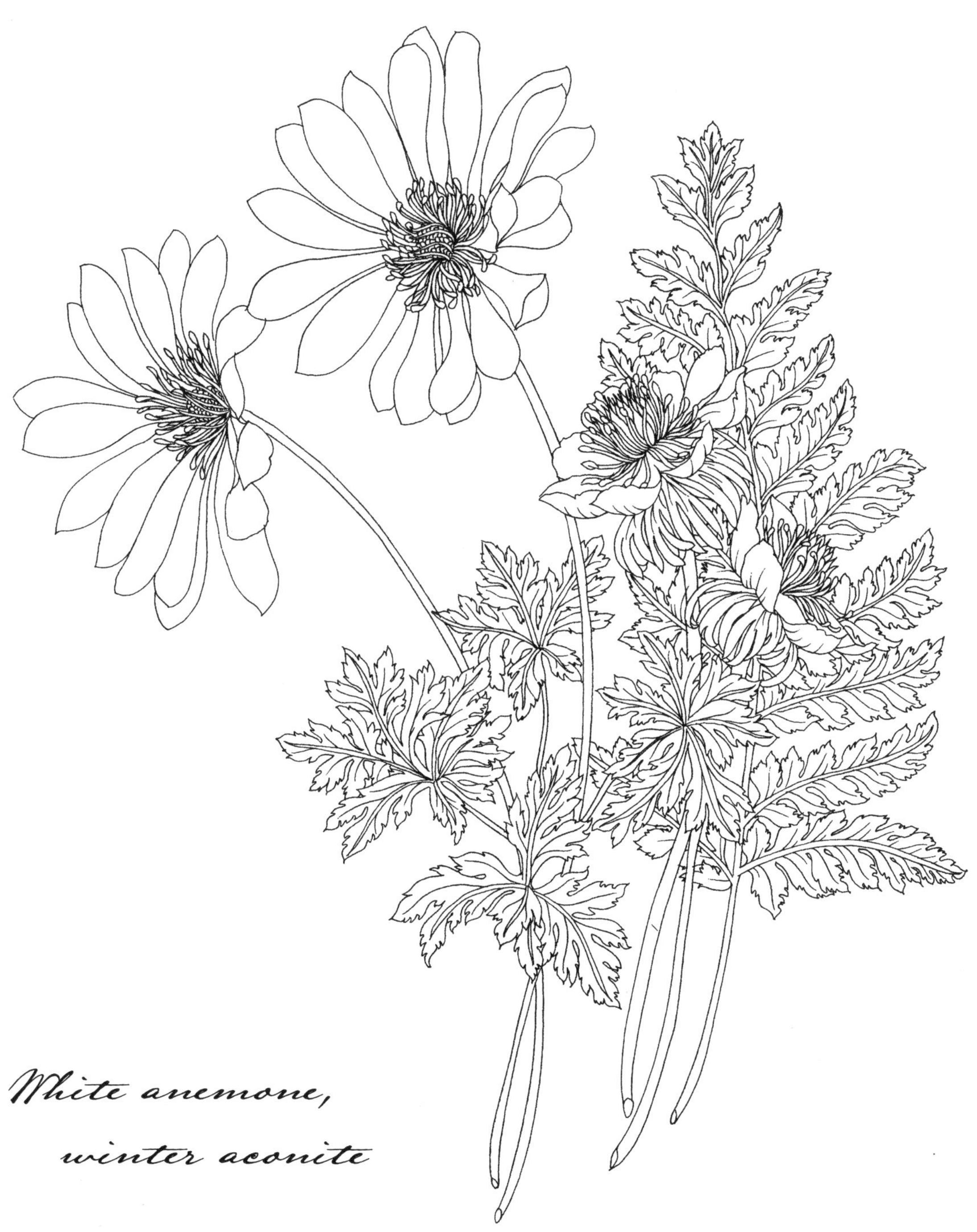

White anemone,
winter aconite

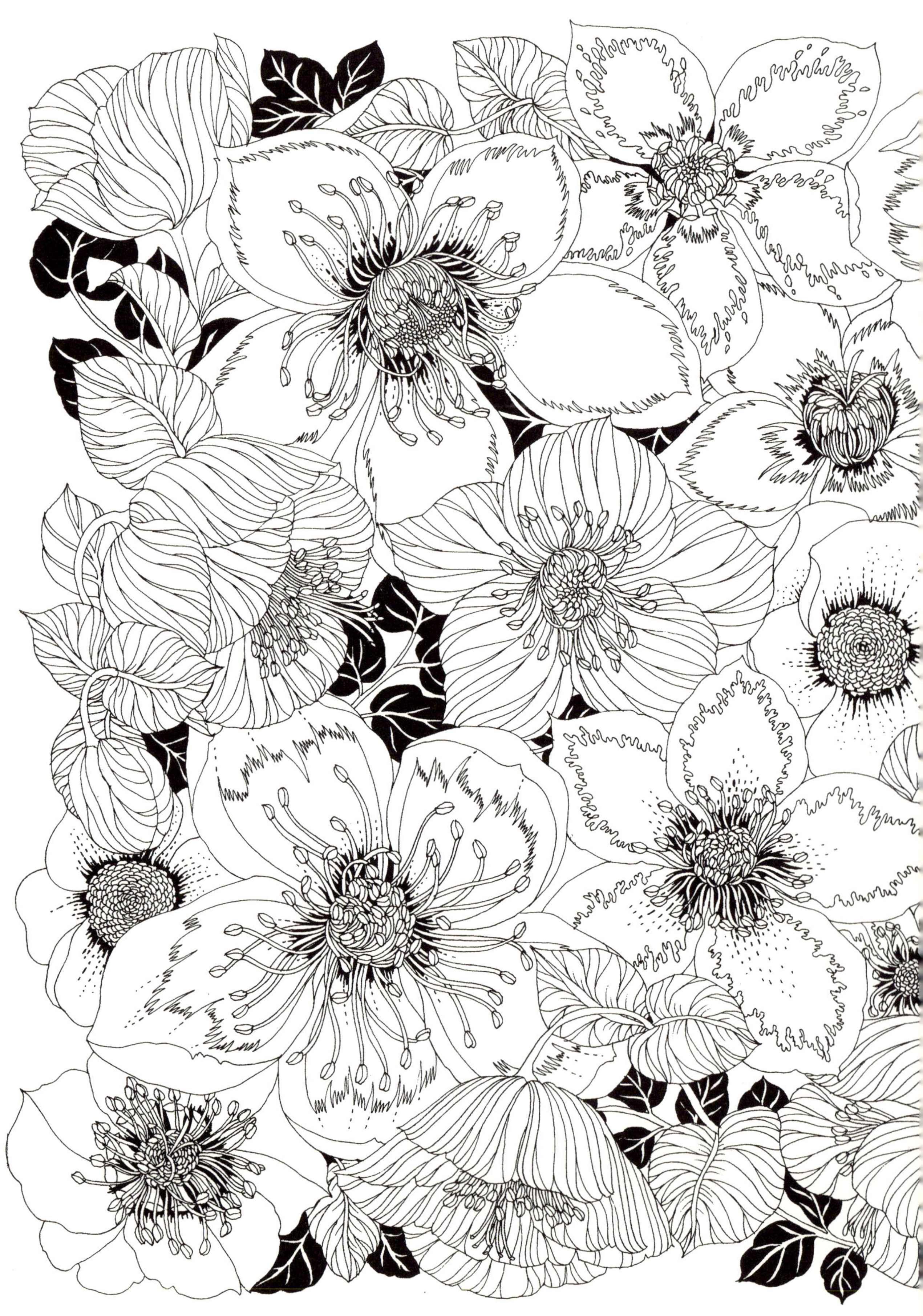

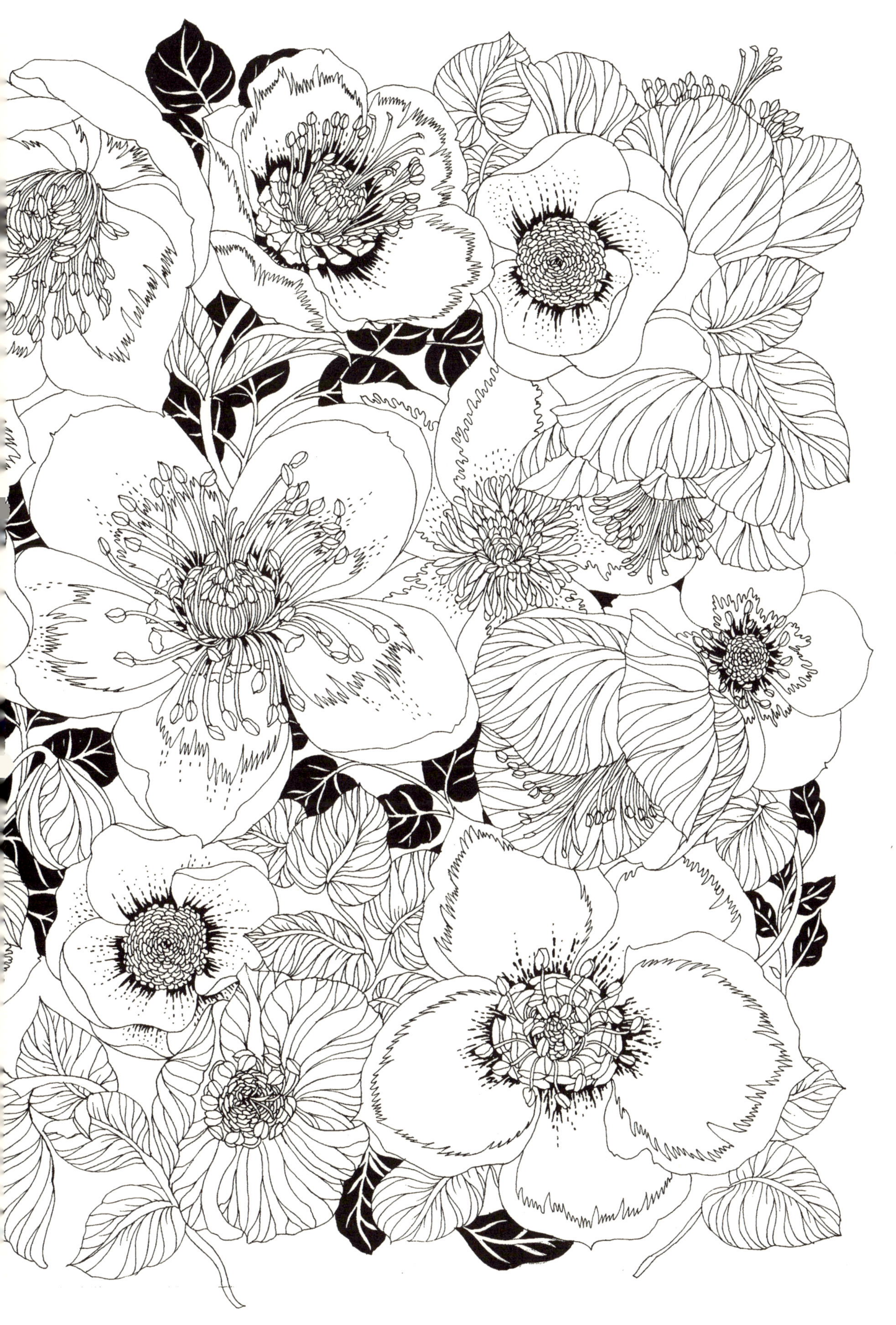

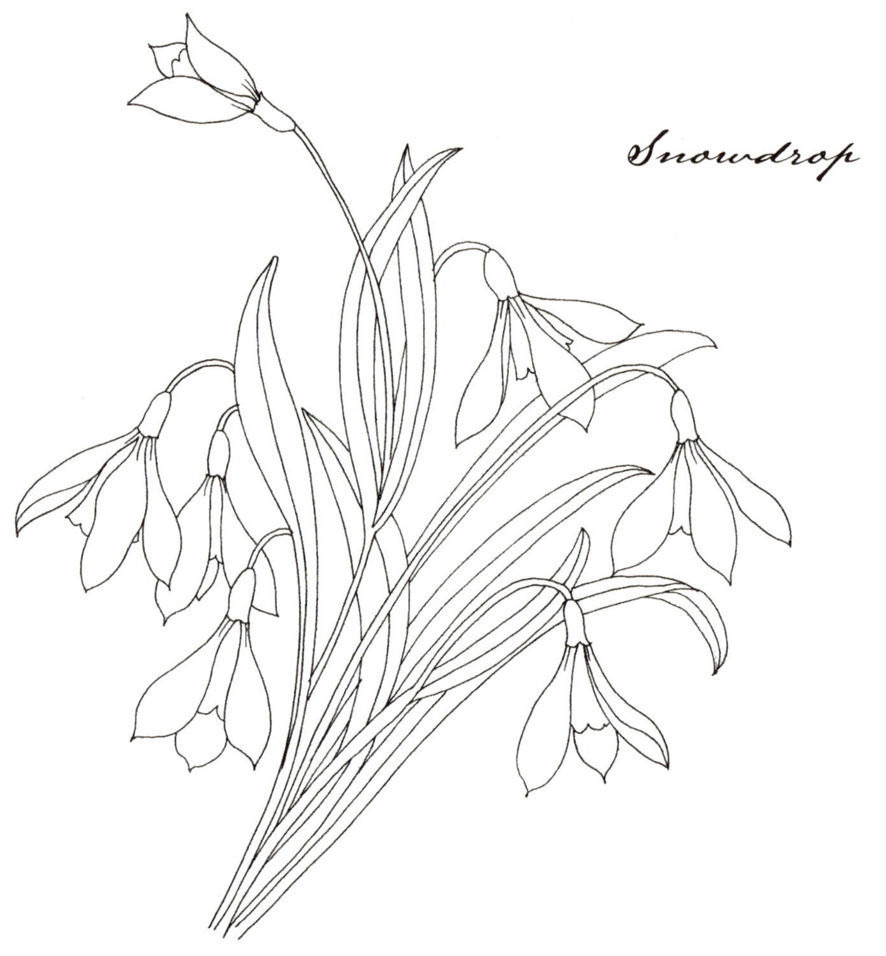
Snowdrop

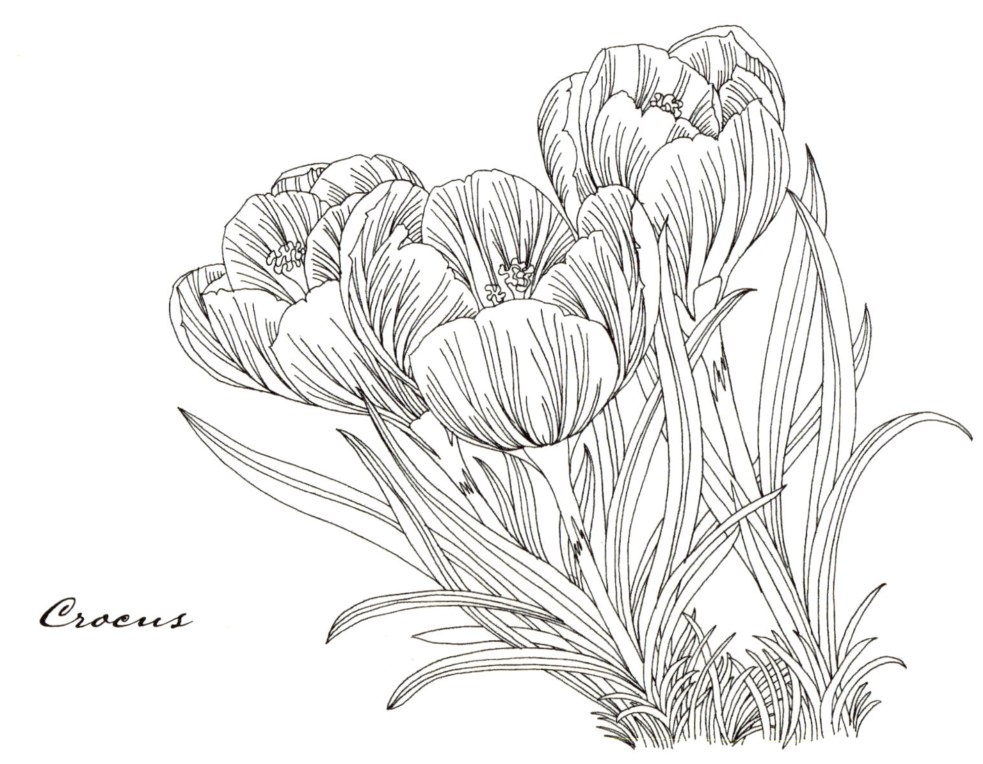
Crocus

FEBRUARY

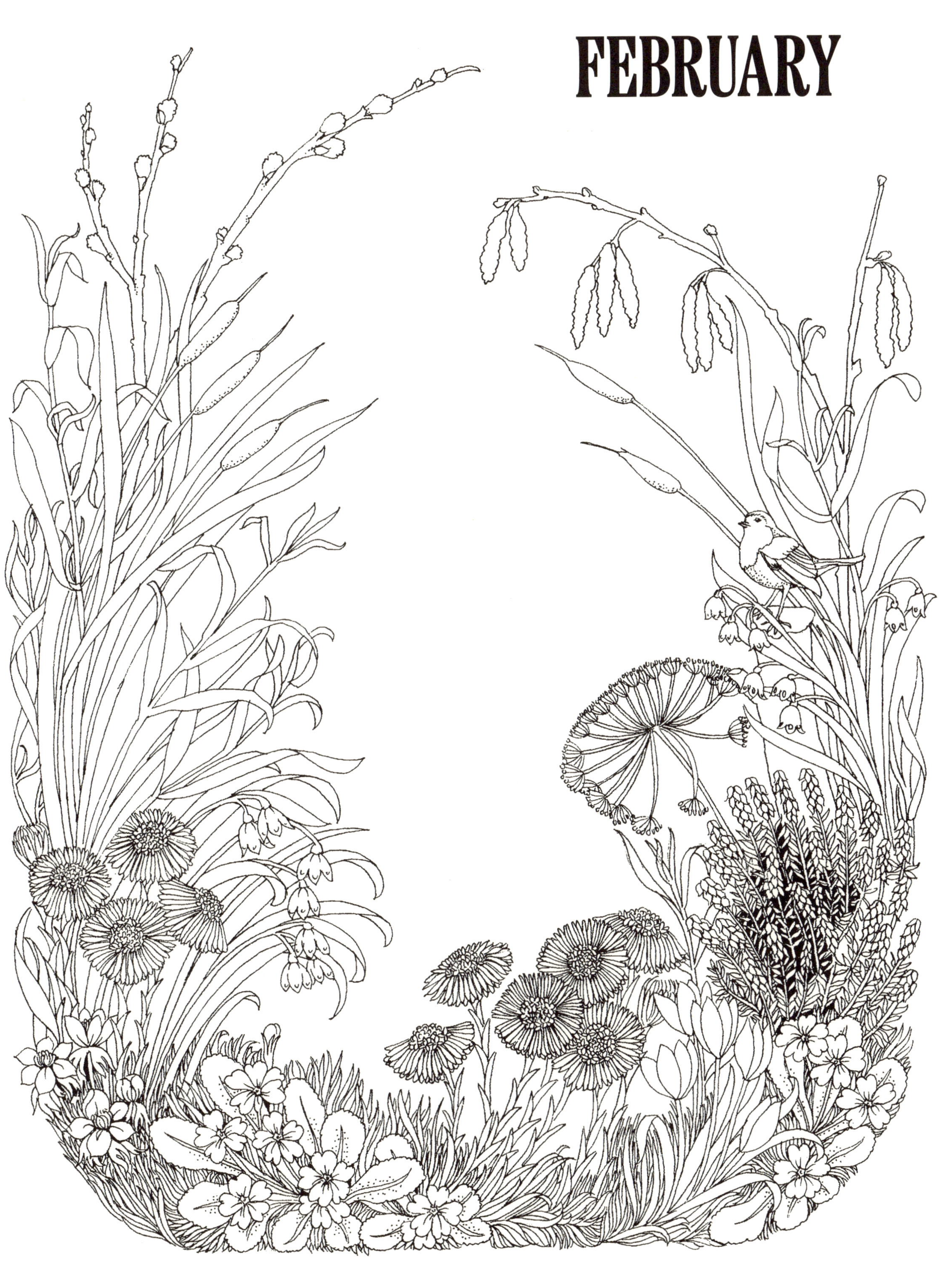

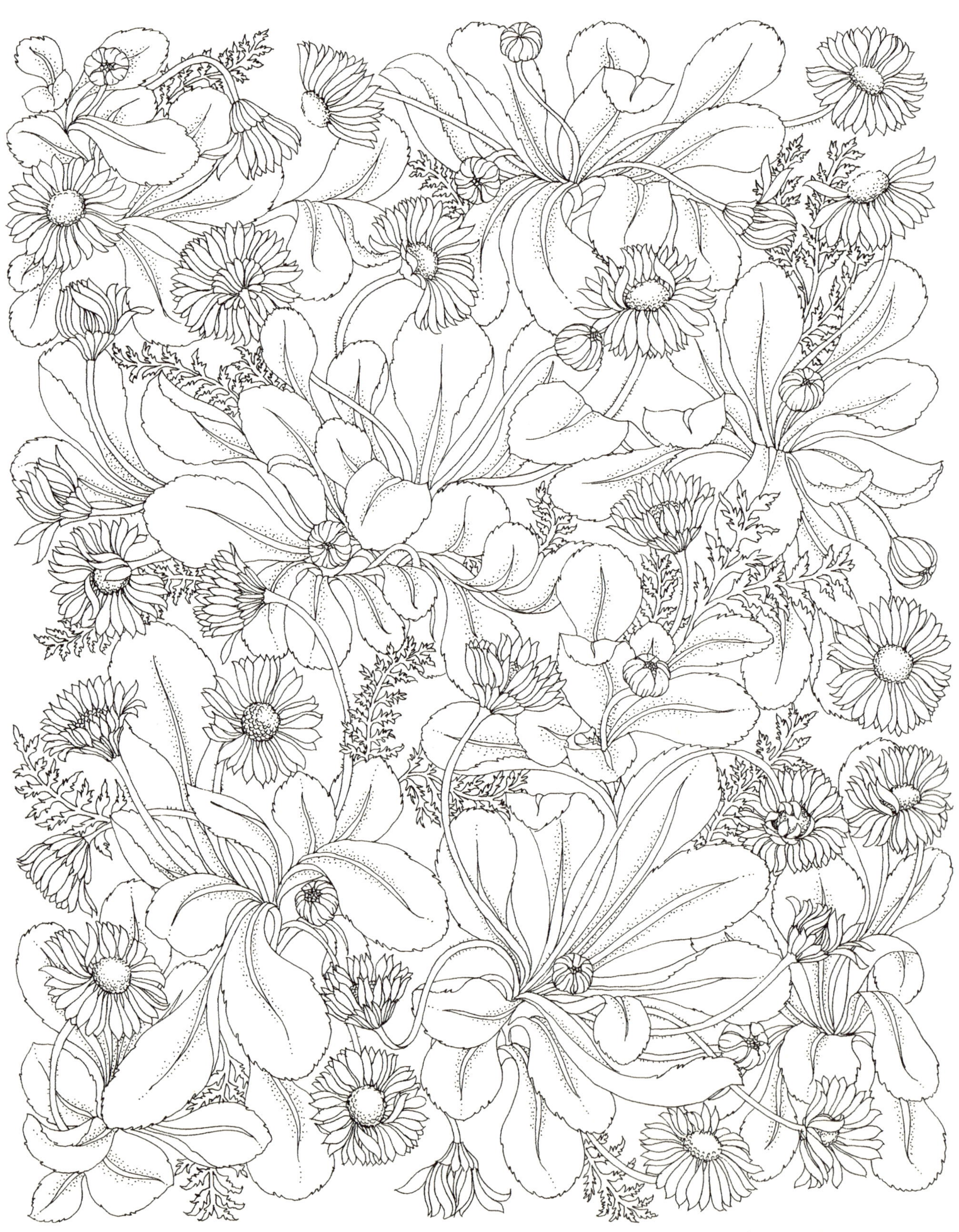

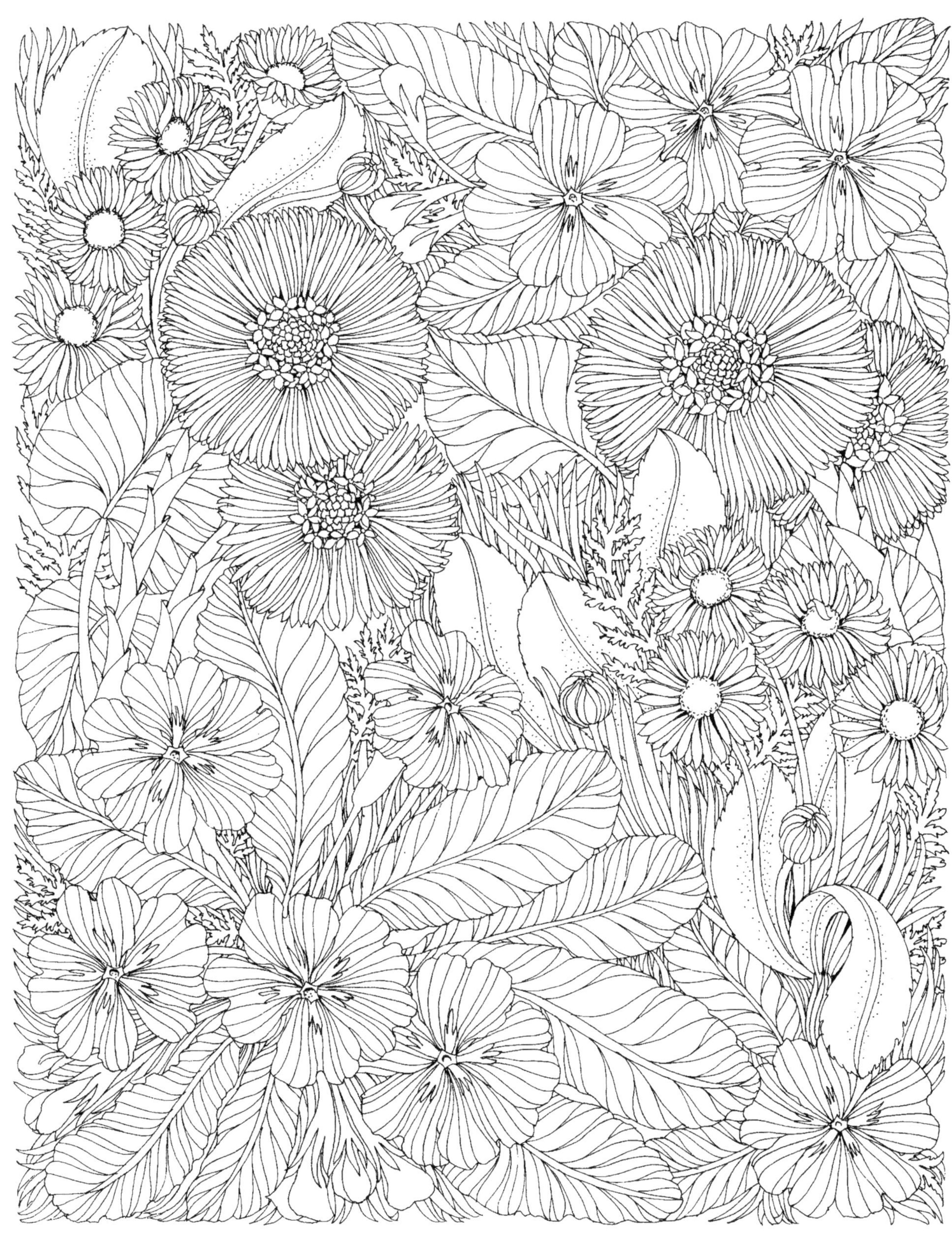

Berried Ivy, Hazel Catkins, Blue Tits

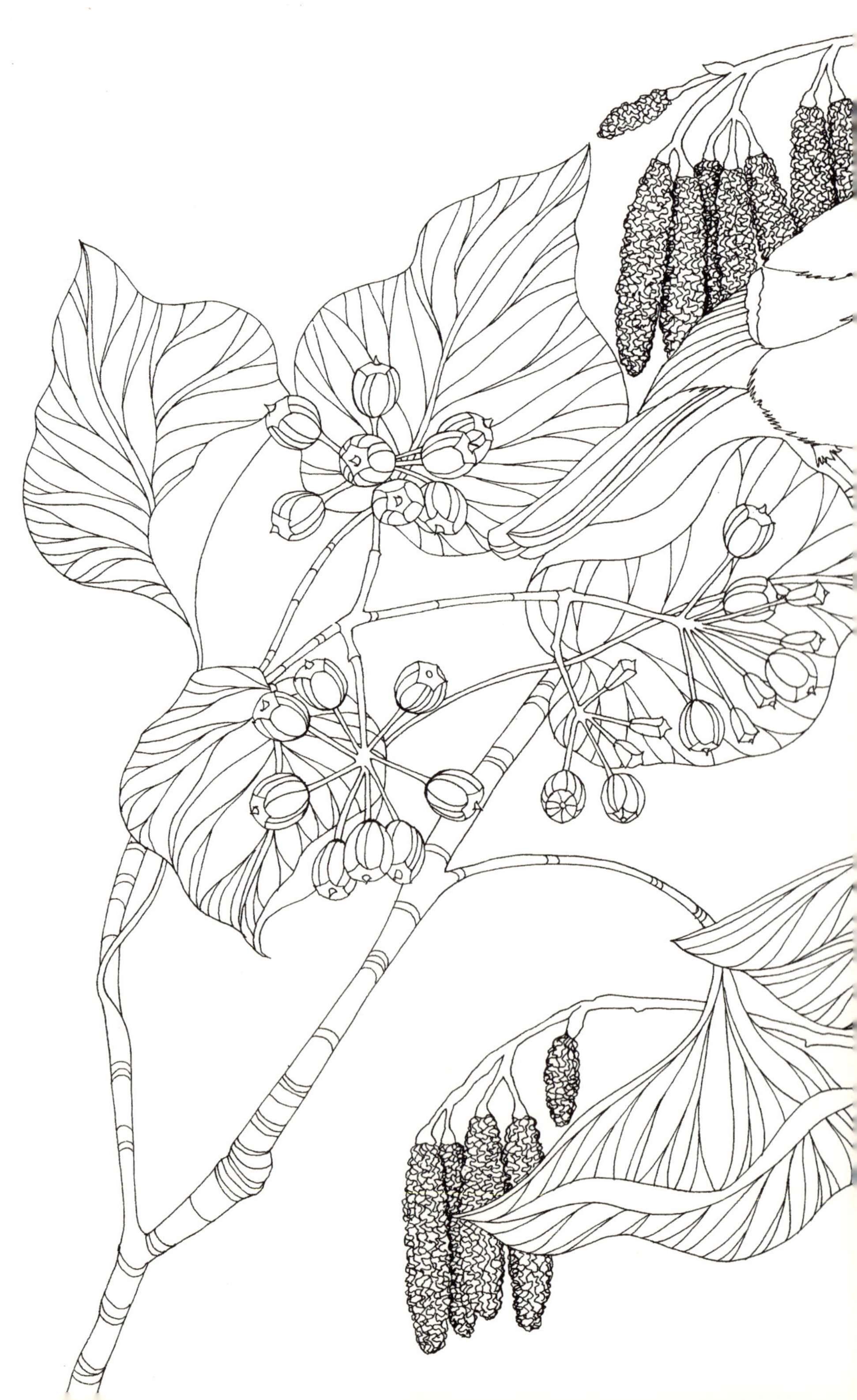

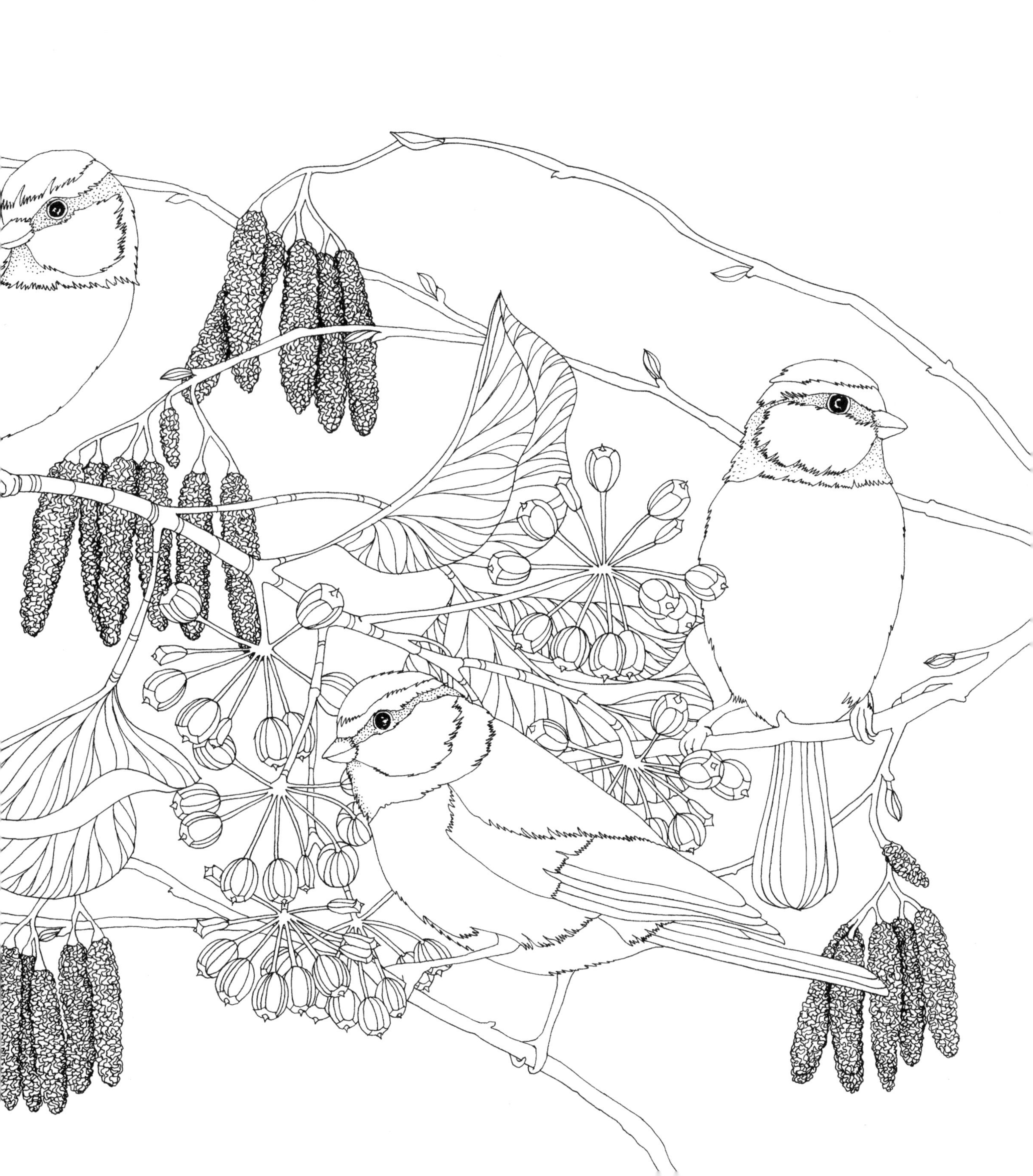

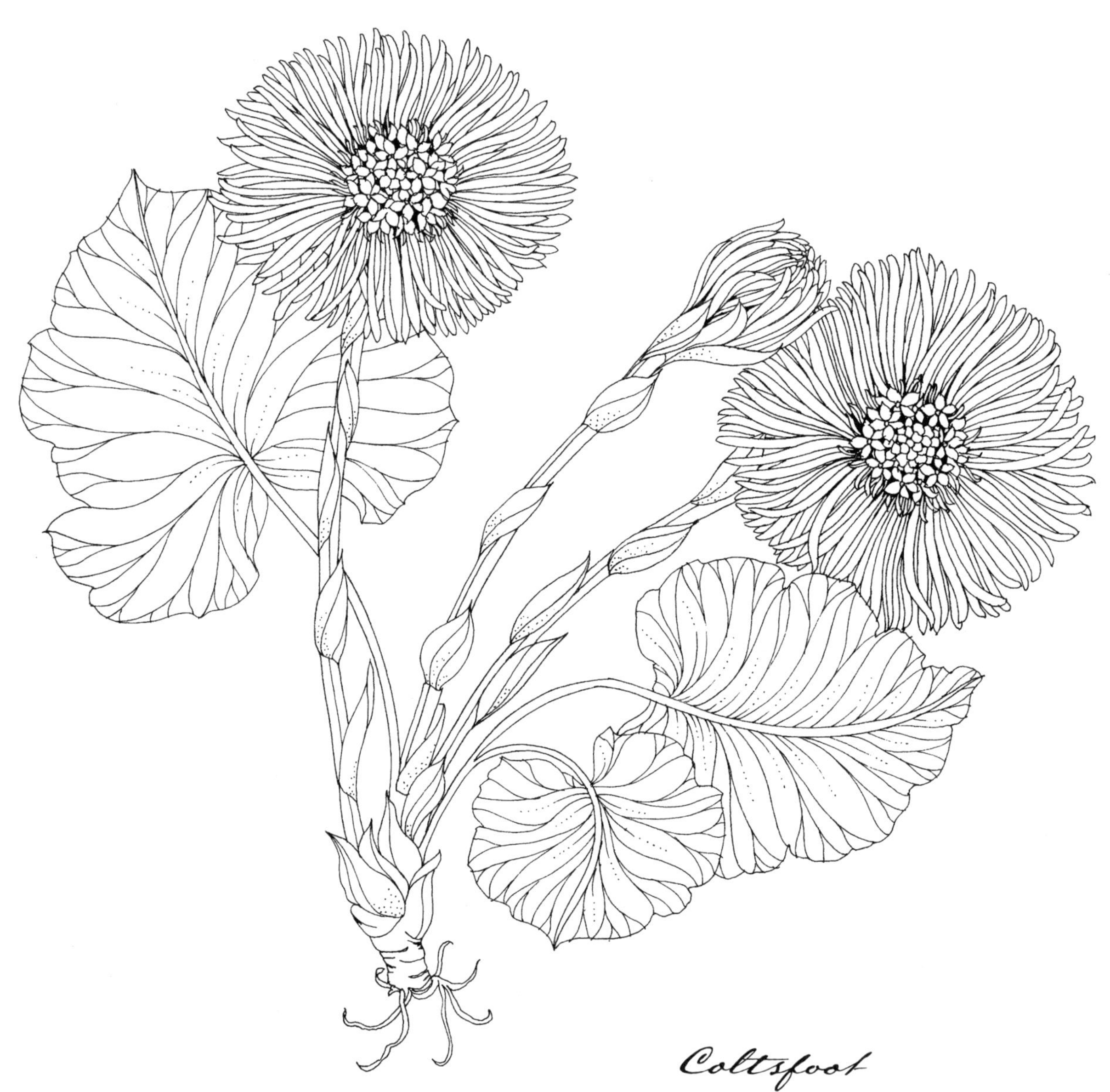
Coltsfoot

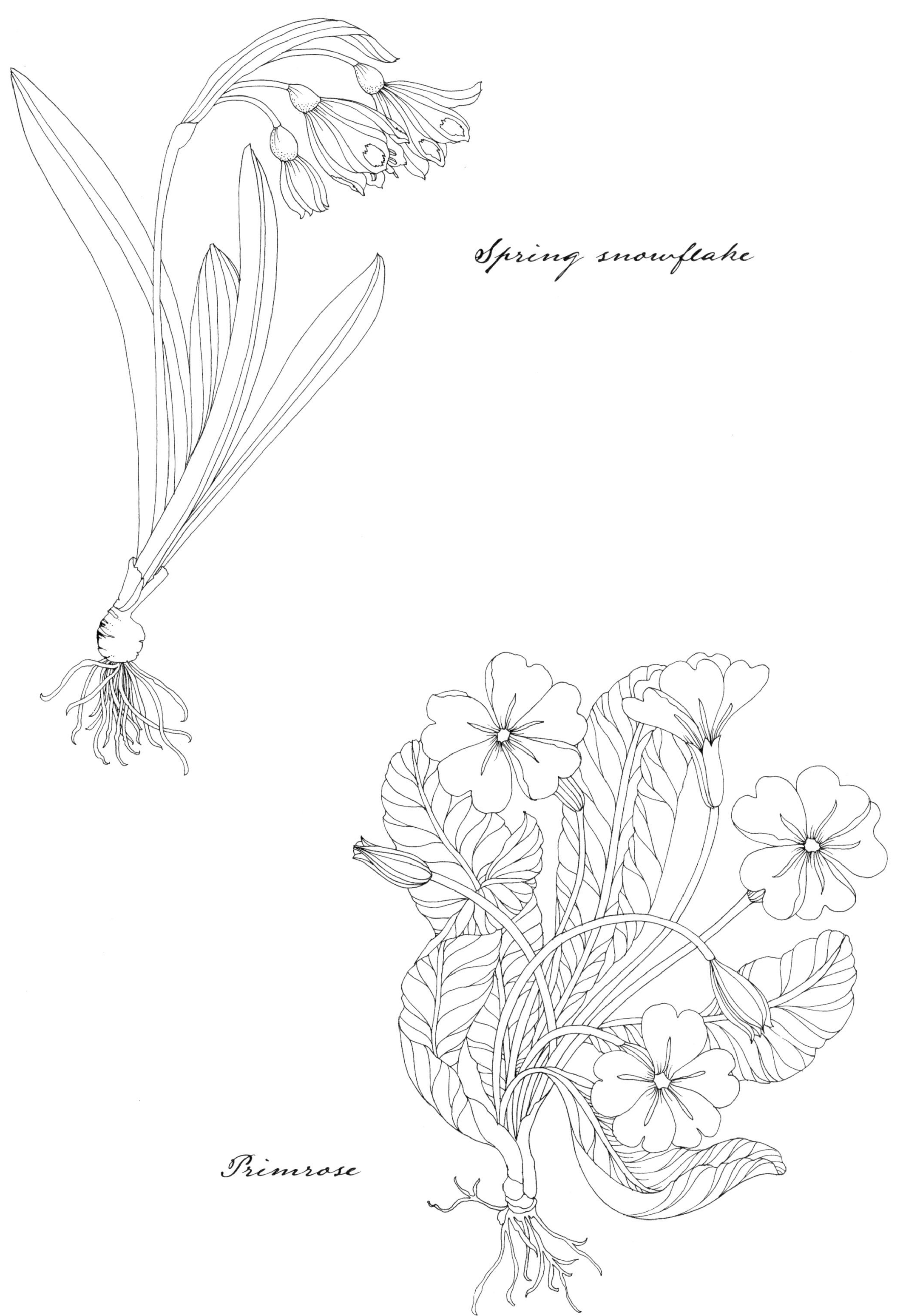
Spring snowflake
Primrose

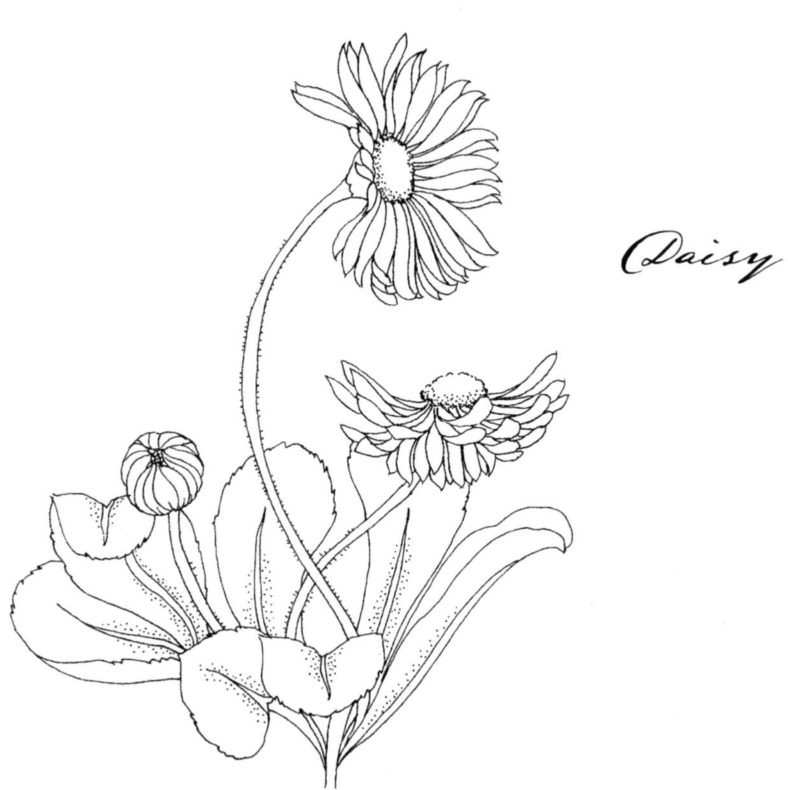
Daisy

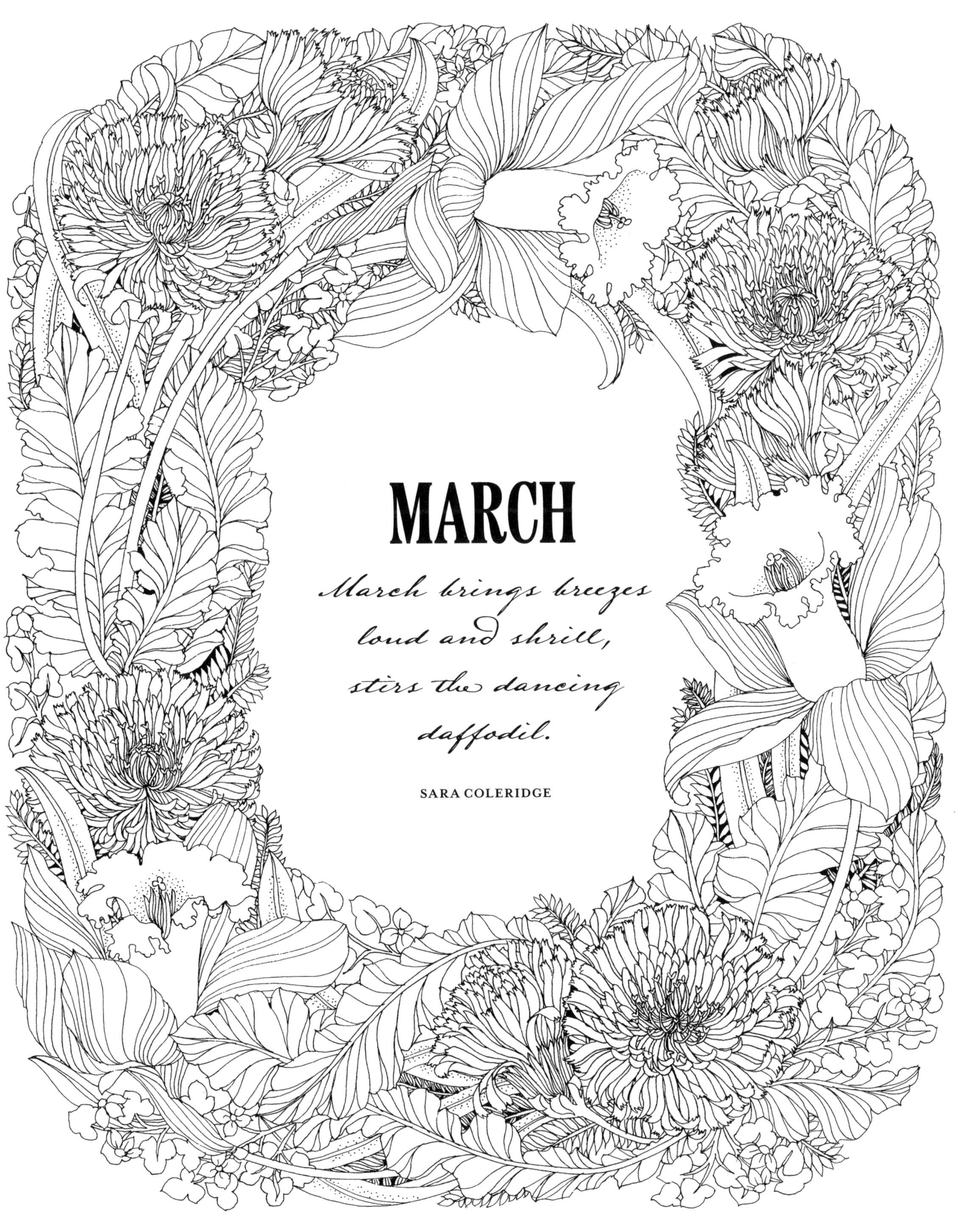

MARCH

March brings breezes
loud and shrill,
stirs the dancing
daffodil.

SARA COLERIDGE

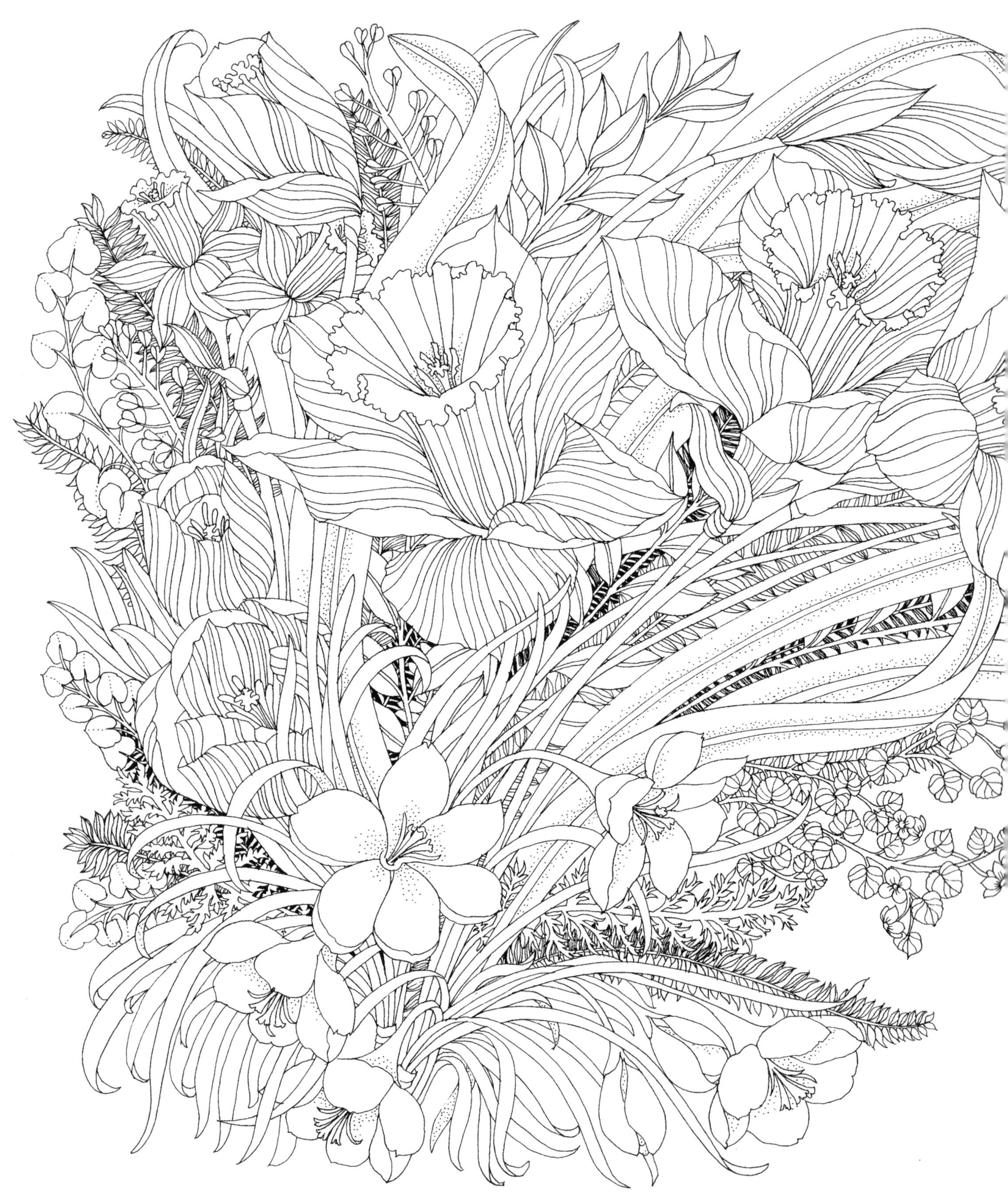

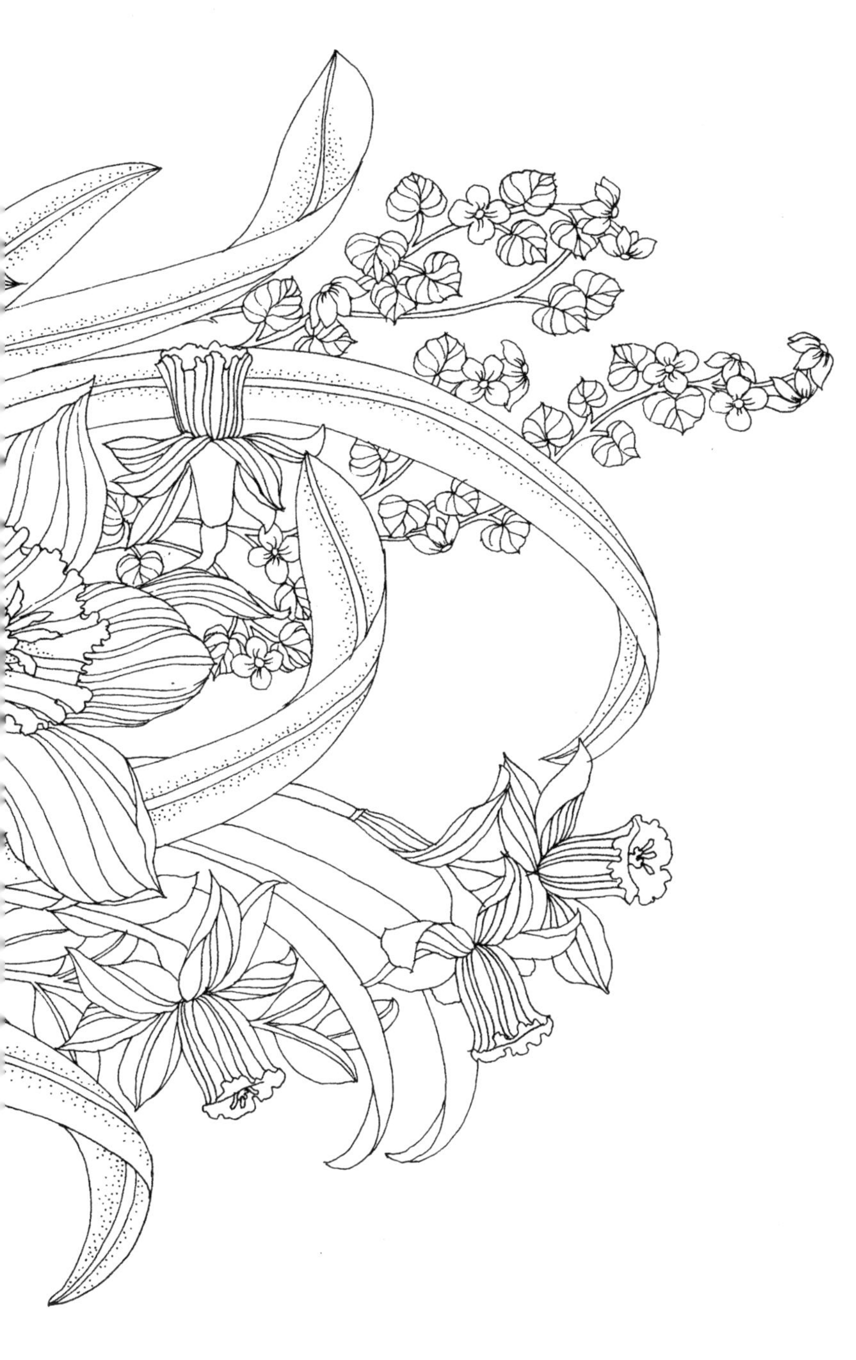

Creeping Speedwell, Crocus, Daffodil

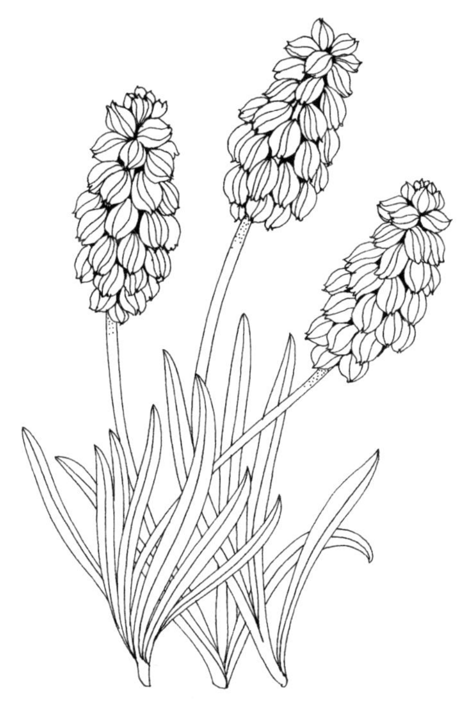

Along these blushing borders bright with dew,
And in your mingled wilderness of flowers,
Fair-handed spring unbosoms every grace.

JAMES THOMSON

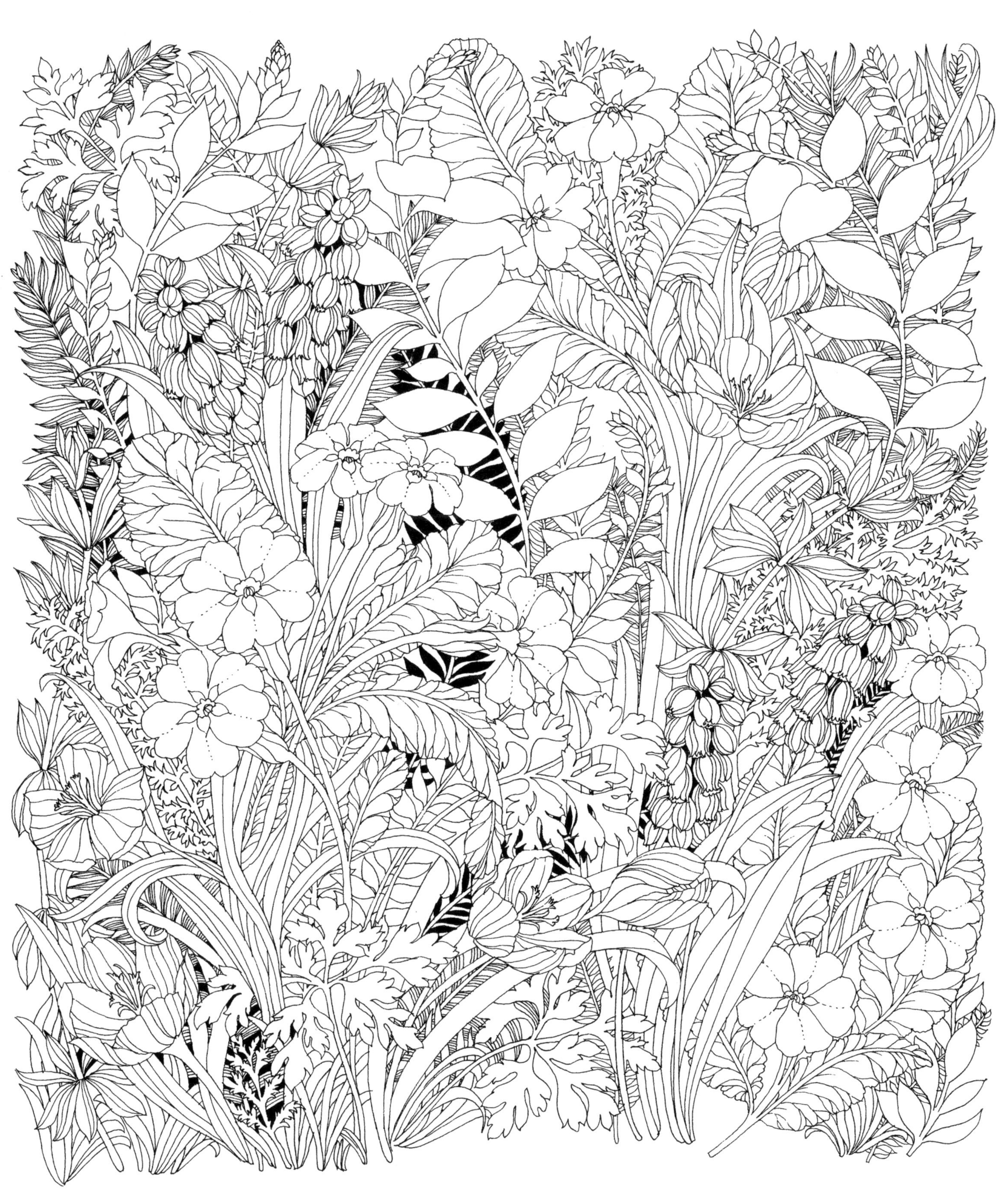

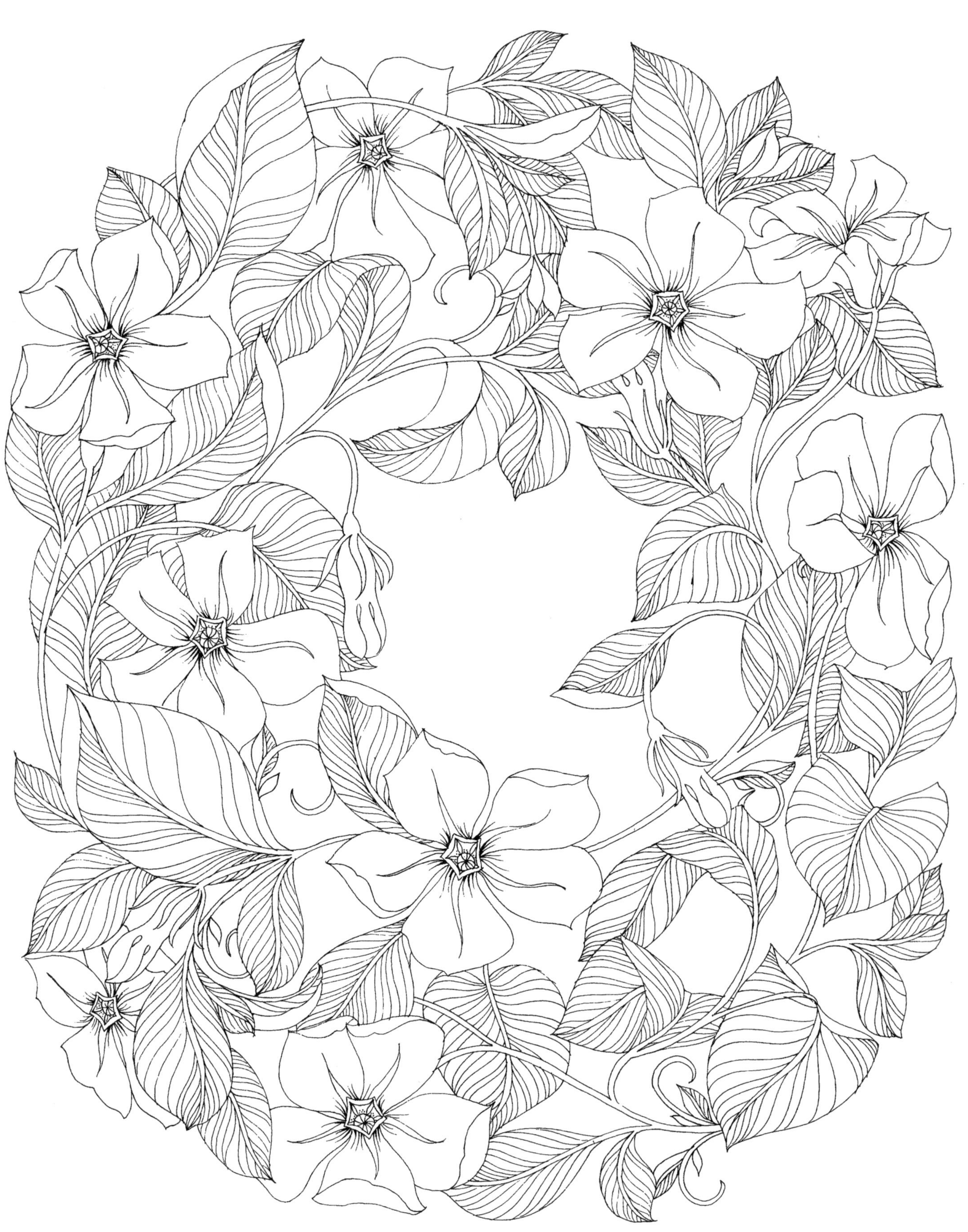

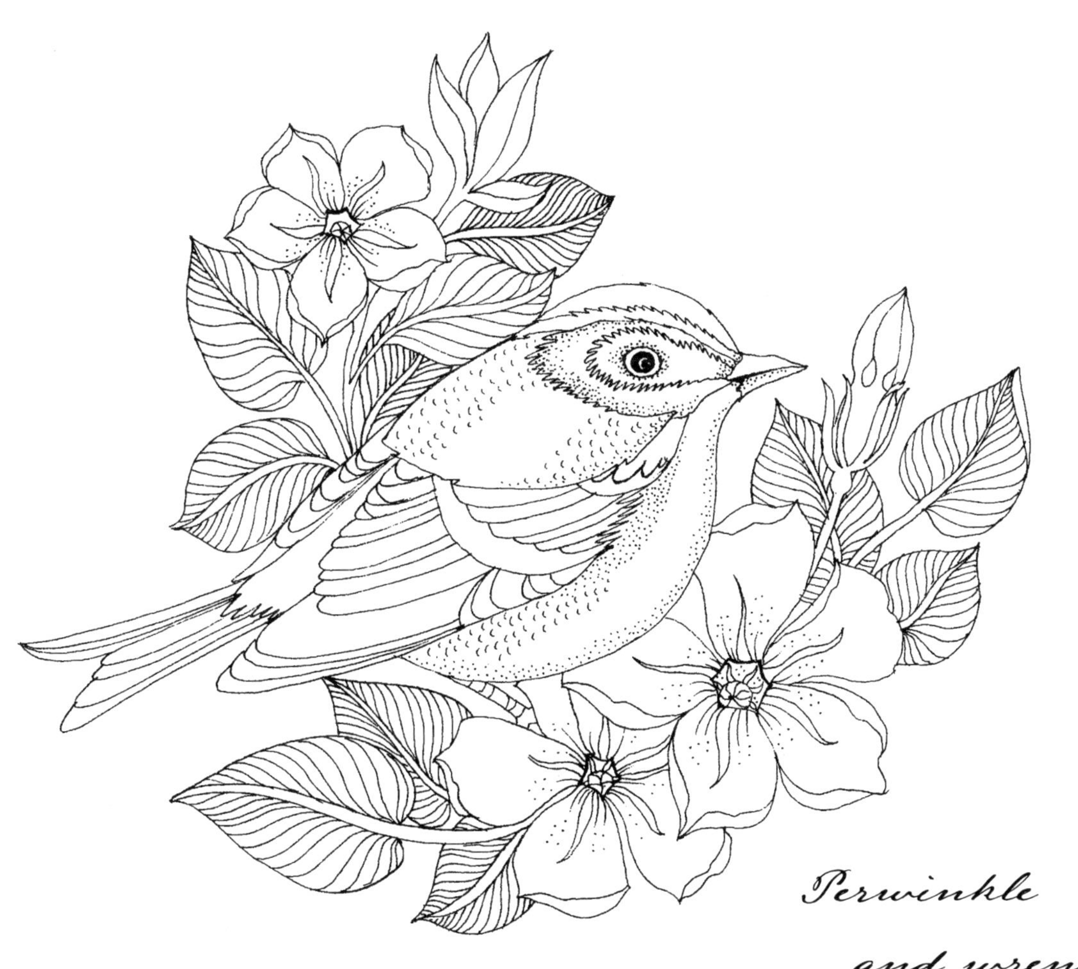

Periwinkle

and wren

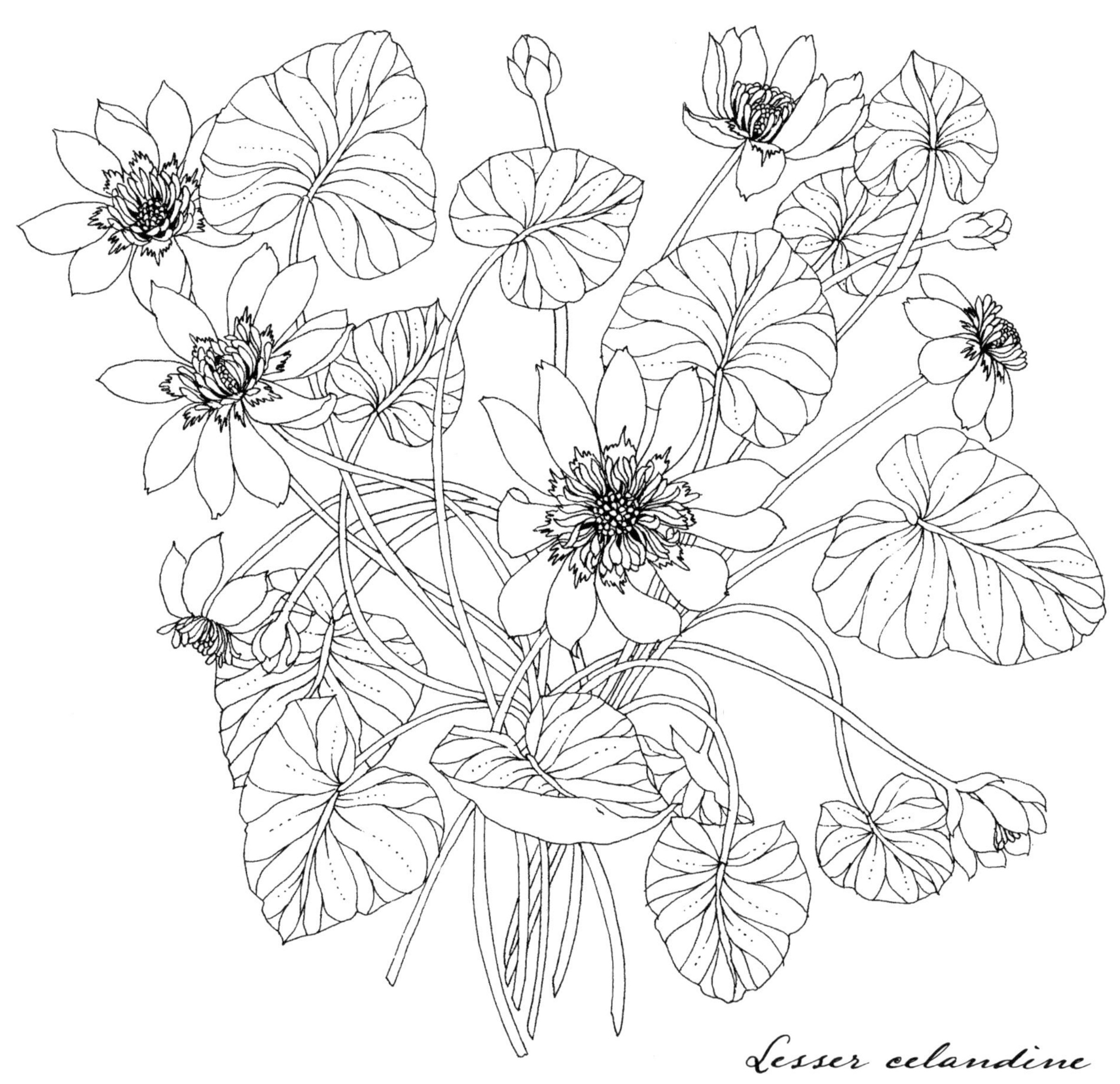

Lesser celandine

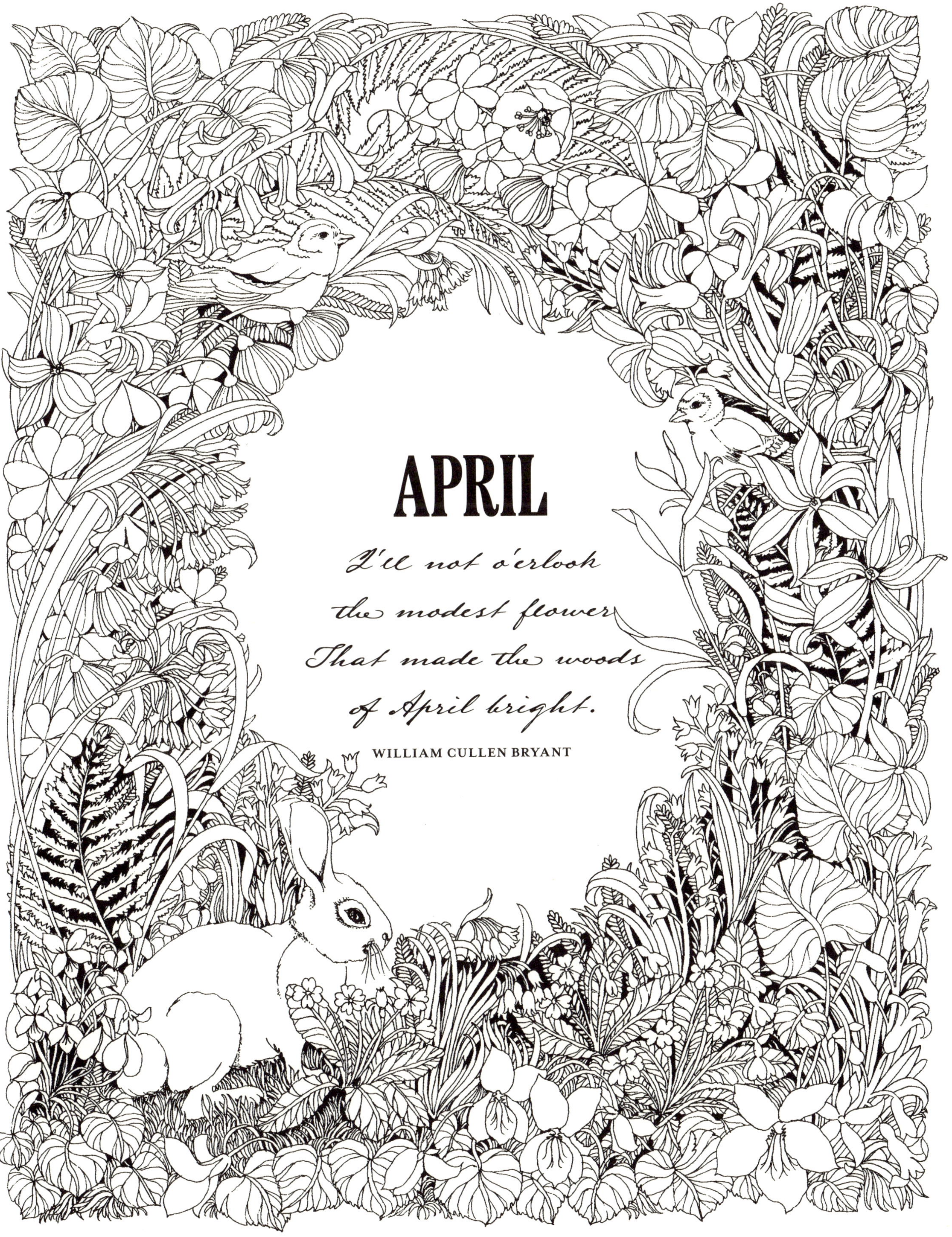
APRIL
I'll not o'erlook
the modest flower
That made the woods
of April bright.
WILLIAM CULLEN BRYANT

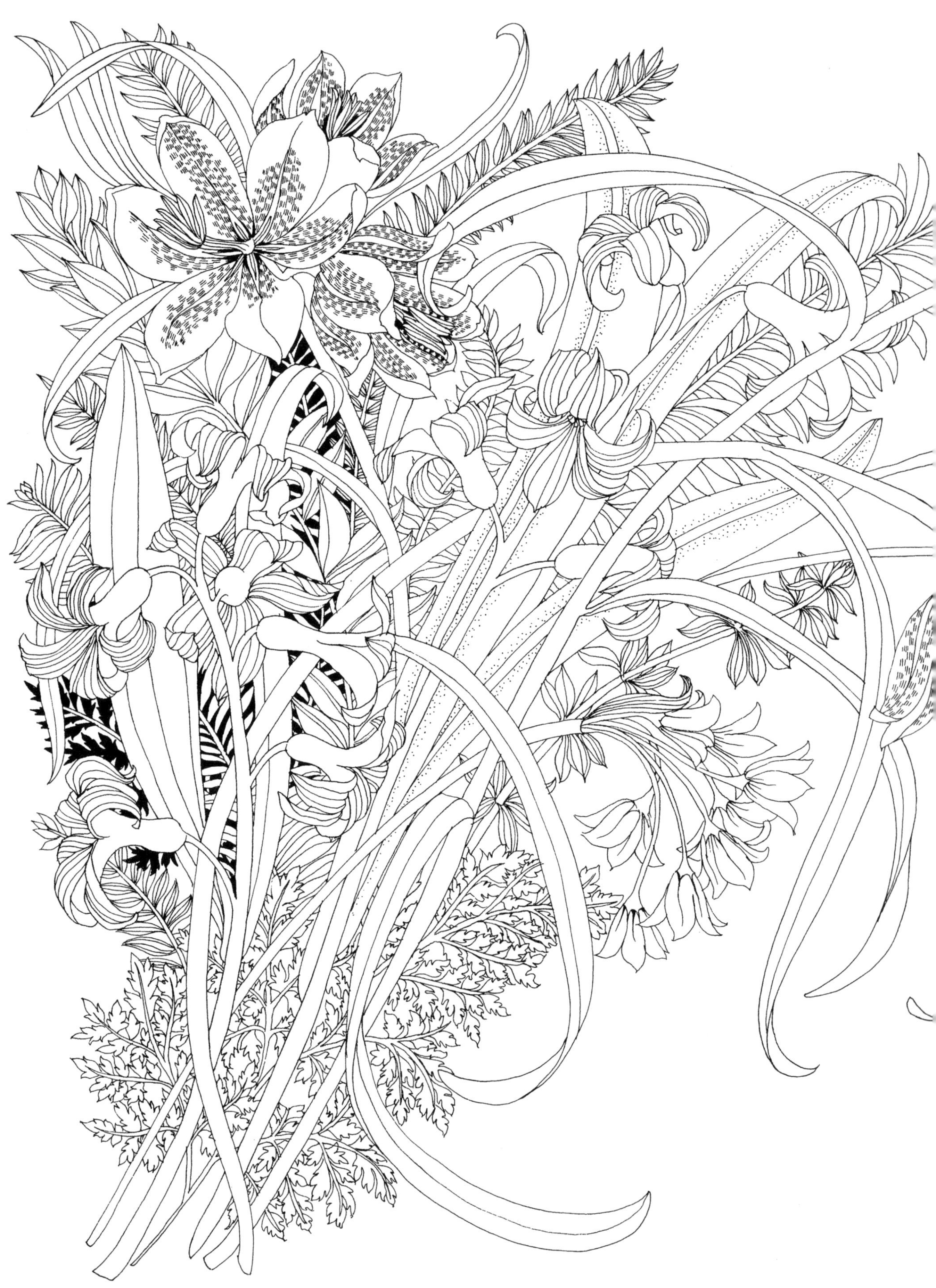

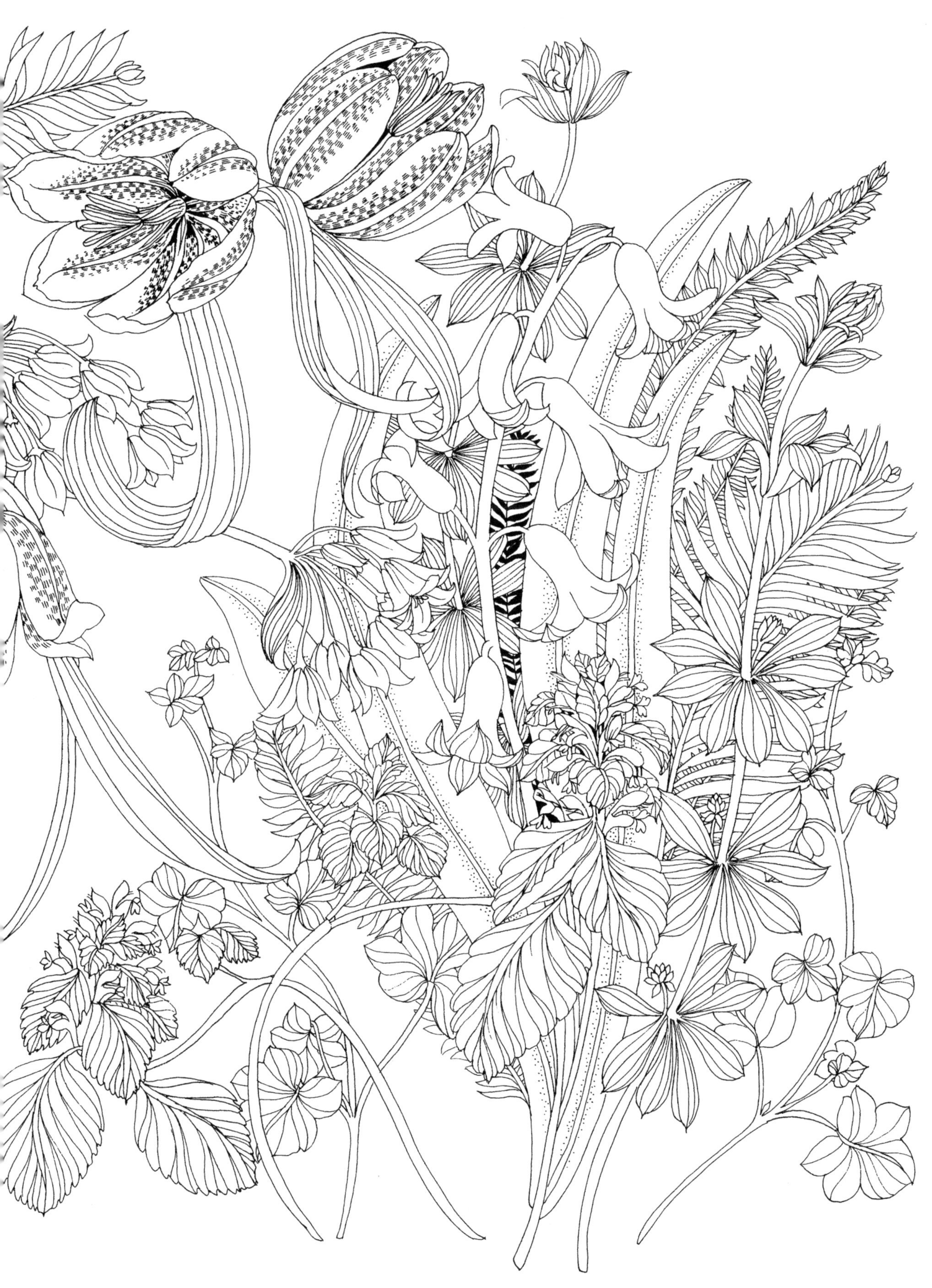

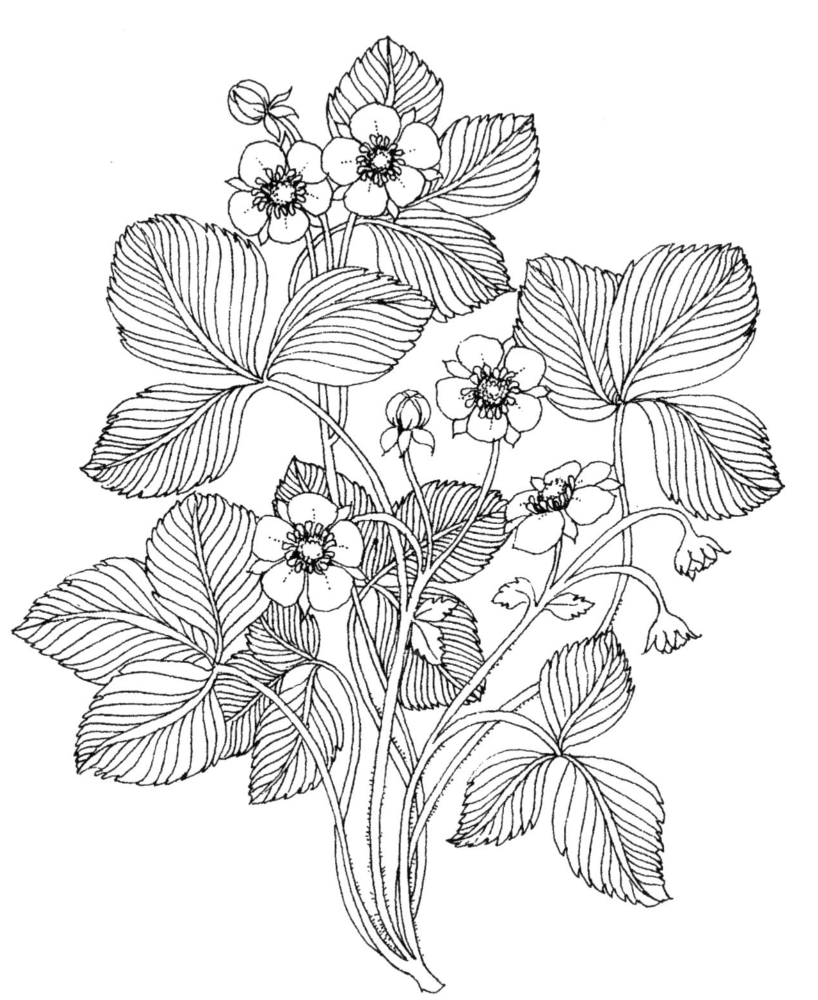

Wild strawberry

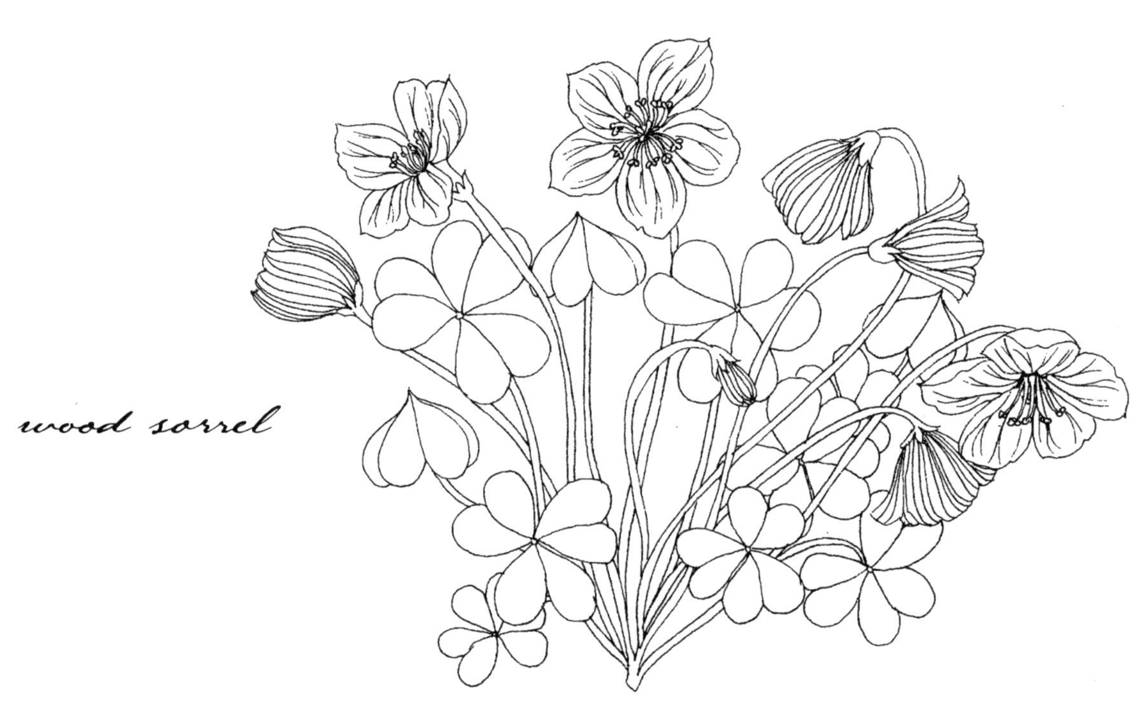

wood sorrel

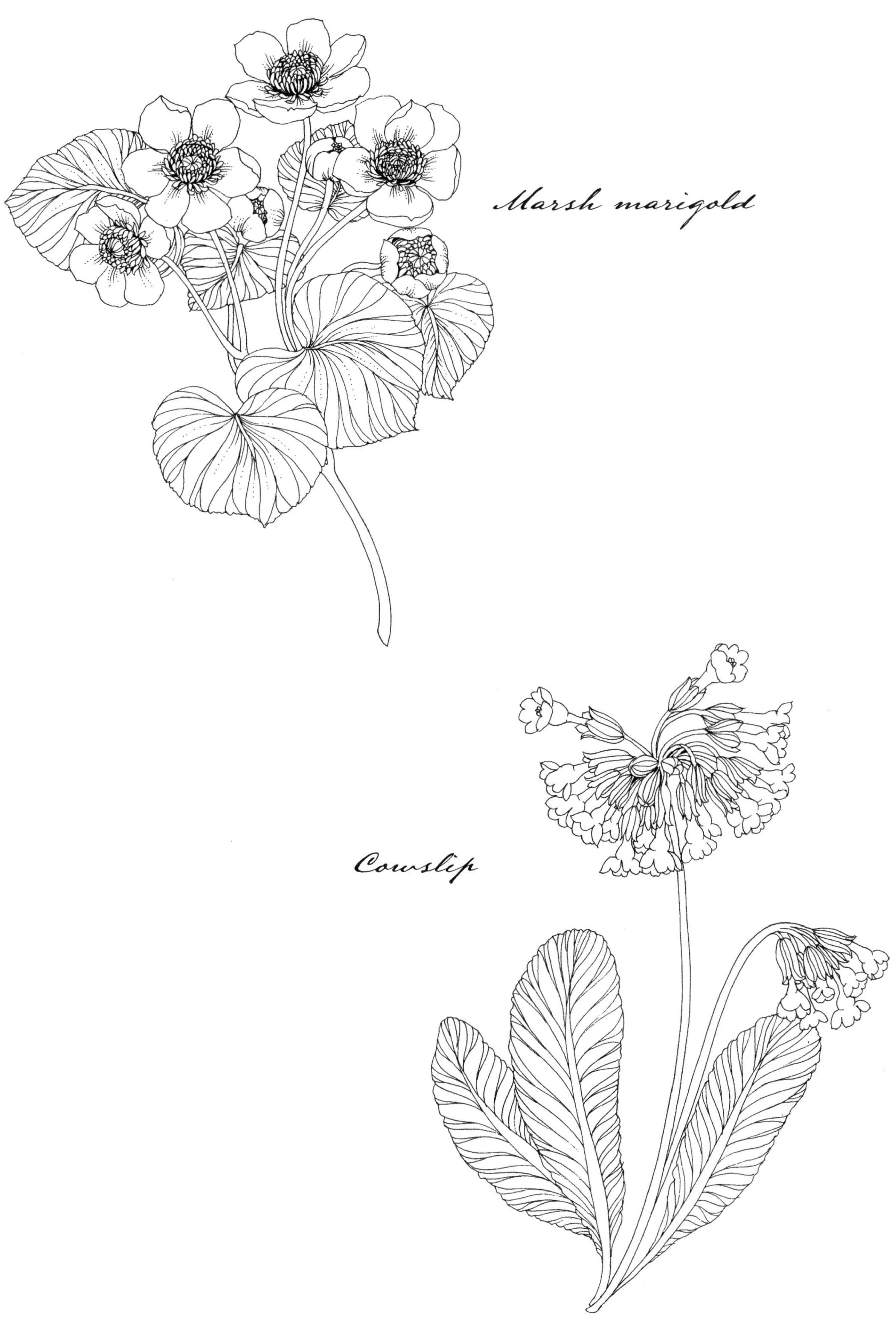
Marsh marigold
Cowslip

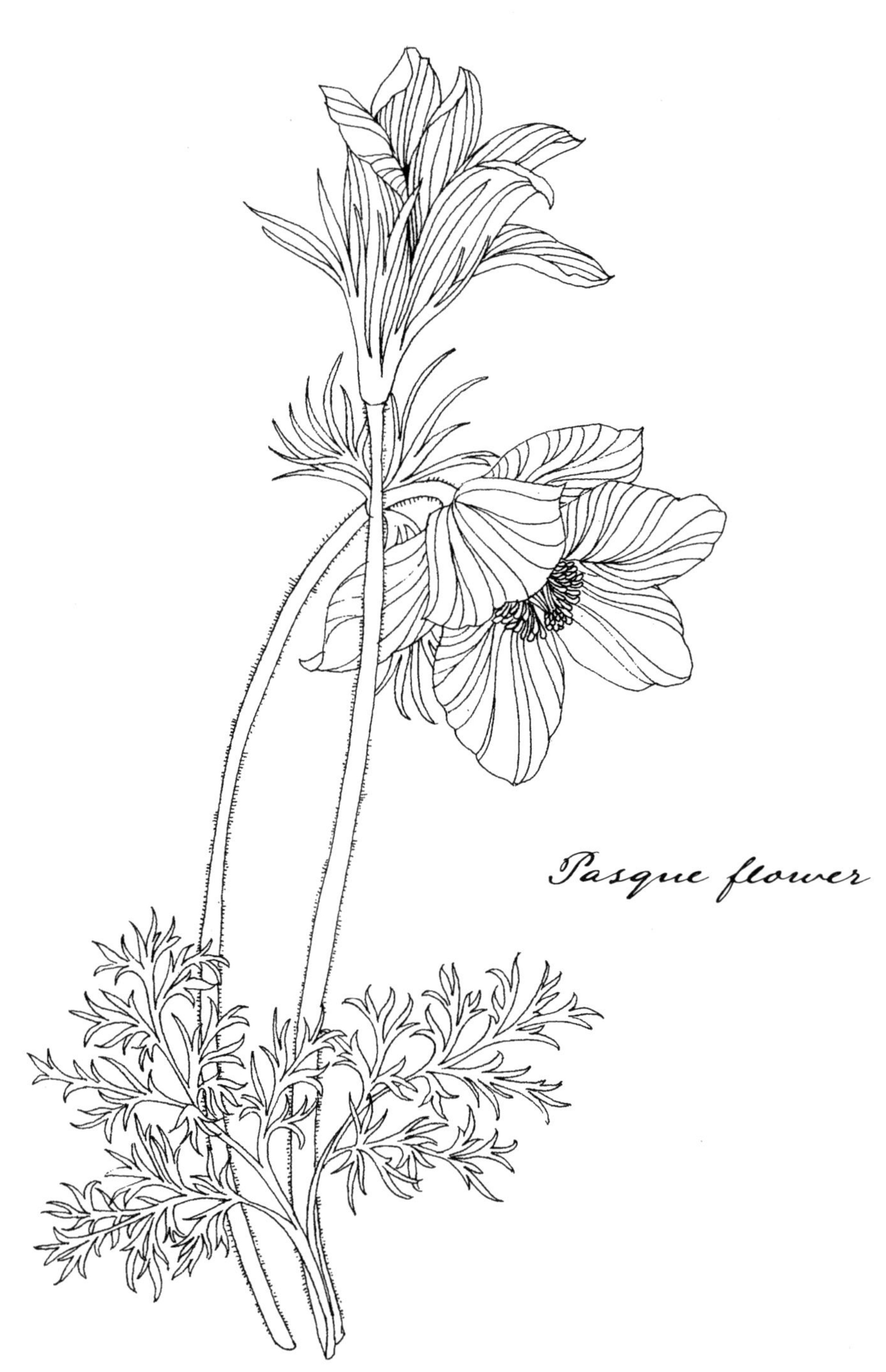
Pasque flower

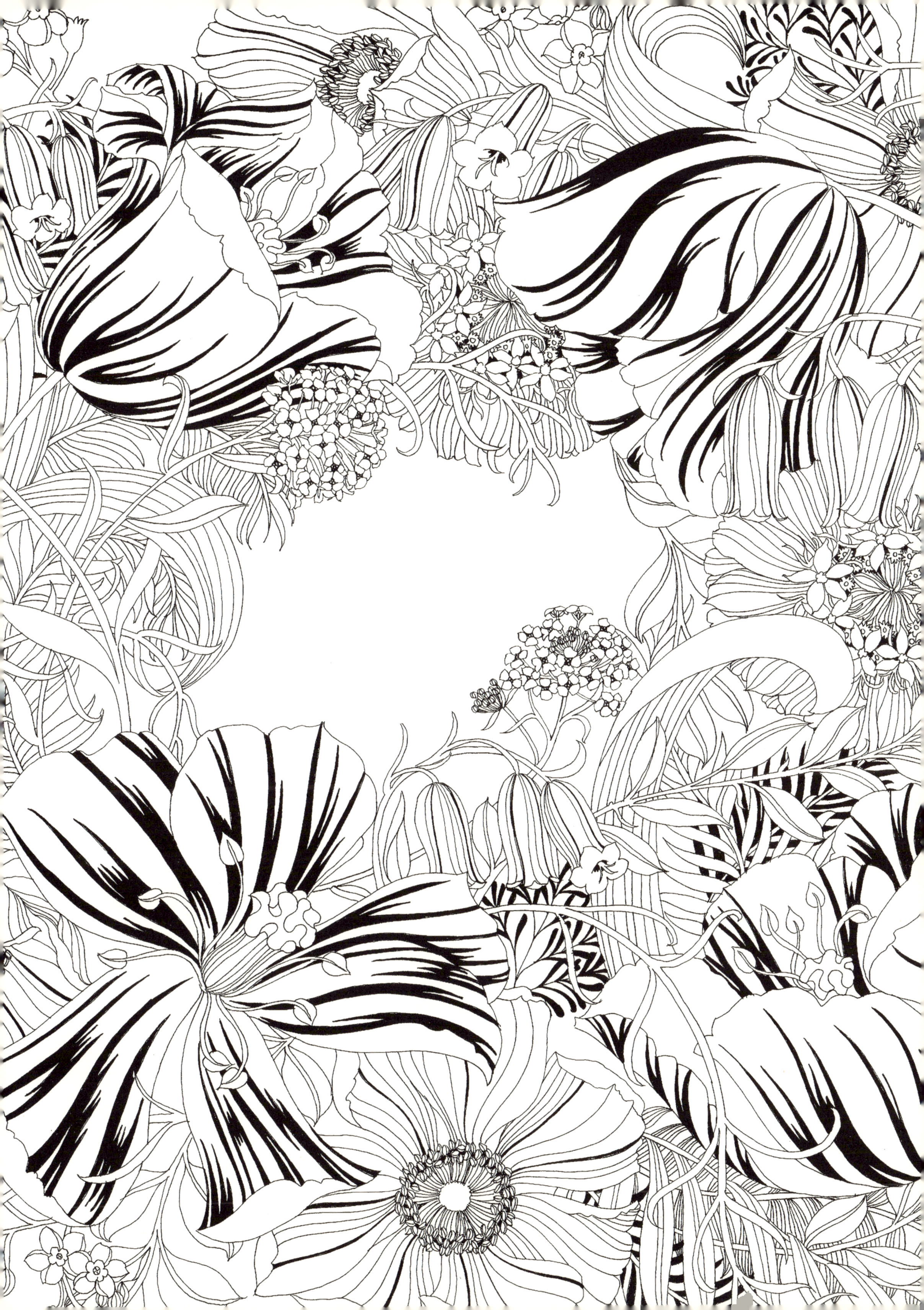

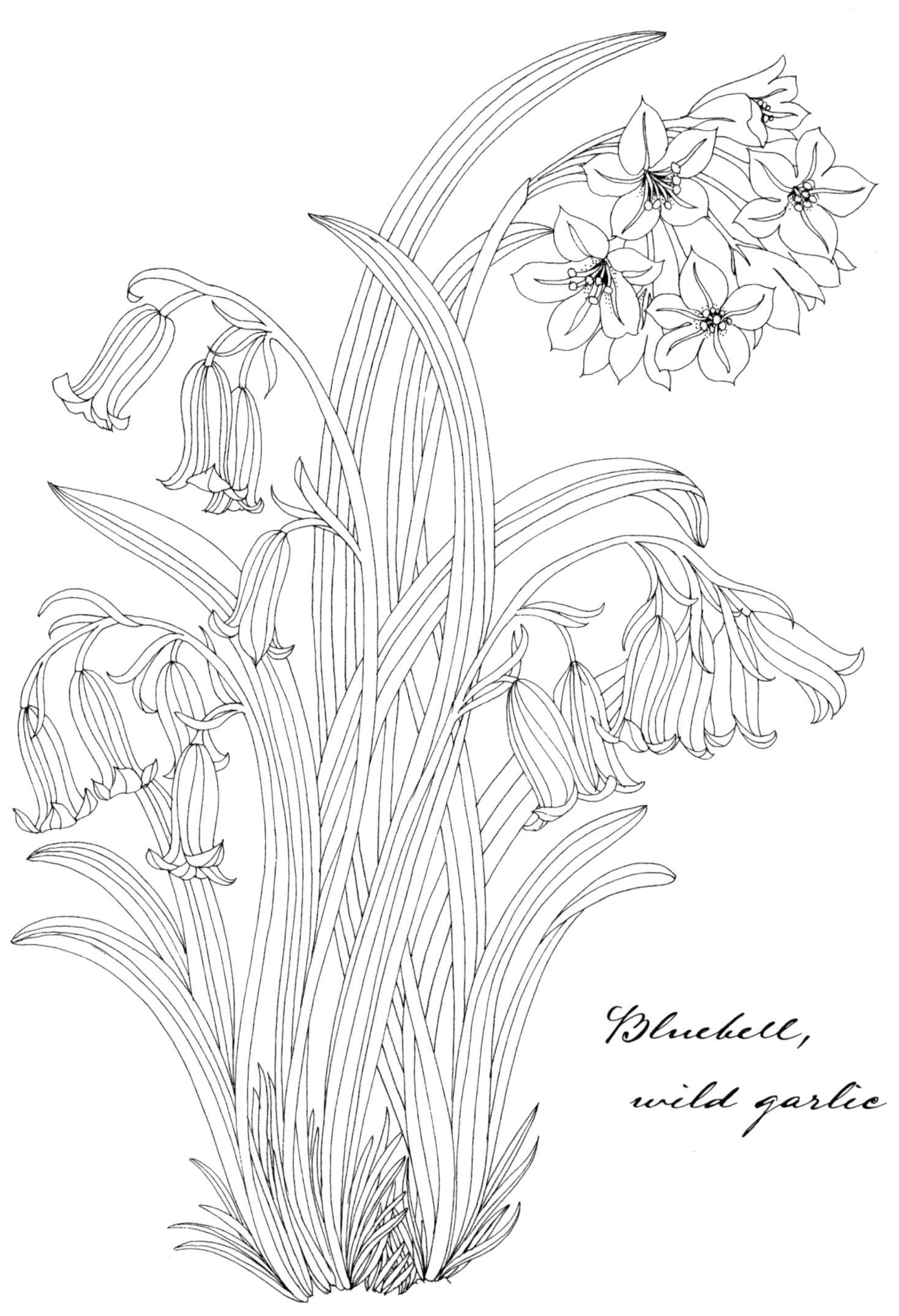

Bluebell, wild garlic

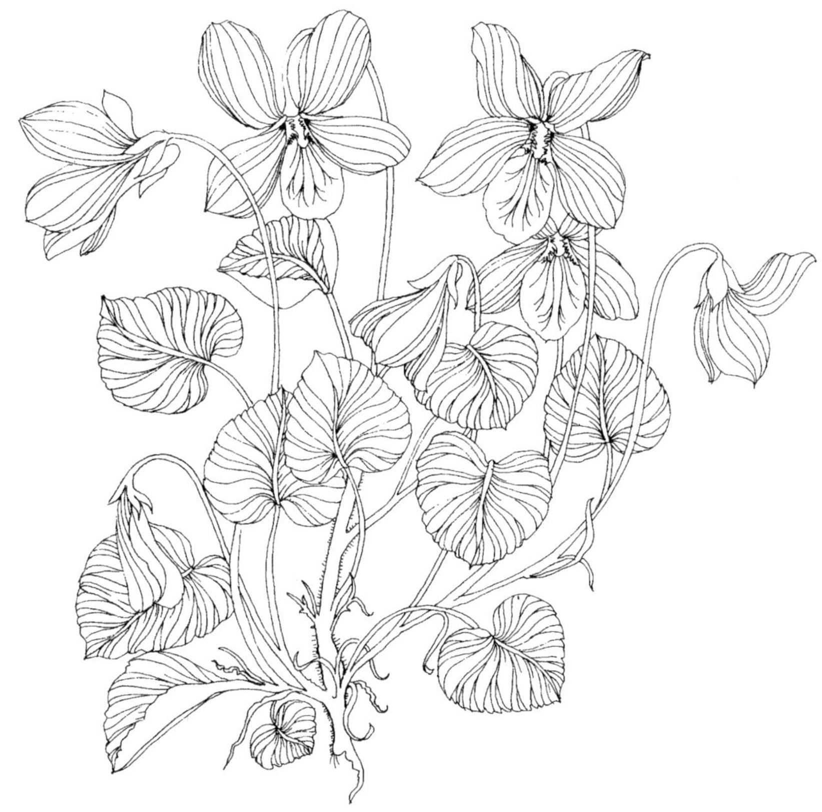

Common dog-violet

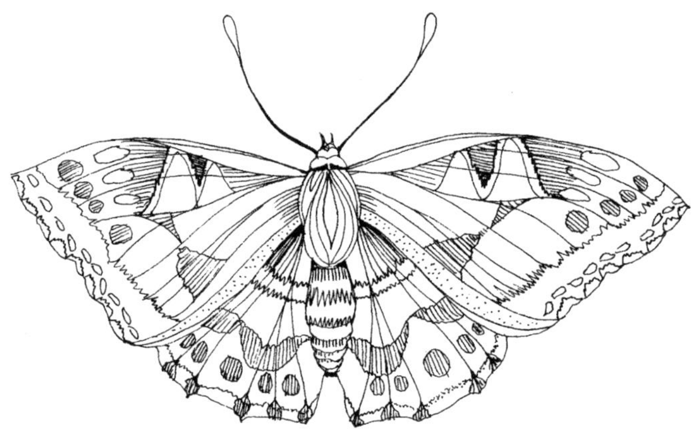

Painted Lady butterfly

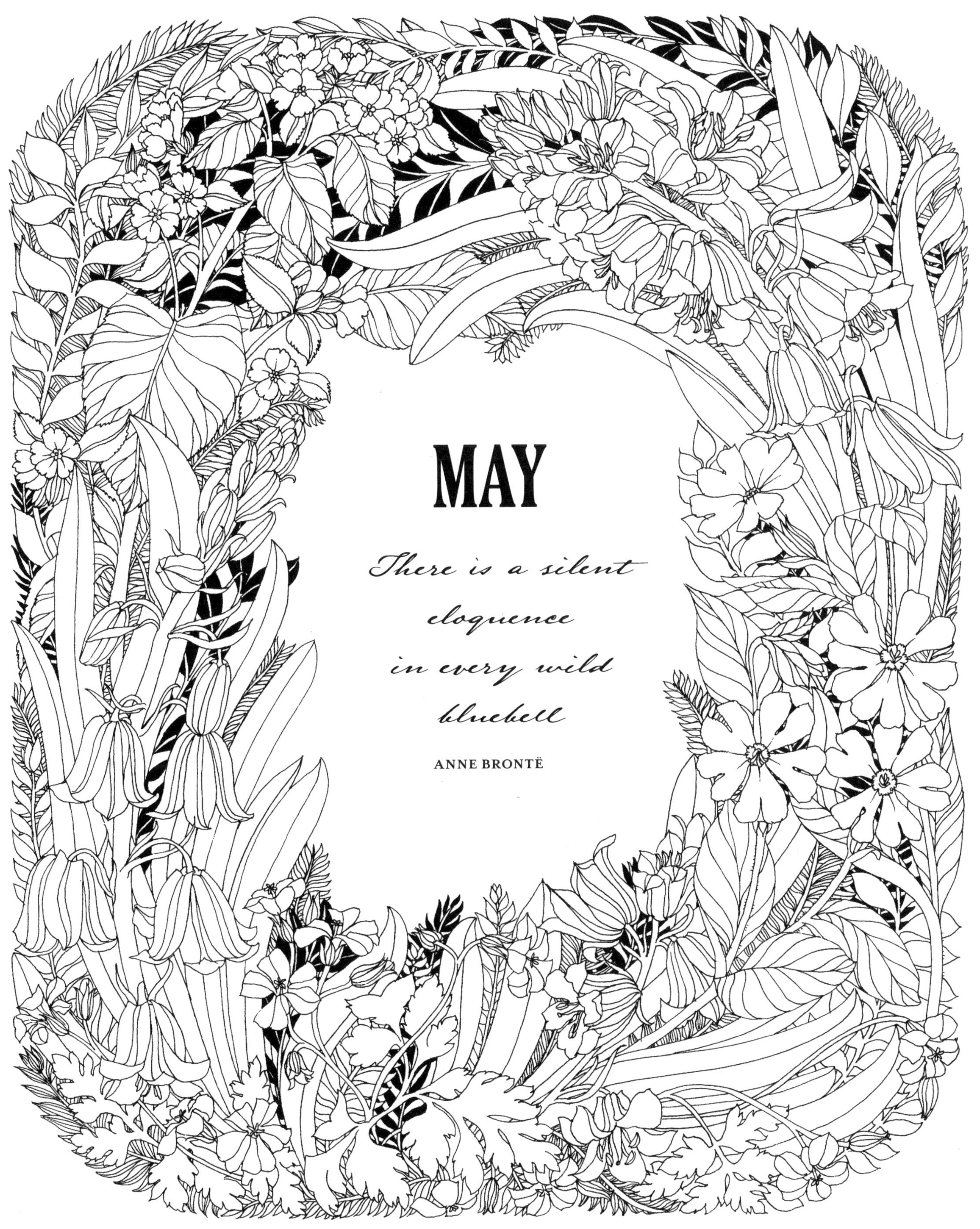

MAY

There is a silent eloquence in every wild bluebell

ANNE BRONTË

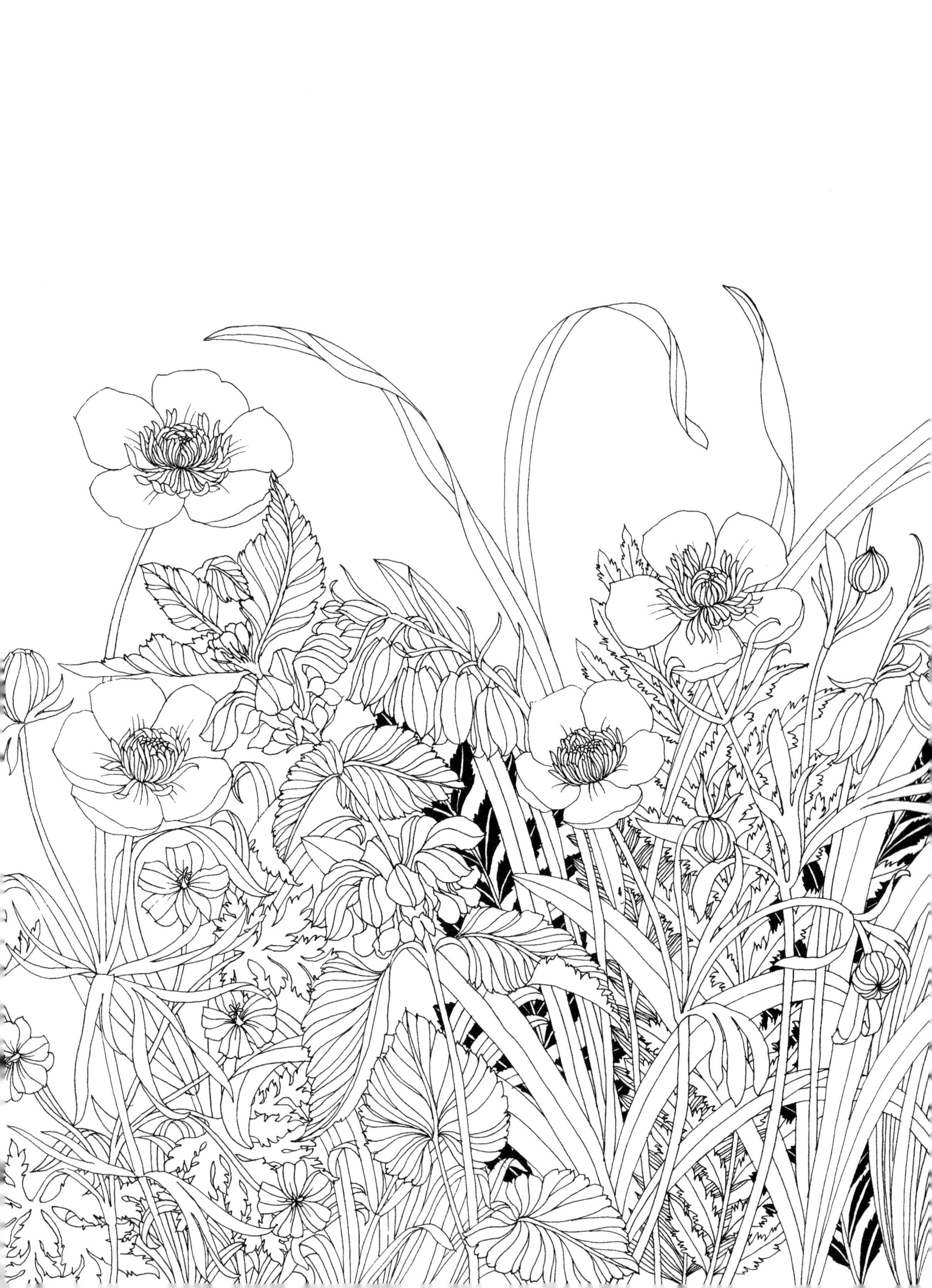

Bluebell, Buttercup, Greater Stitchwort, Herb Robert, Ramsons, White Deadnettle

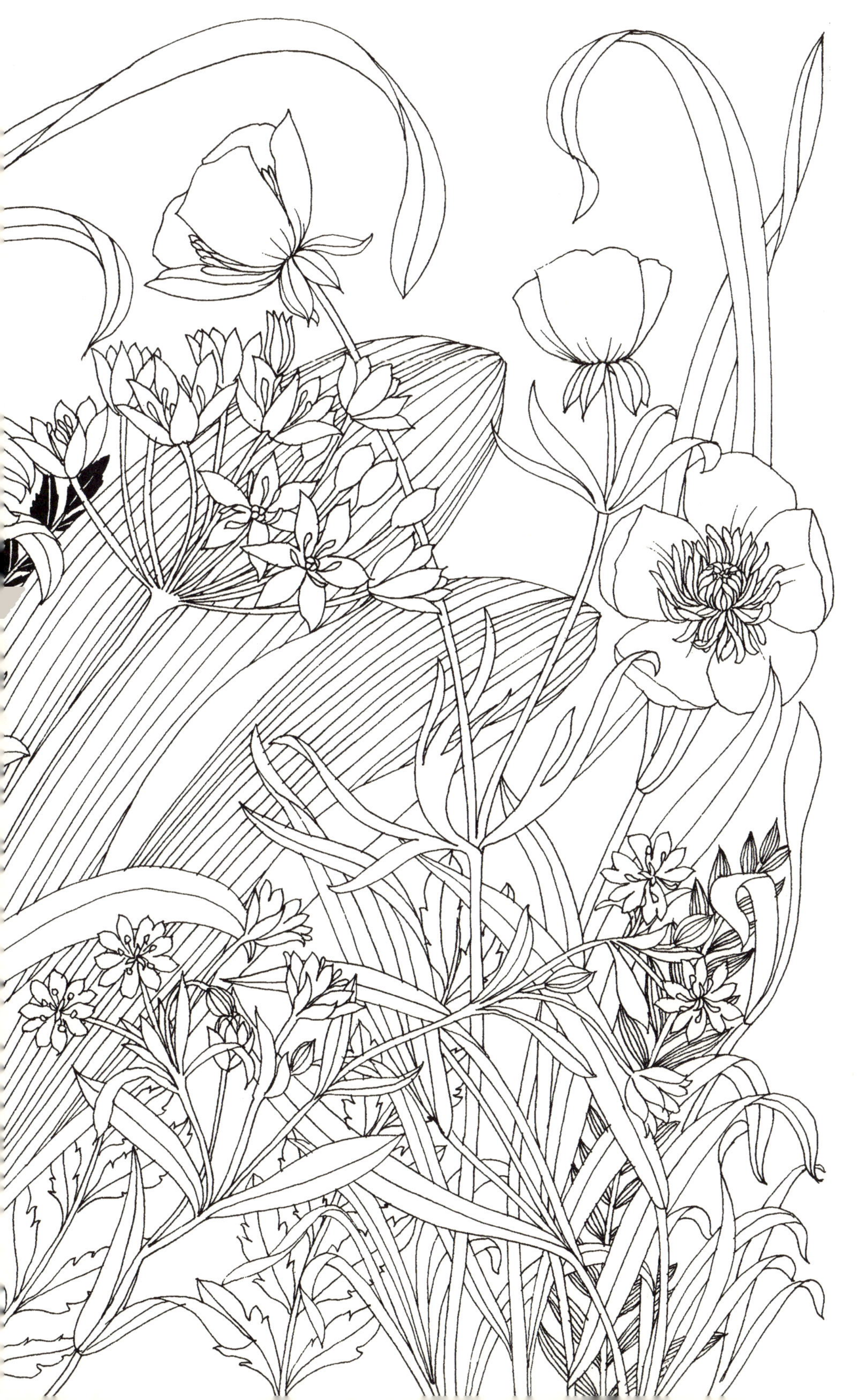

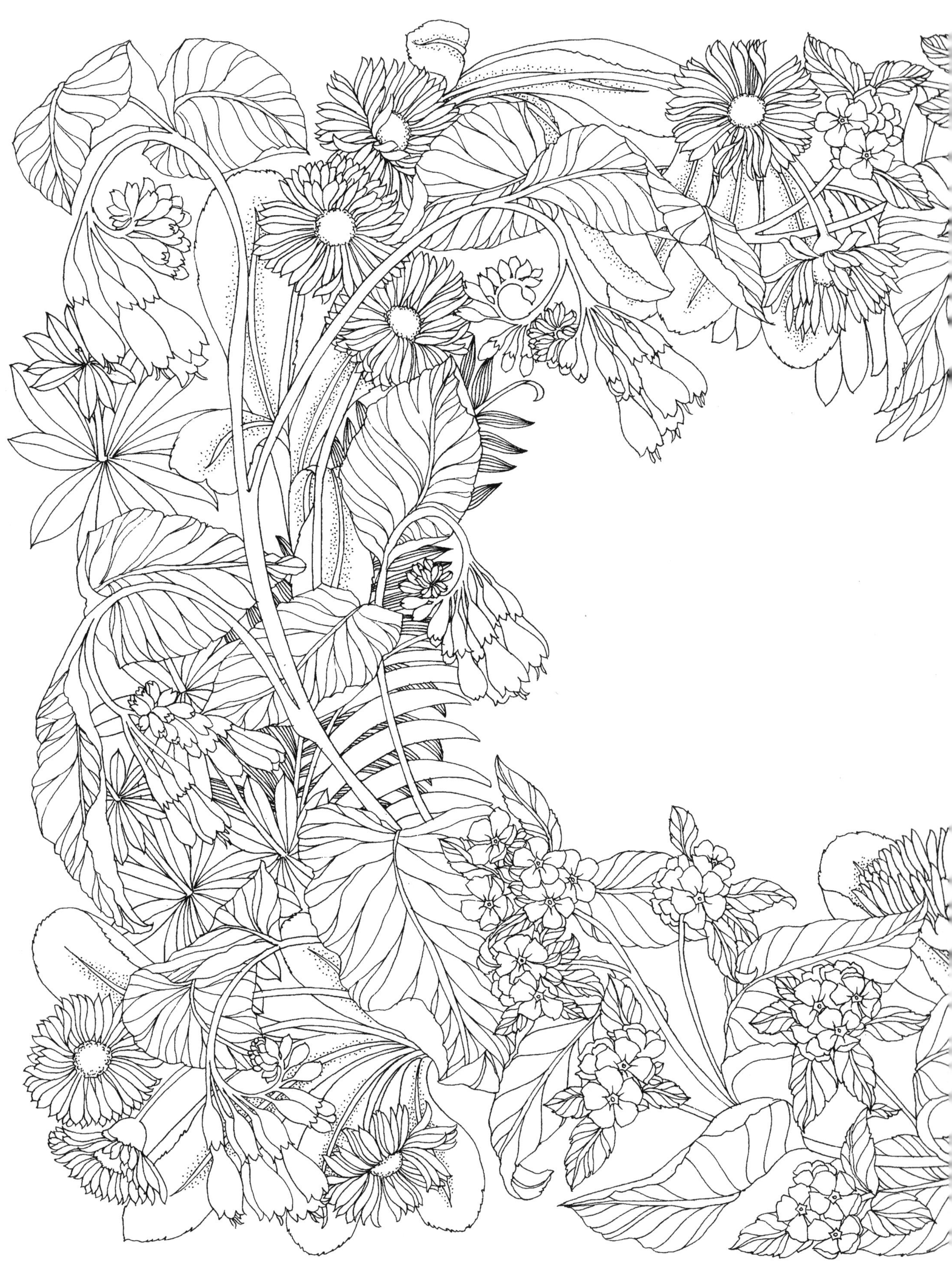

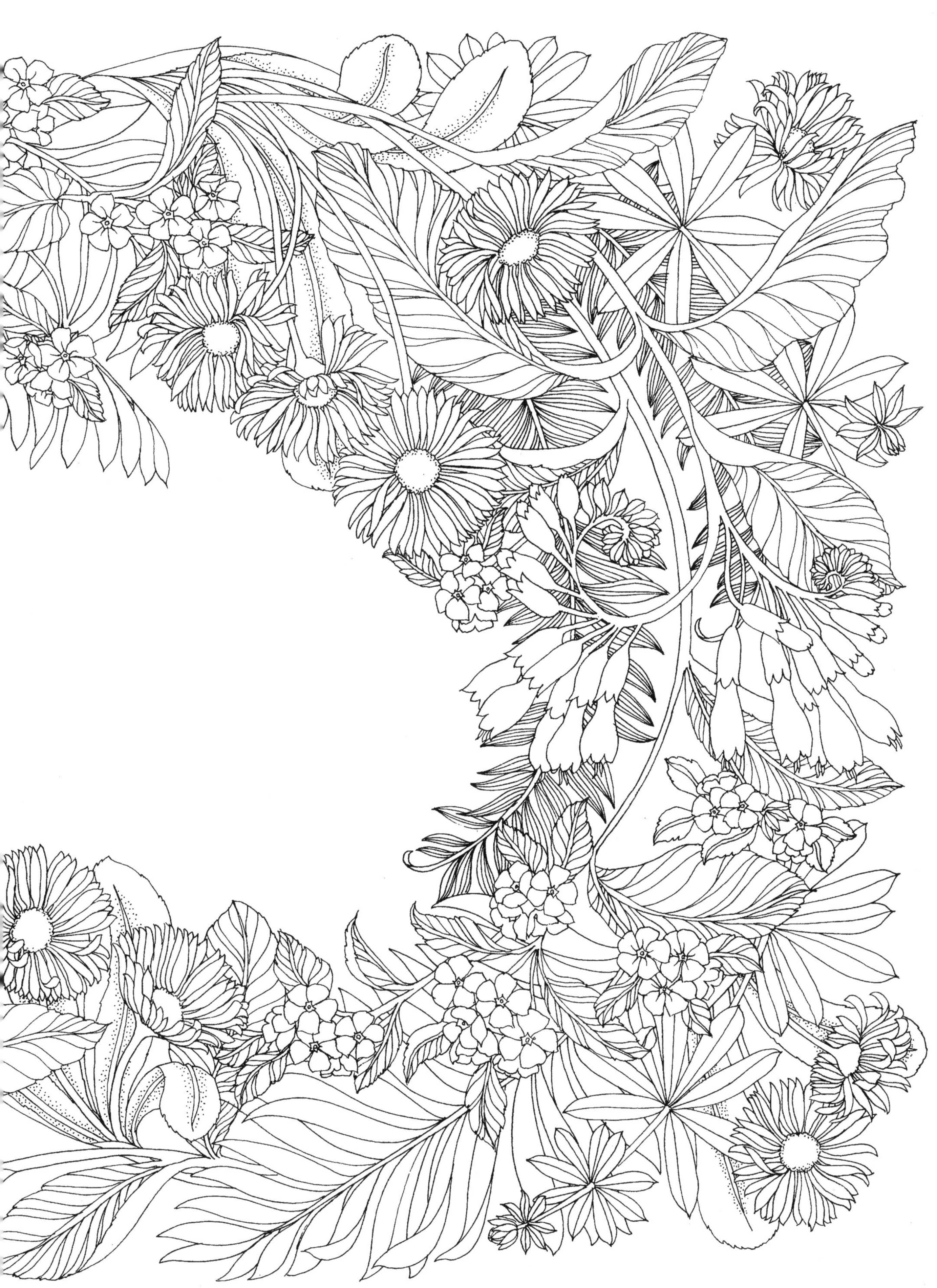

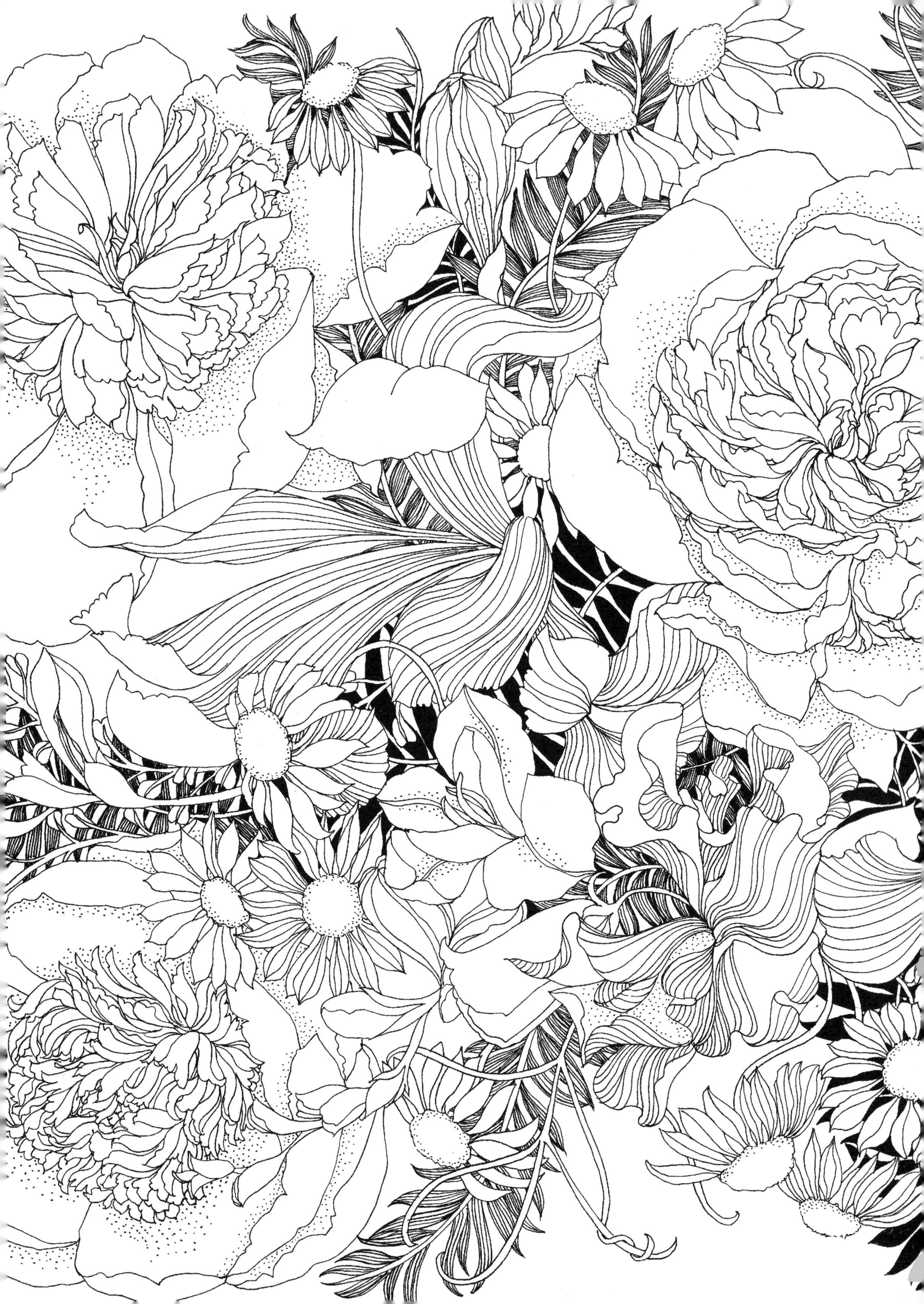

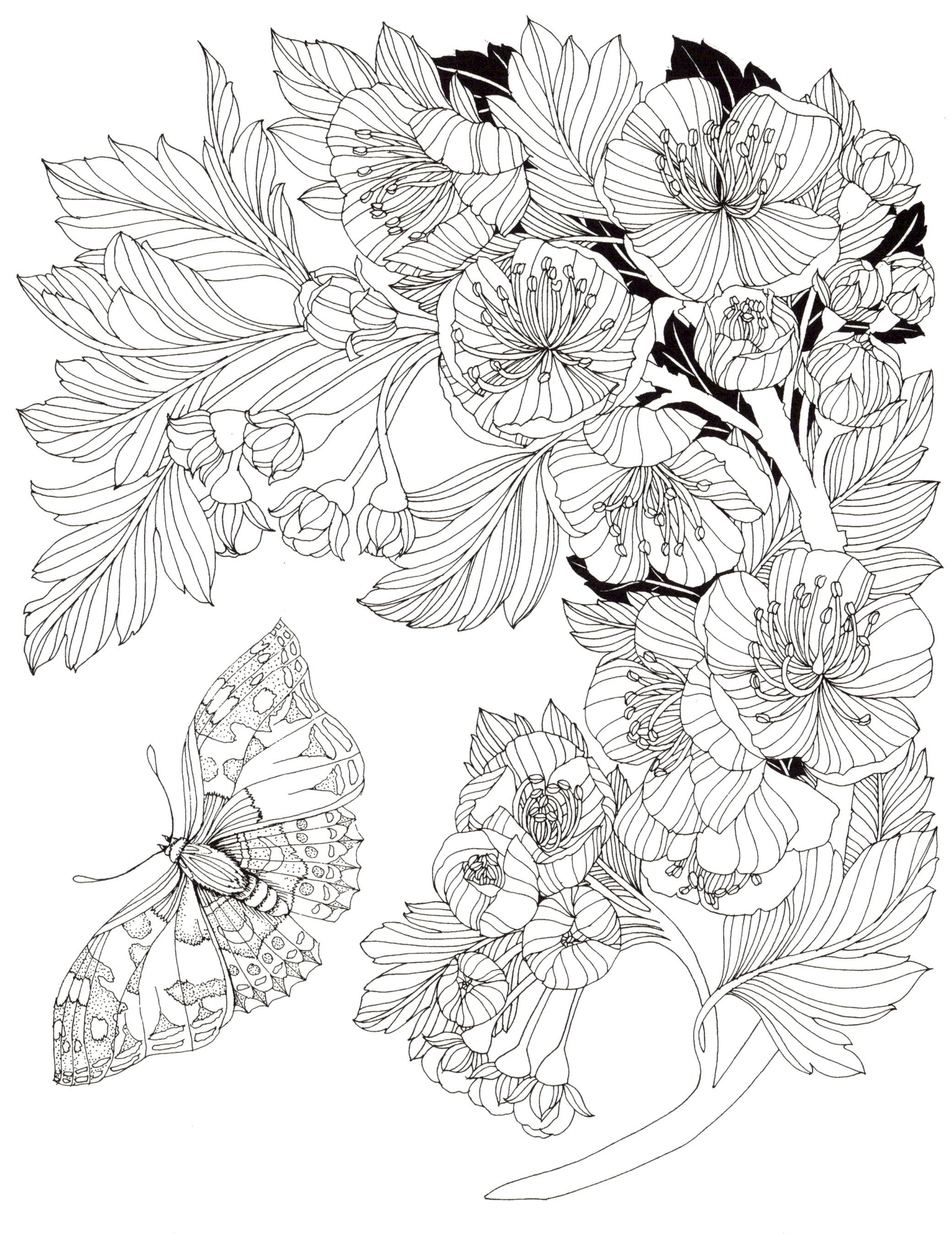

Hawthron,
Painted Lady Butterfly

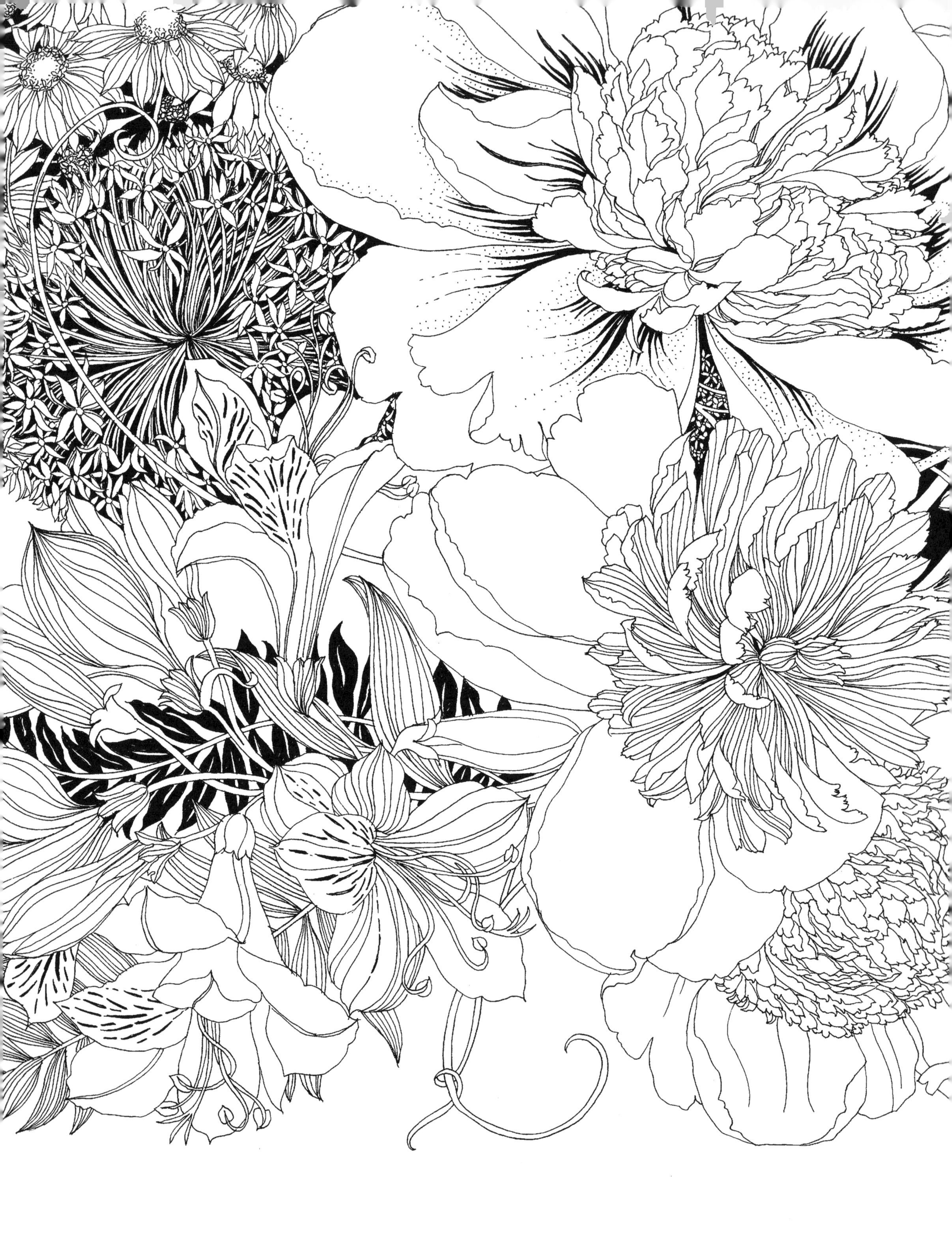

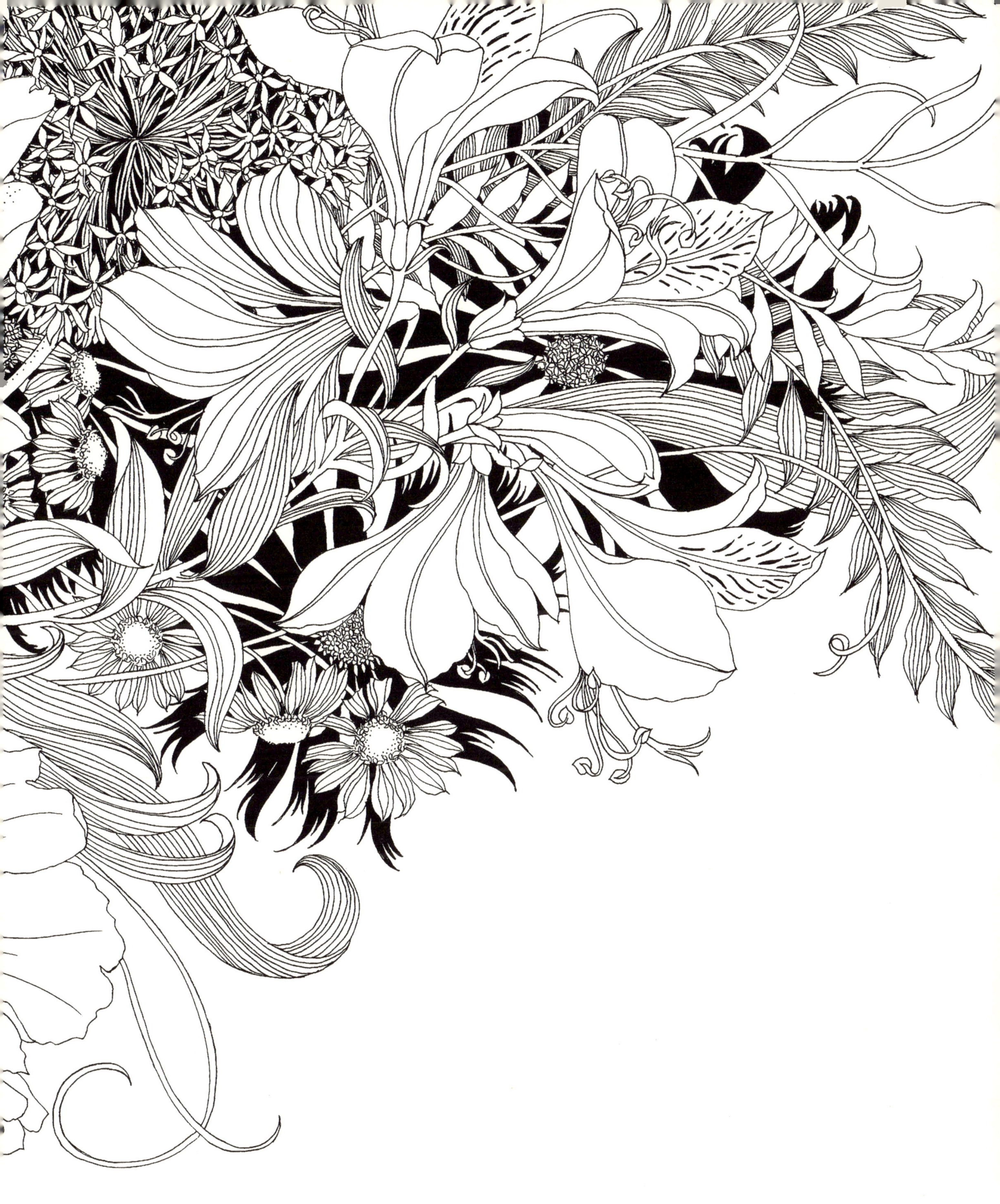

Ornamental Onion, Peony,
Peruvian Lily, Shasta Daisy

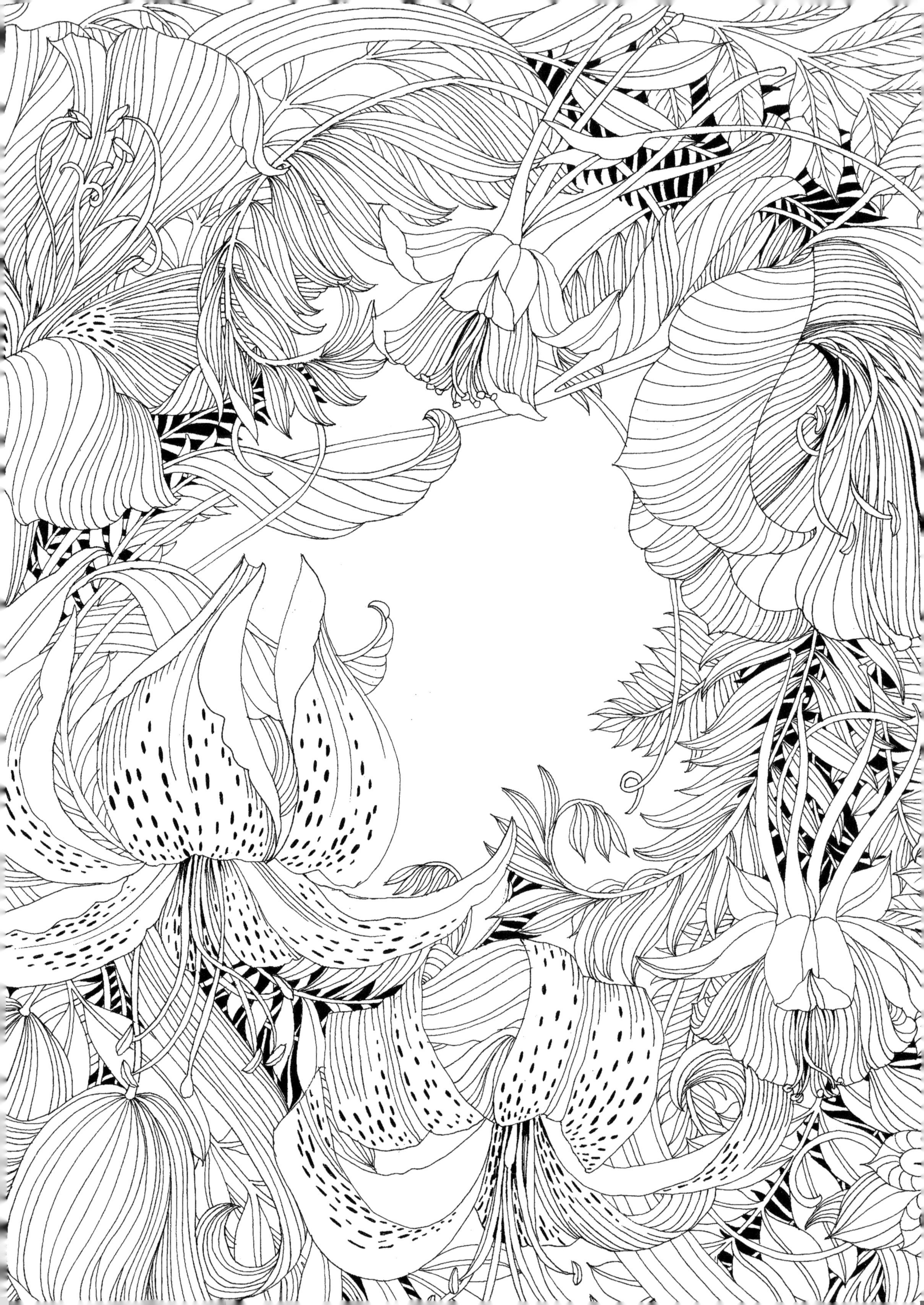

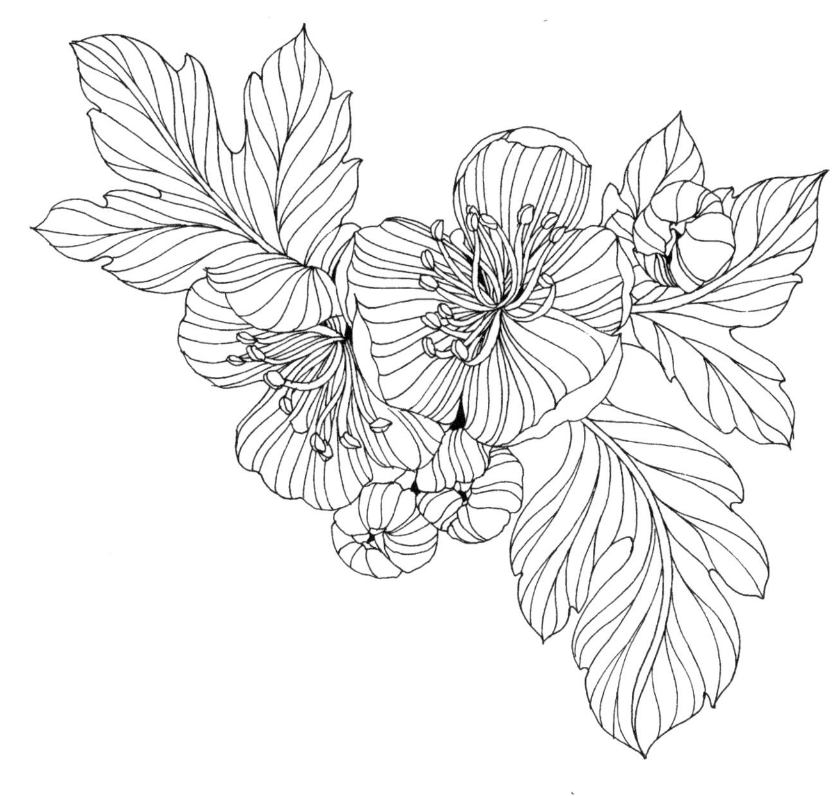

Gives not the hawthorn bush a sweeter shade
To shepherds looking on their silly sheep
Than doth a rich embroider'd canopy
To kings that fear their subjects' treachery?

WILLIAM SHAKESPEARE

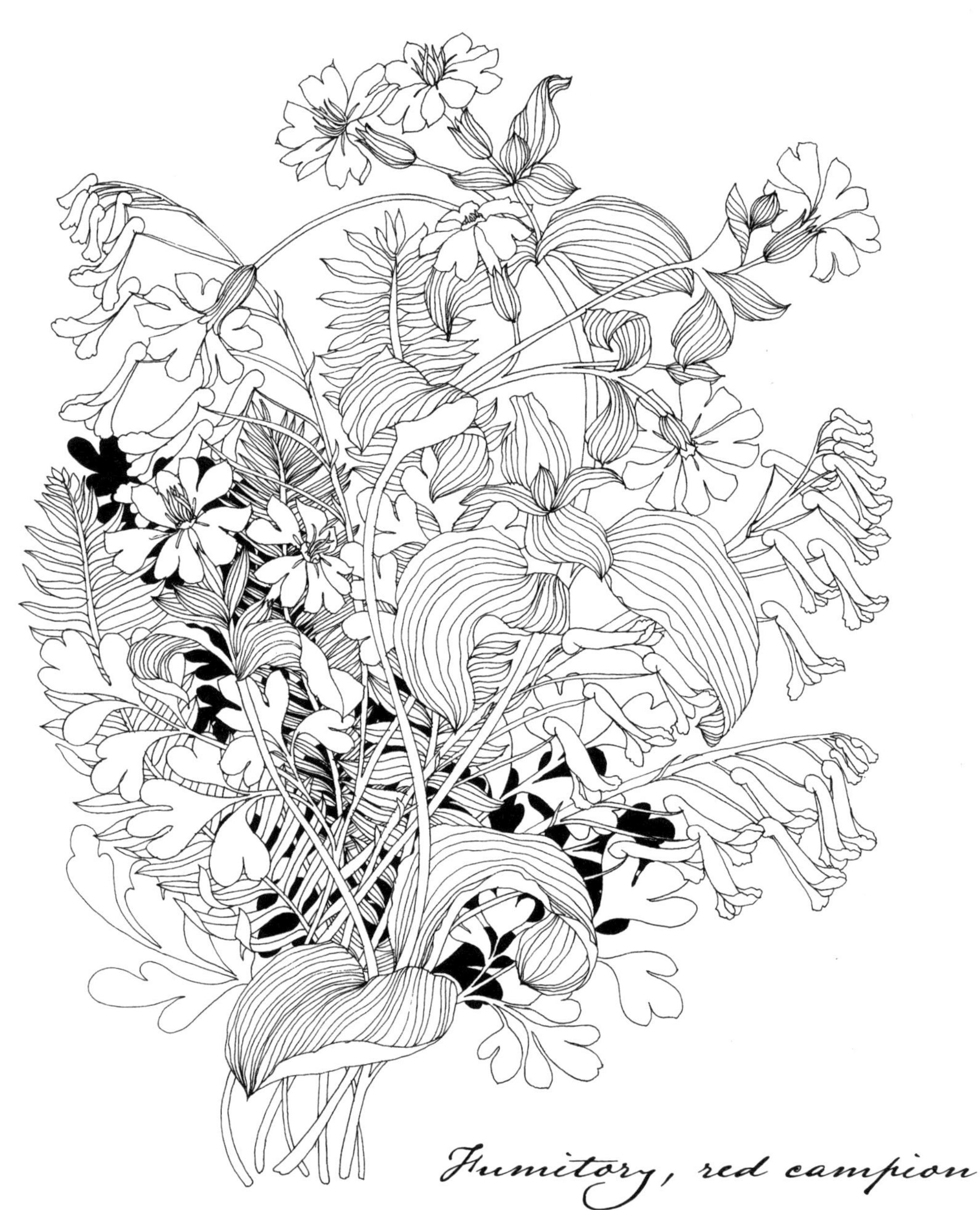

Fumitory, red campion

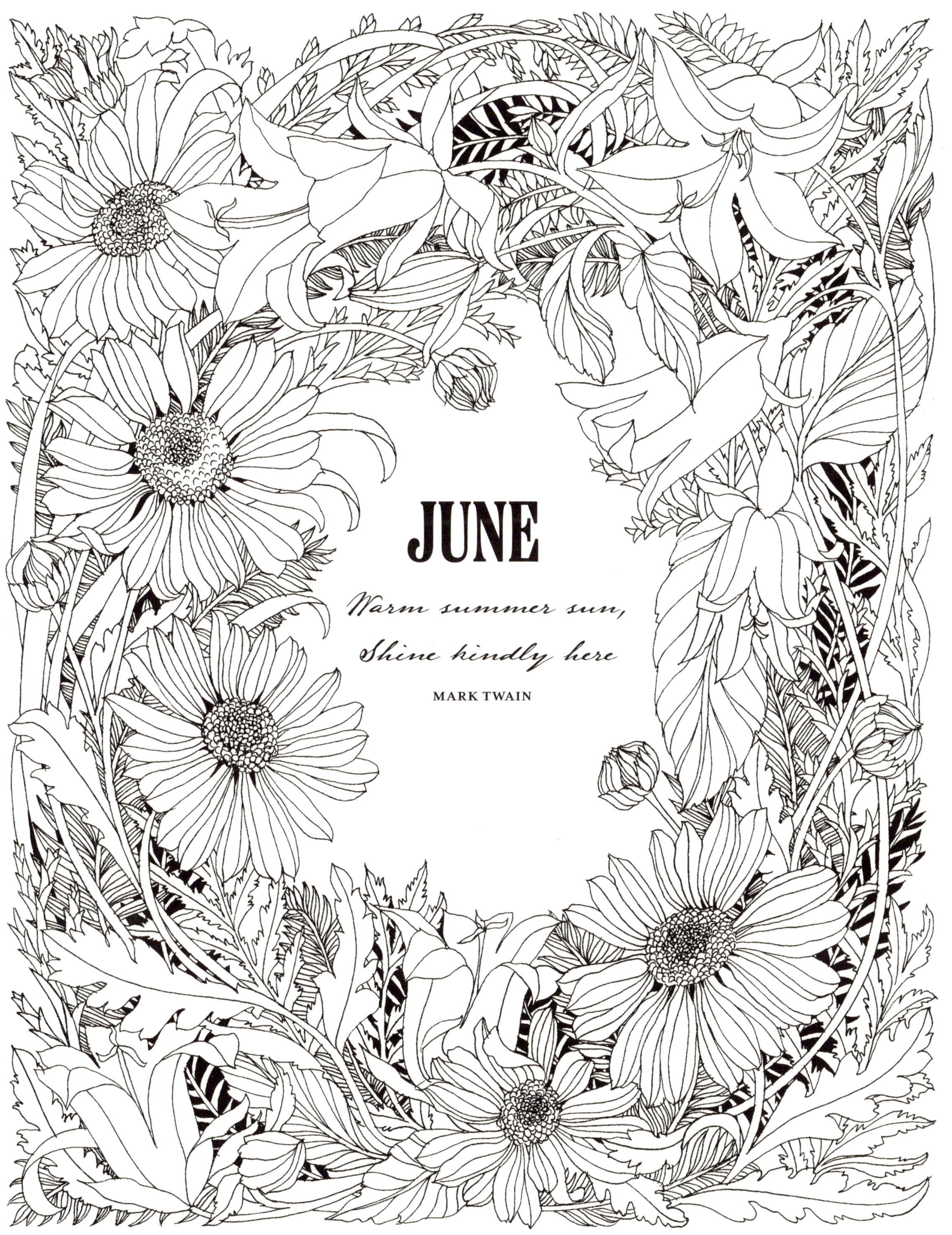
JUNE
Warm summer sun,
Shine kindly here
MARK TWAIN

Field Scabious, Marguerite Daisy,
Tufted Vetch, Zigzag Clover

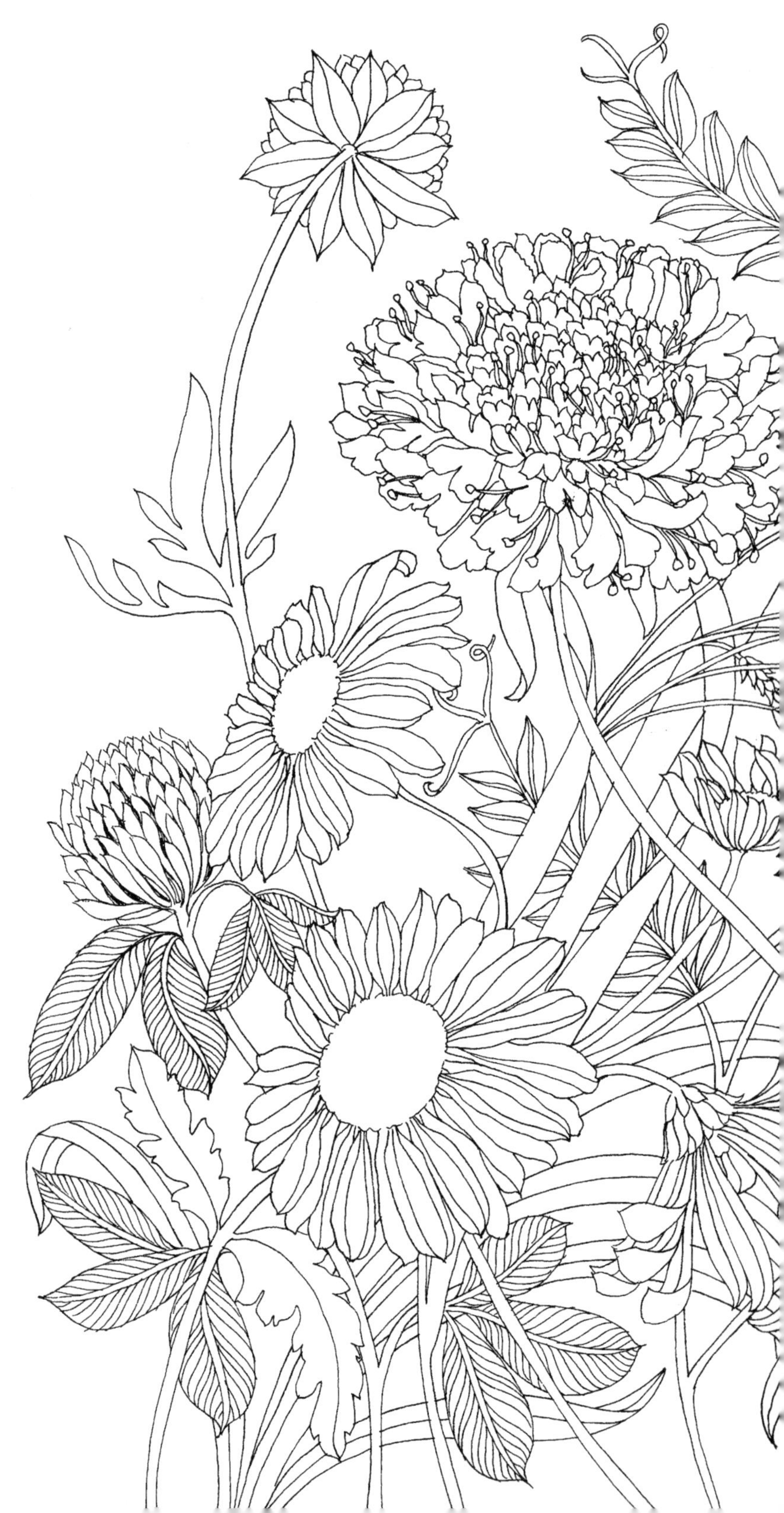

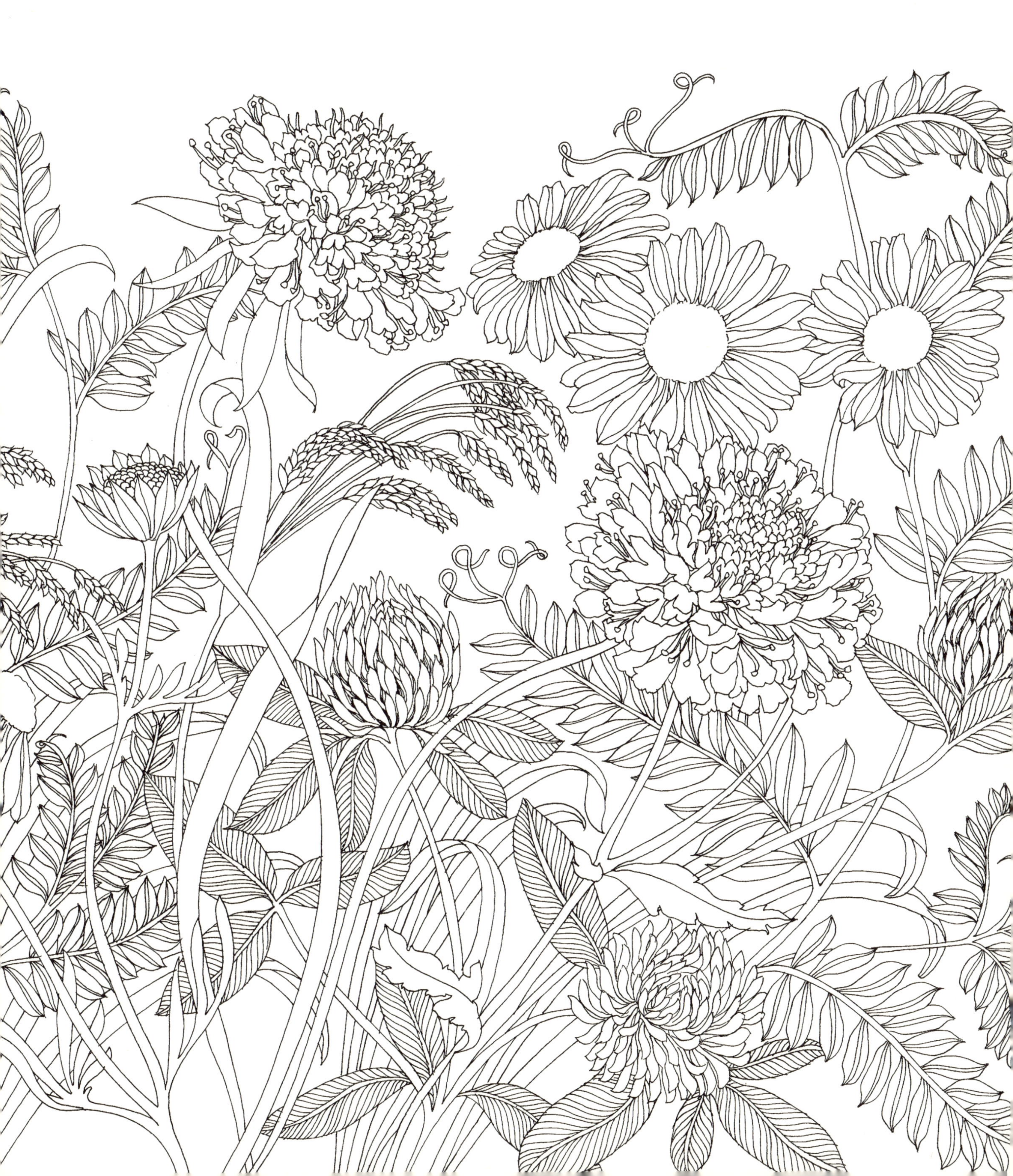

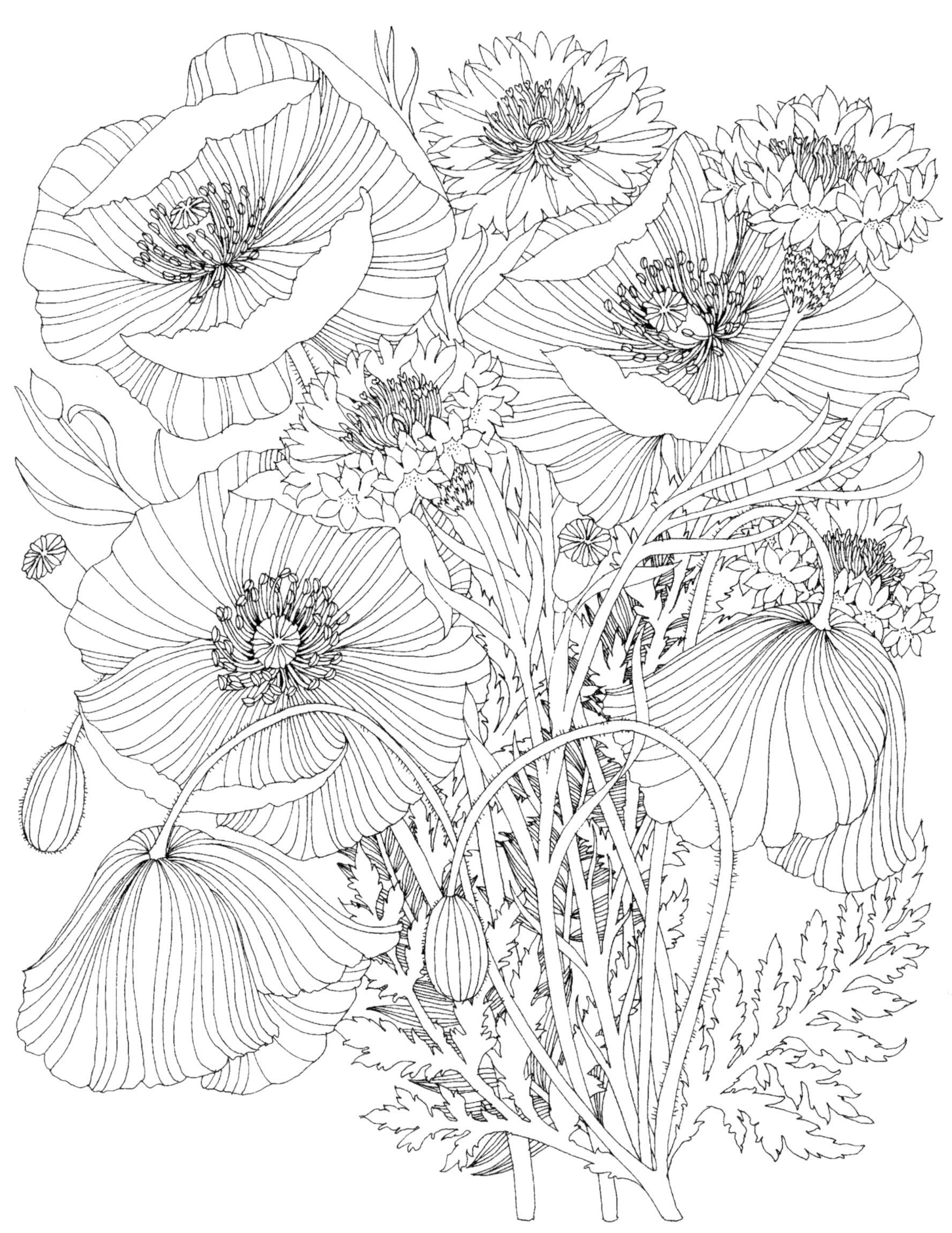

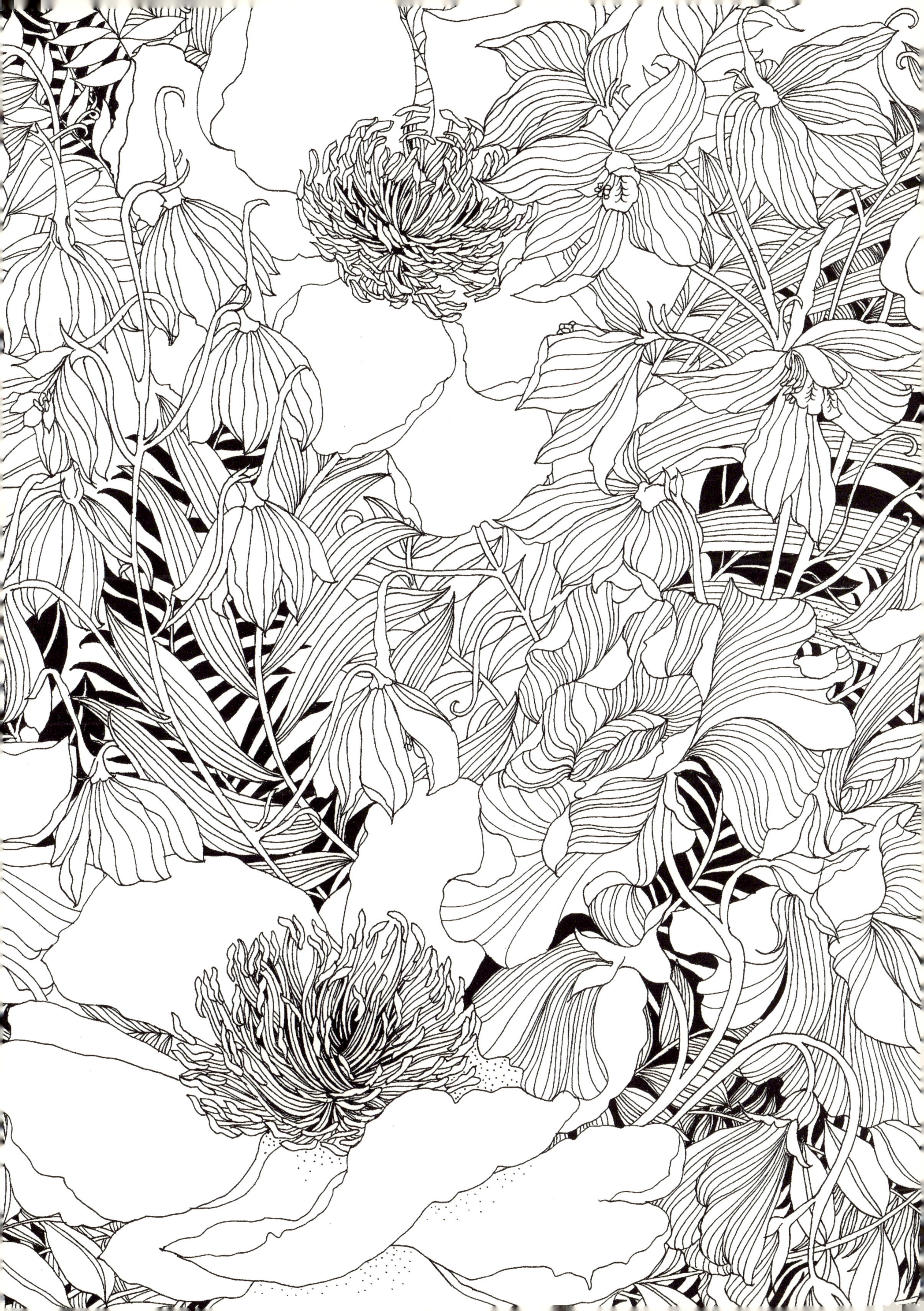

Guelder rose

Lily - of - the - valley

Meadow cranesbill

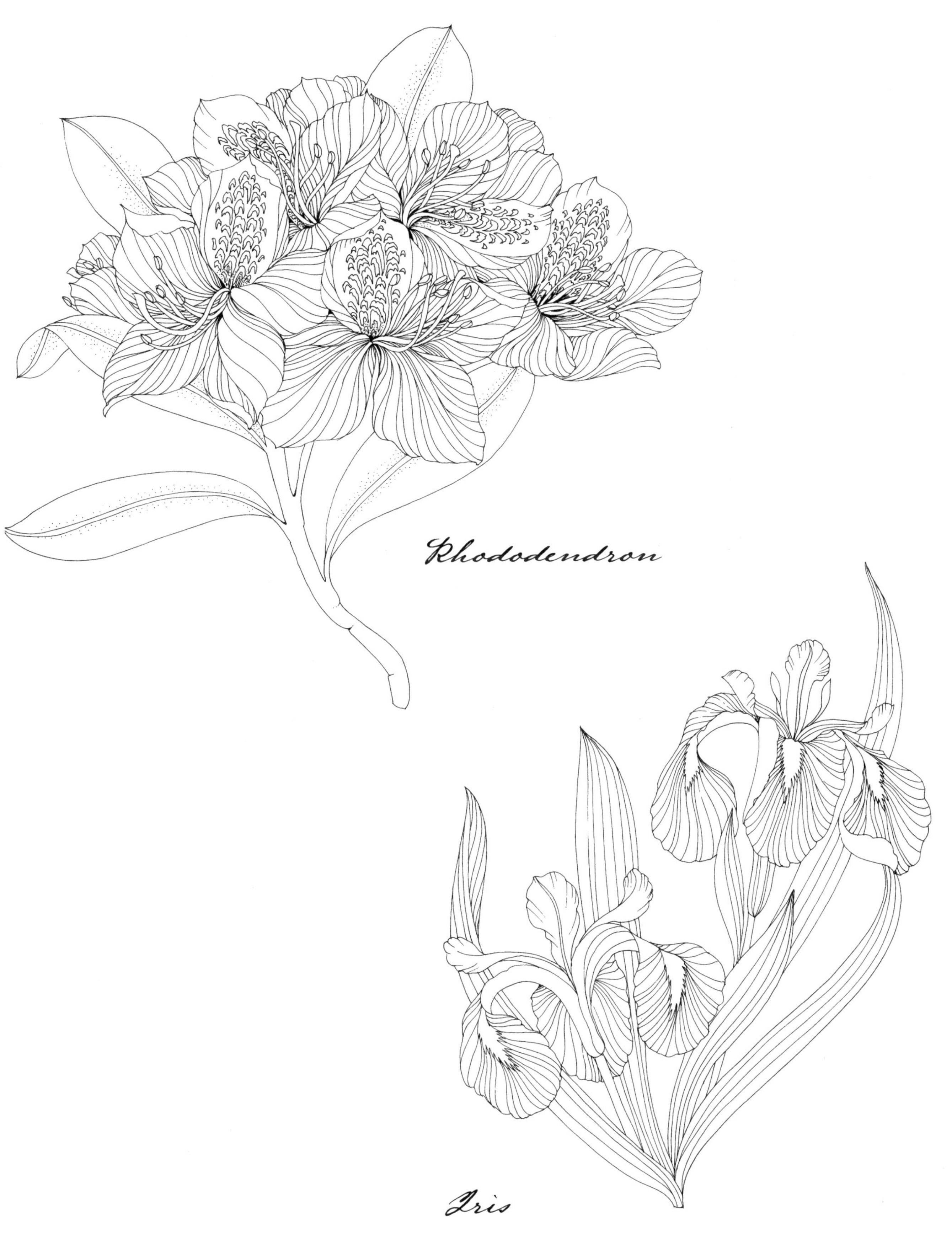
Rhododendron
Iris

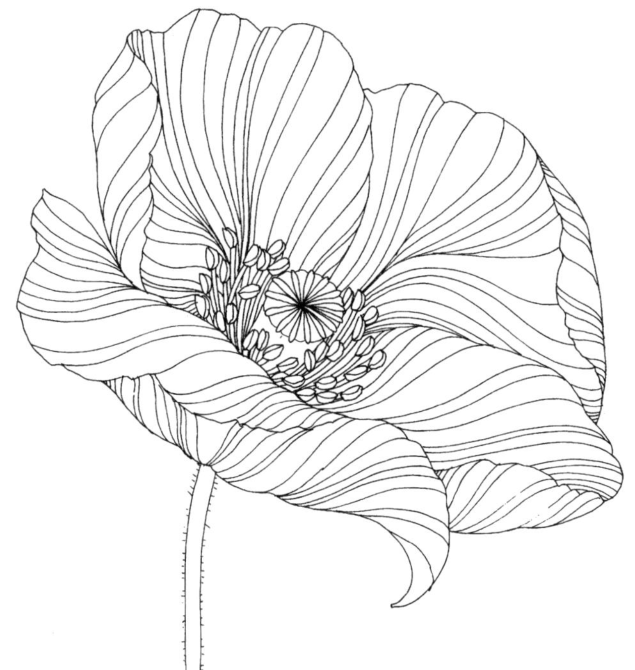

High on a bright sunny bed
A scarlet poppy grew

JANE TAYLOR

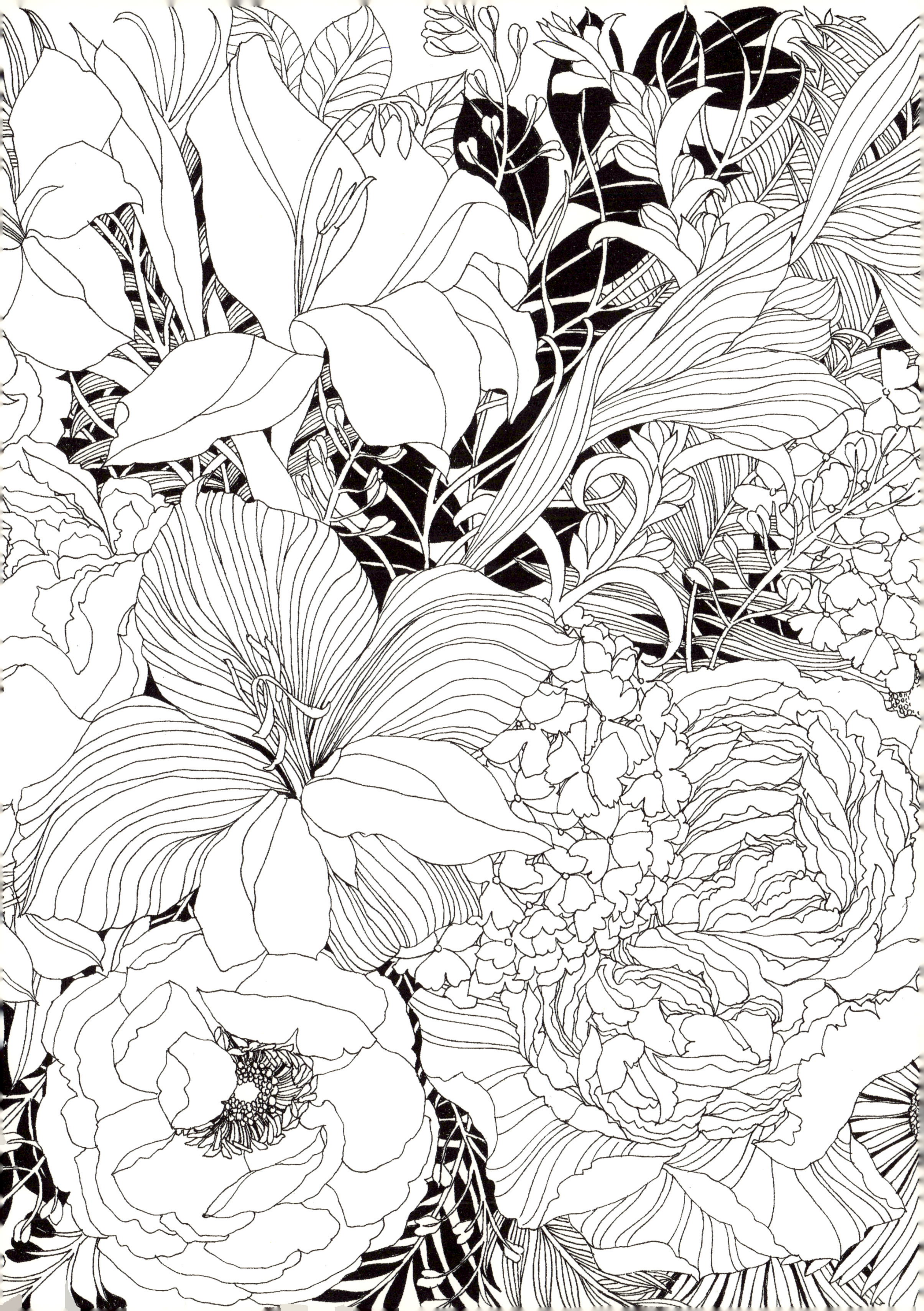

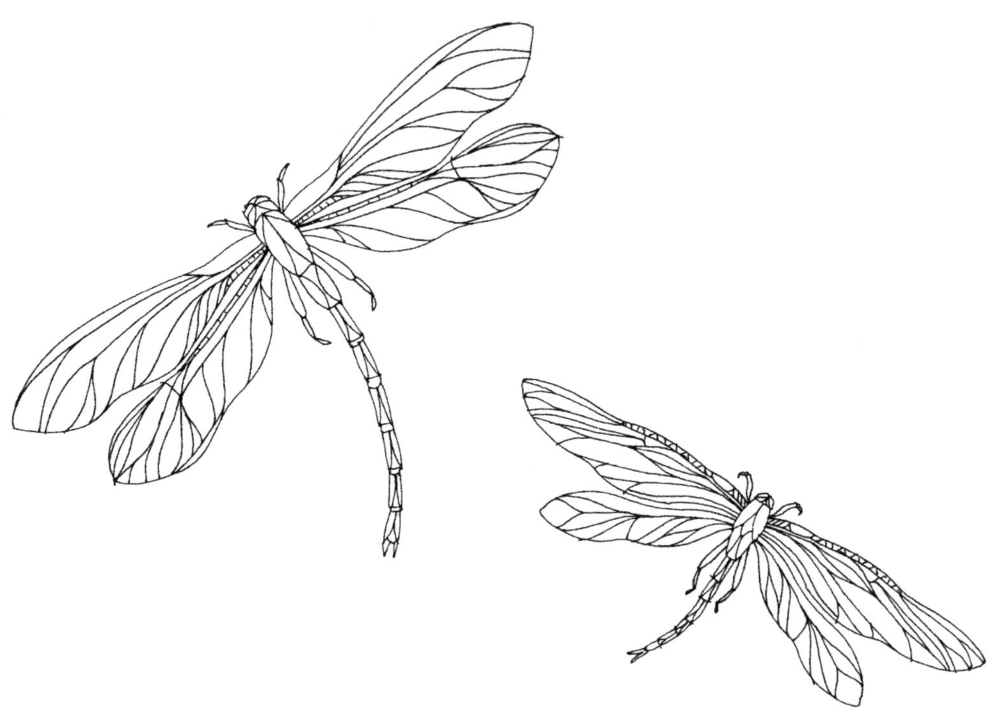

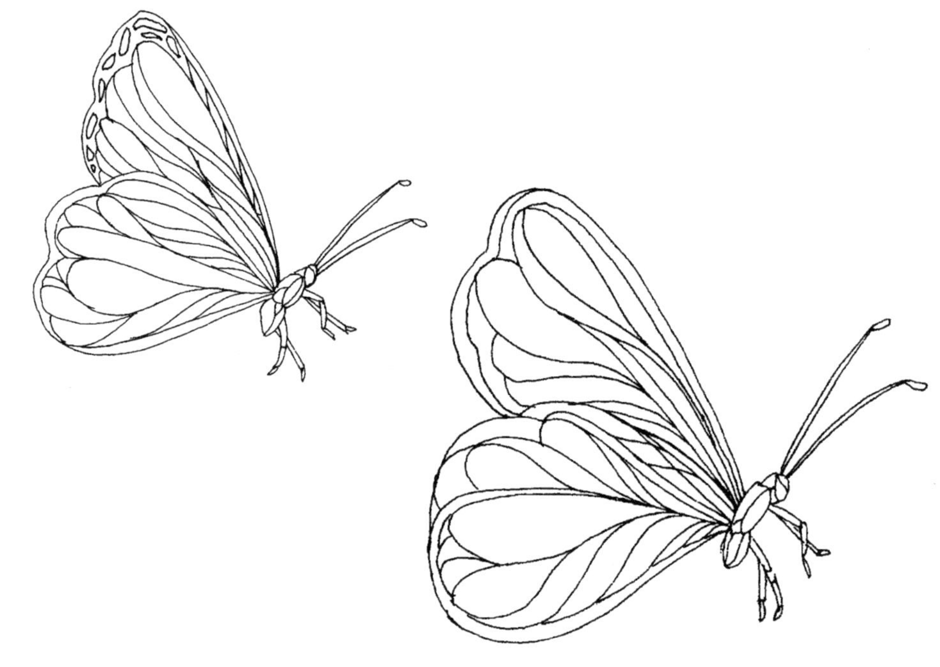

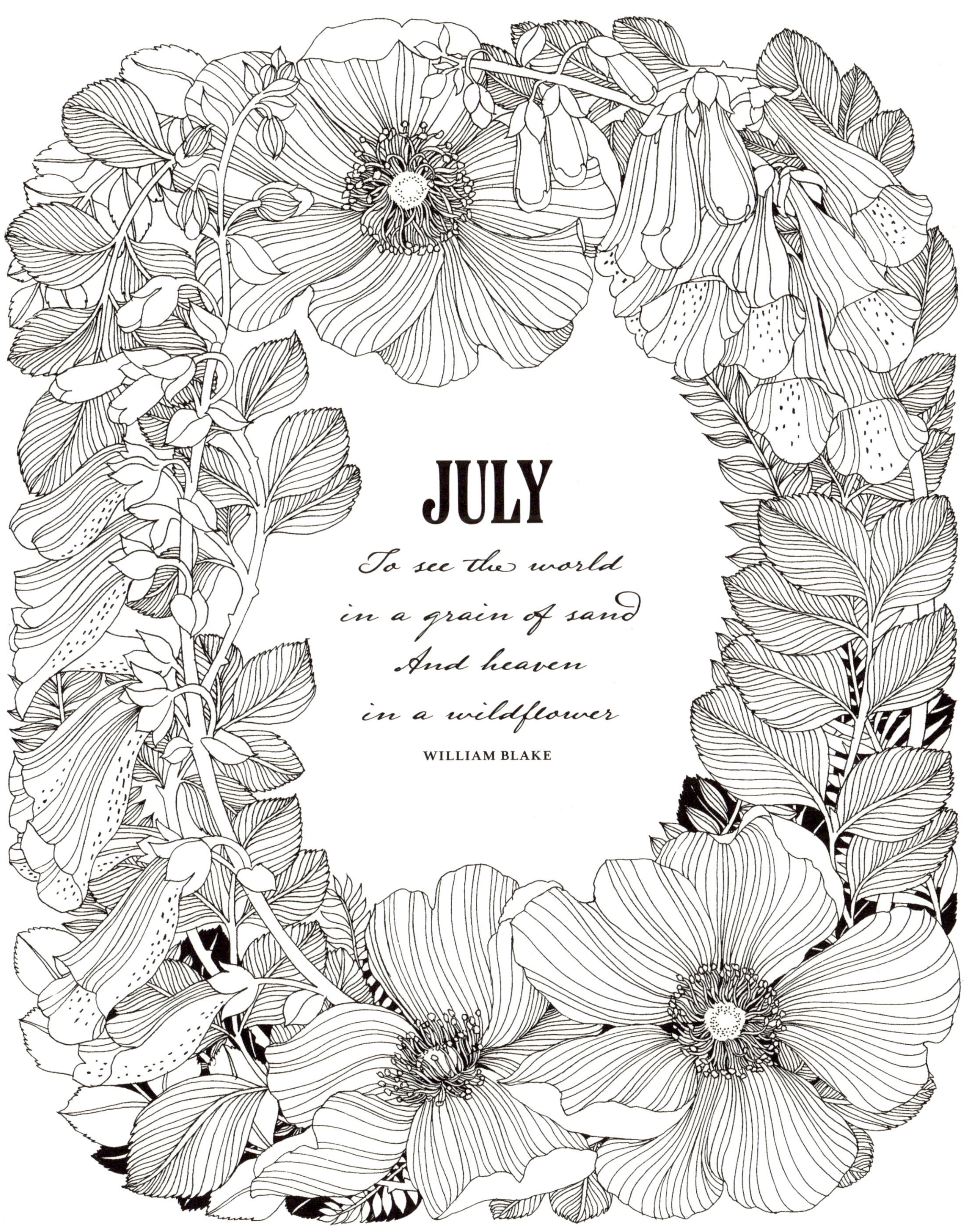

JULY

To see the world
in a grain of sand
And heaven
in a wildflower

WILLIAM BLAKE

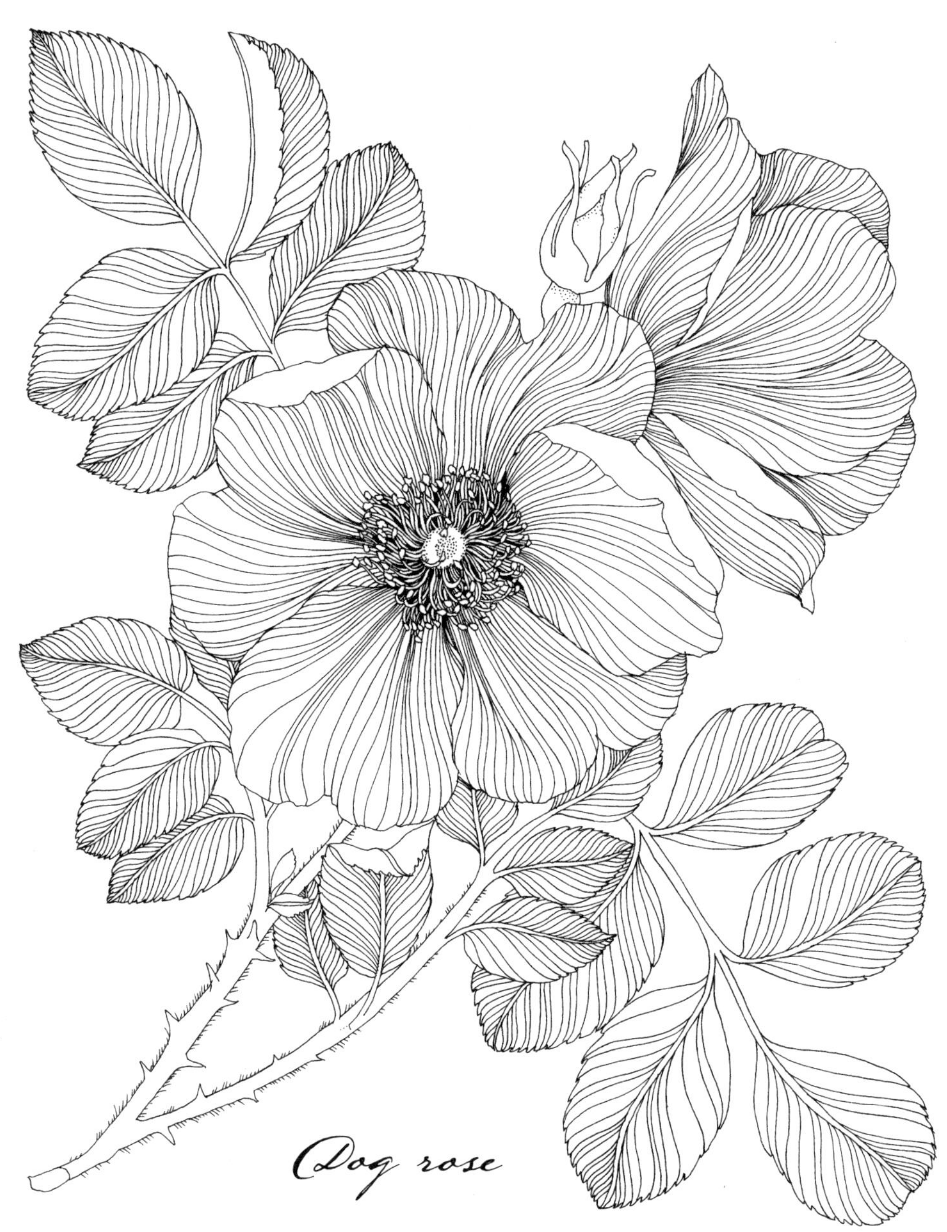
Dog rose

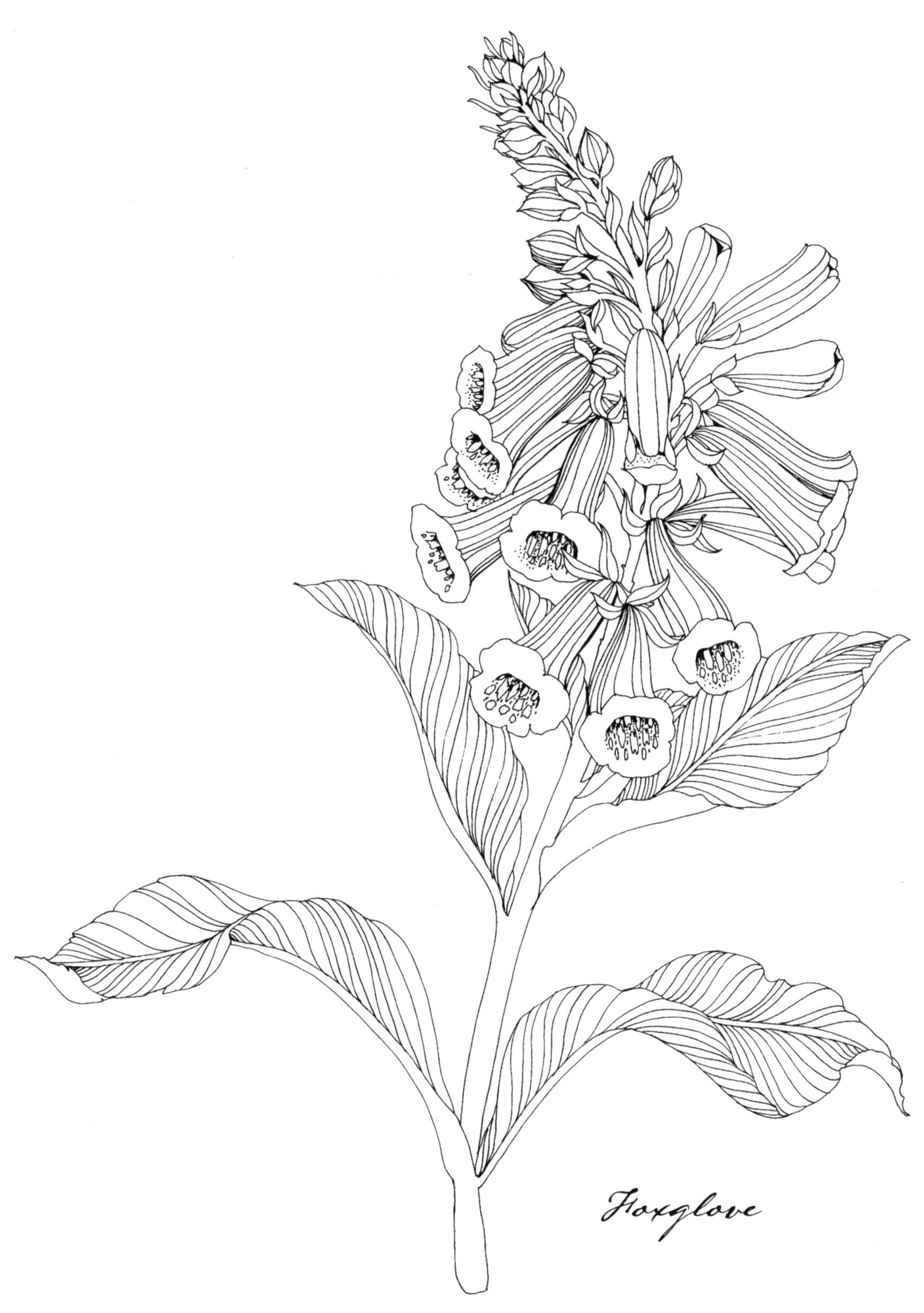
Foxglove

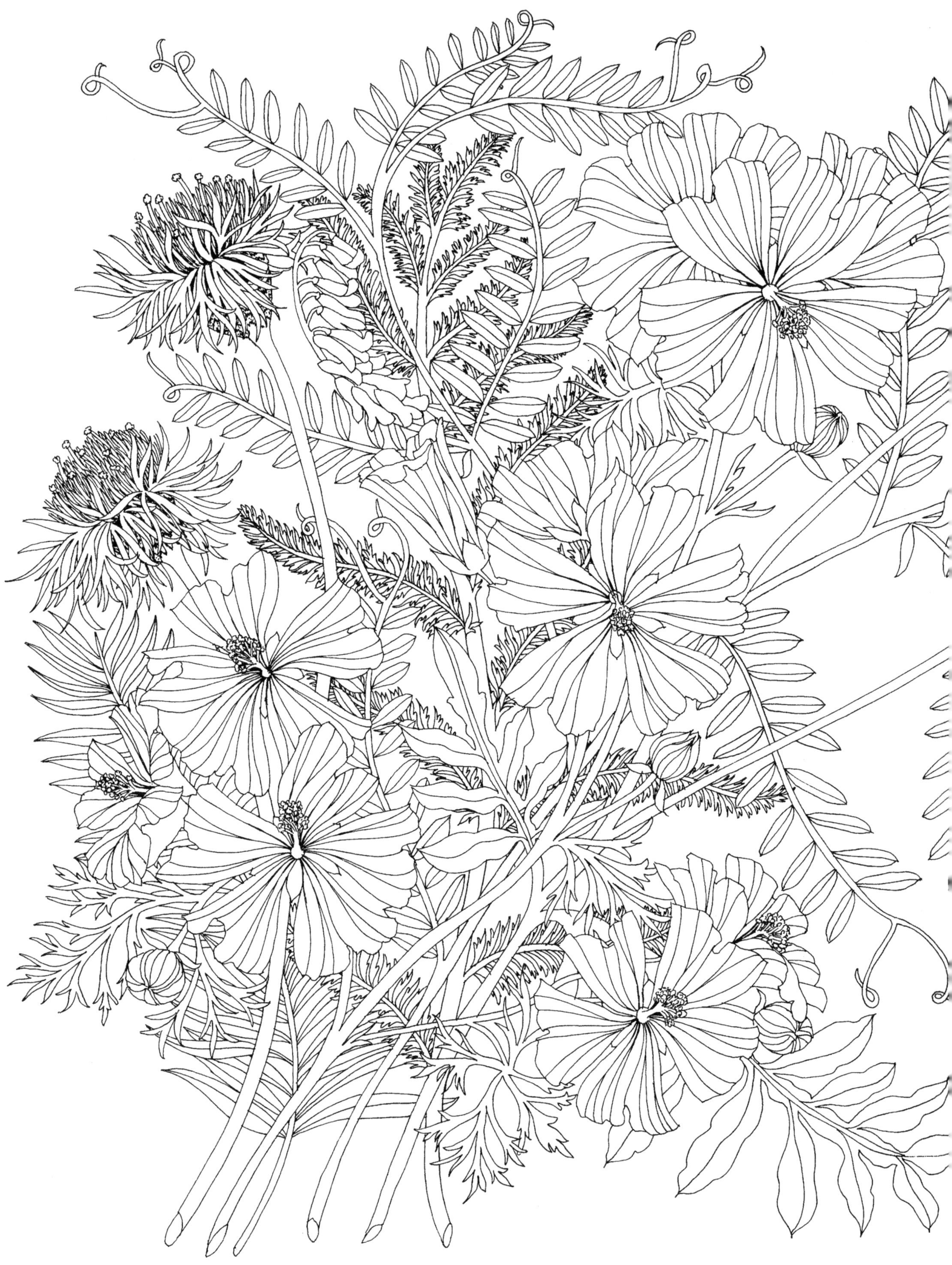

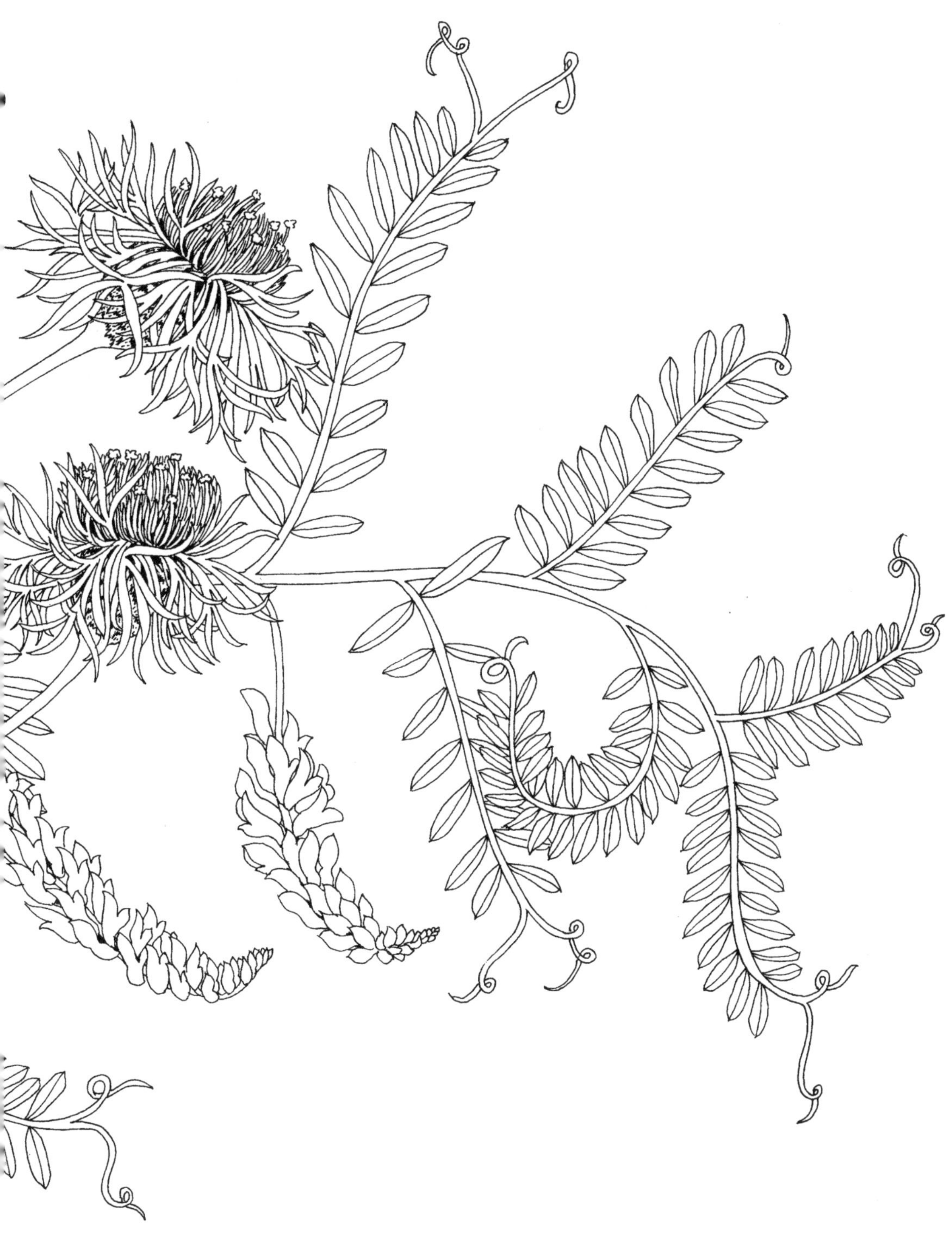

Lesser Knapweed,
Musk Mallow, Tufted Vetch

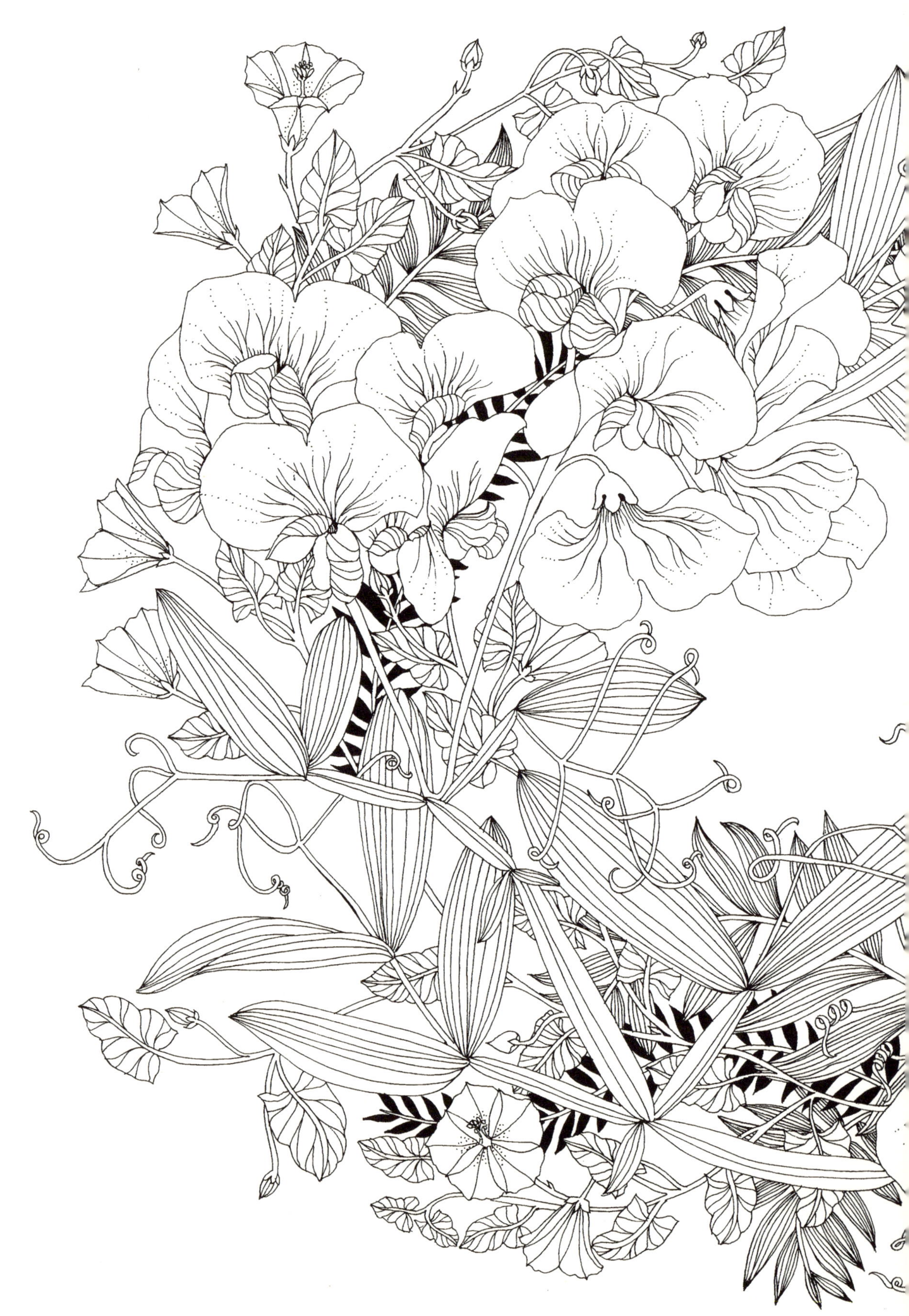

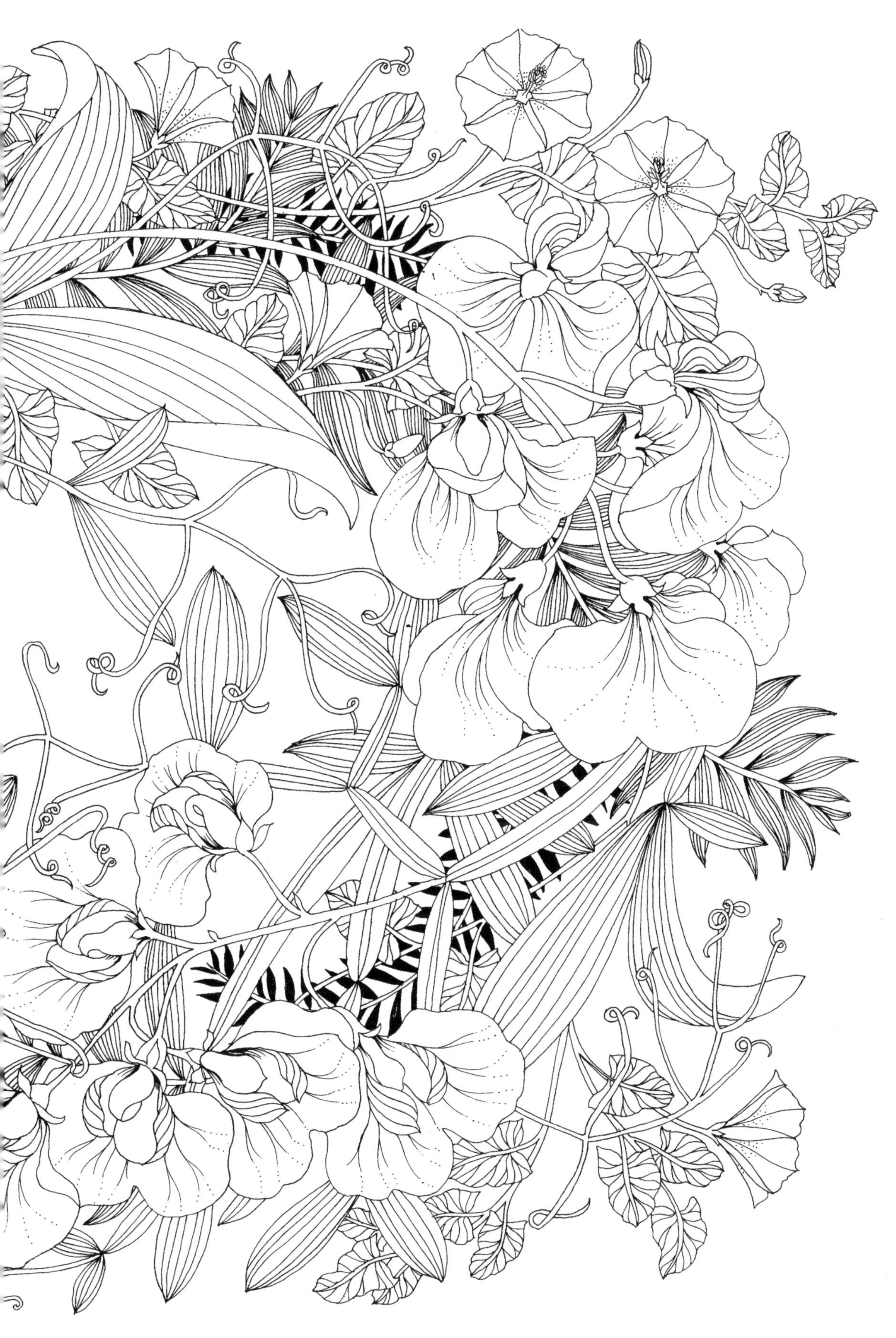

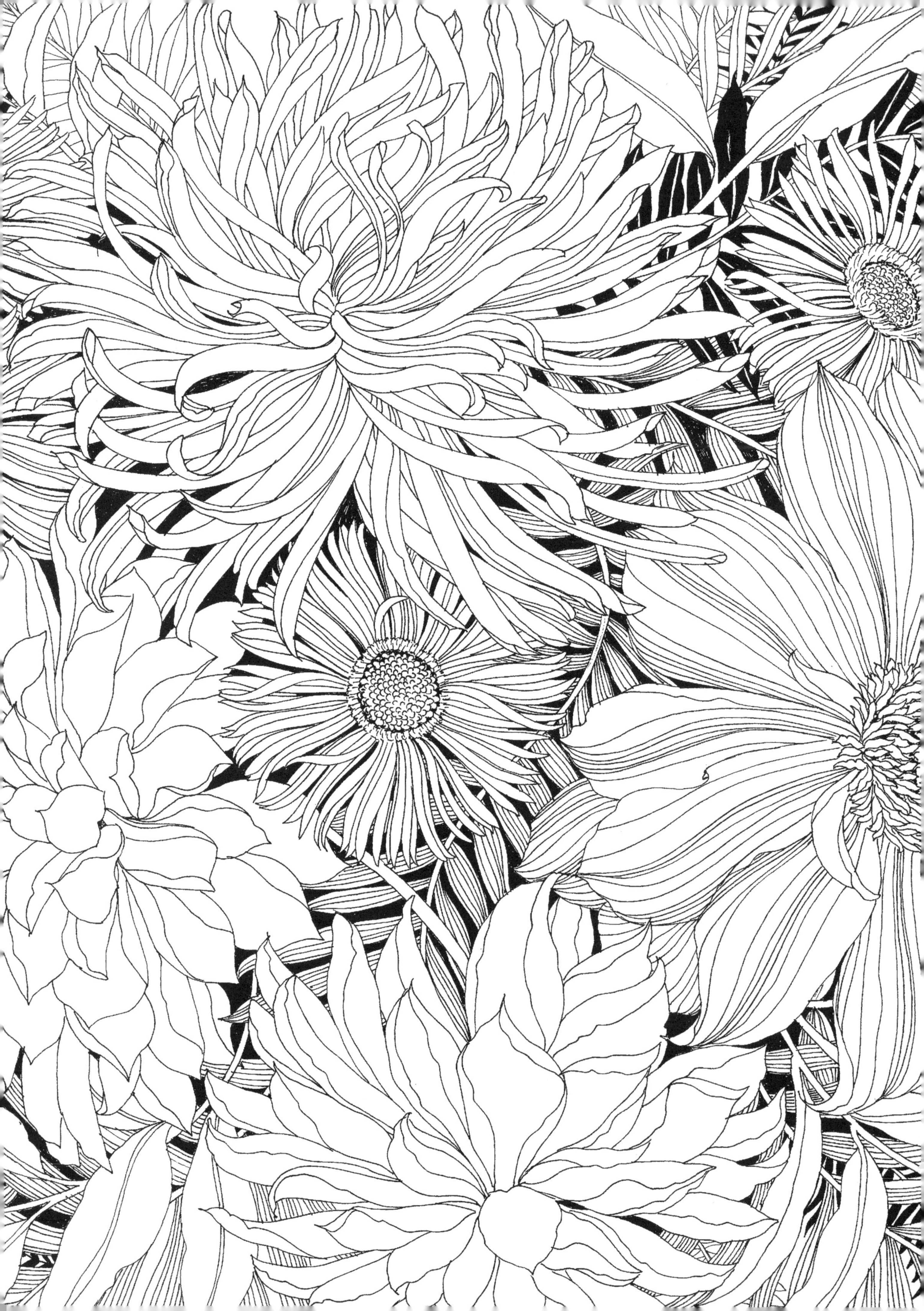

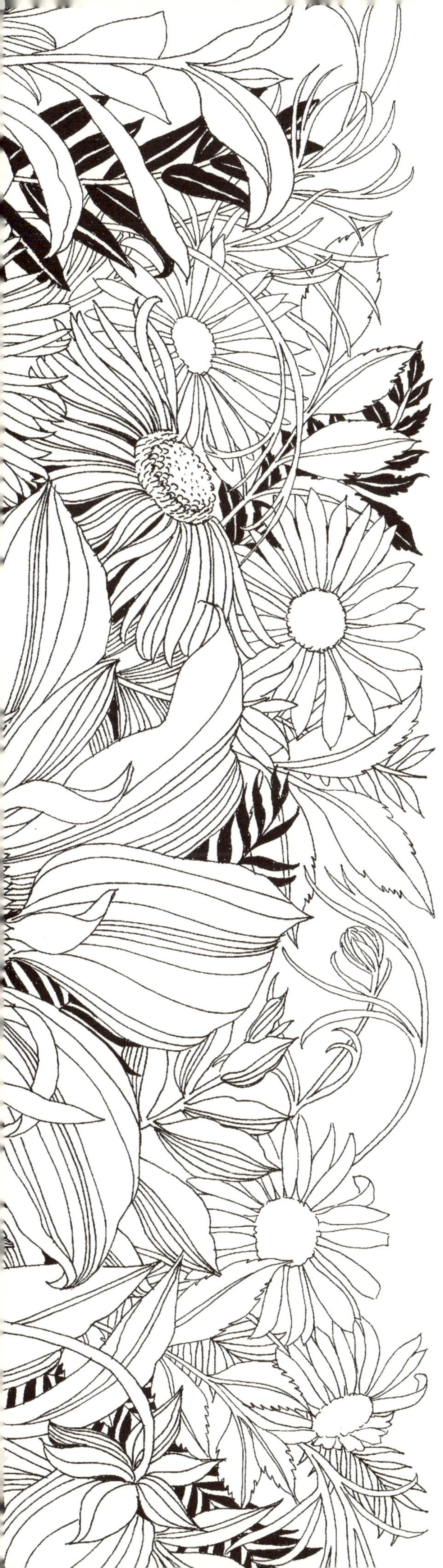

Dahlia, English Daisy,
Michaelmas Daisy

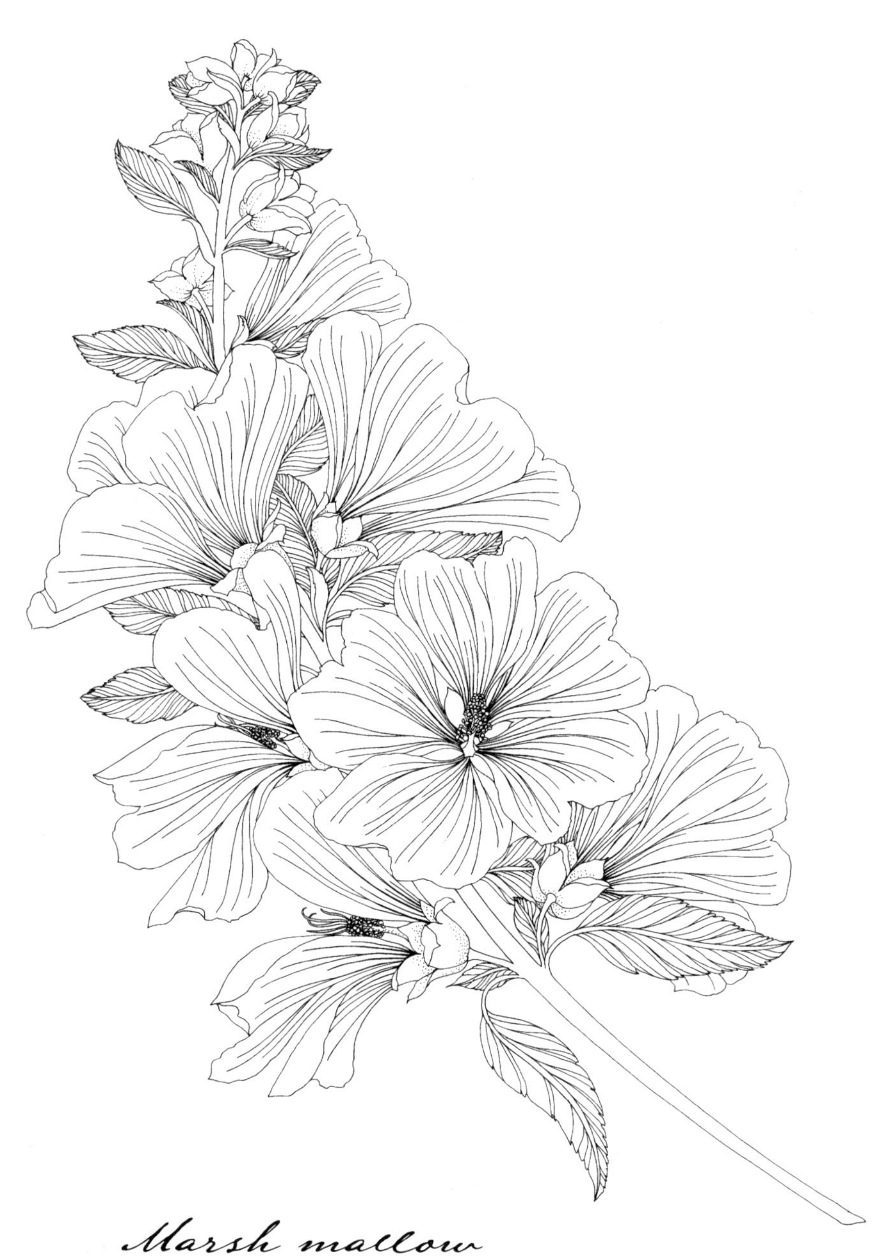

Marsh mallow

AUGUST

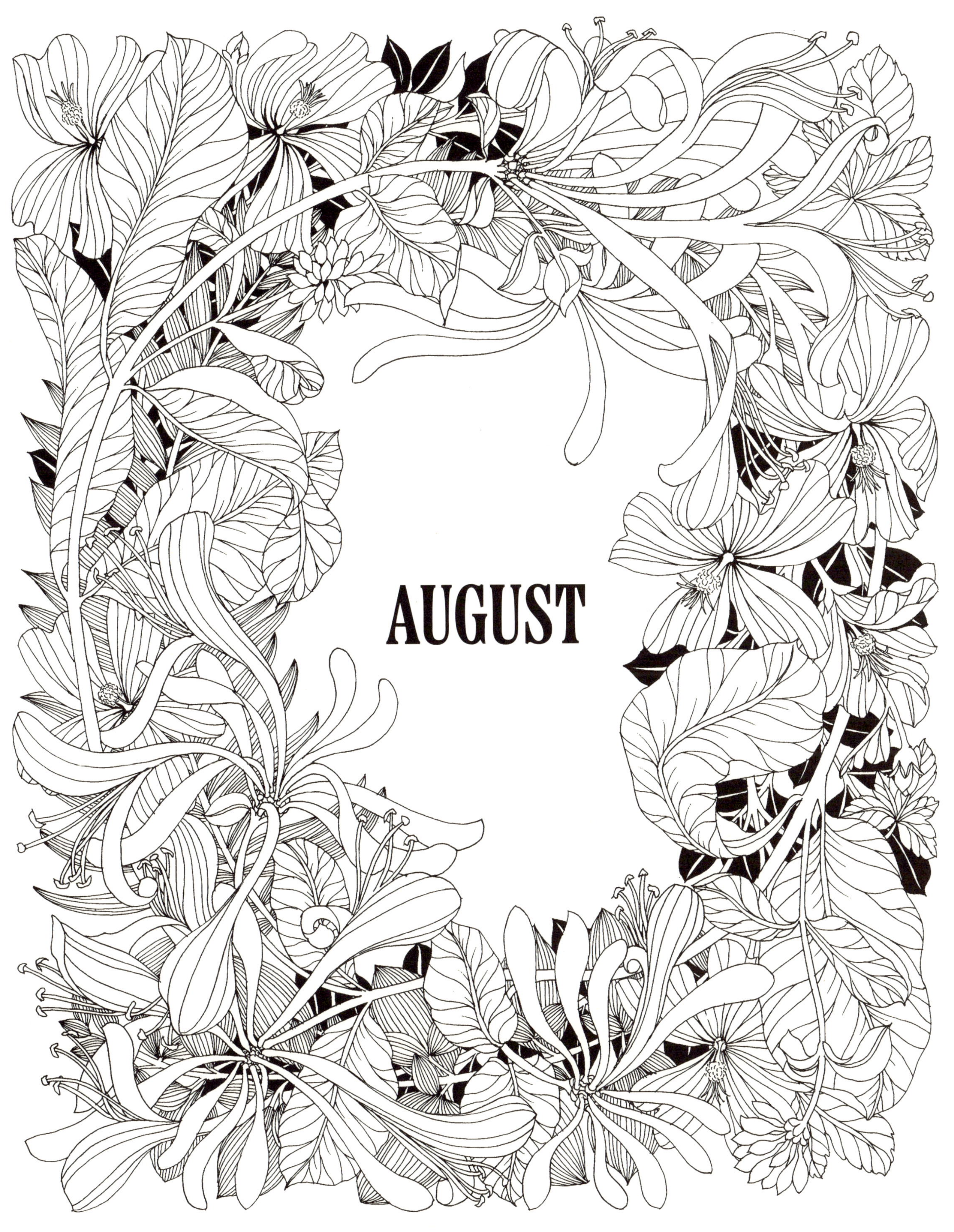

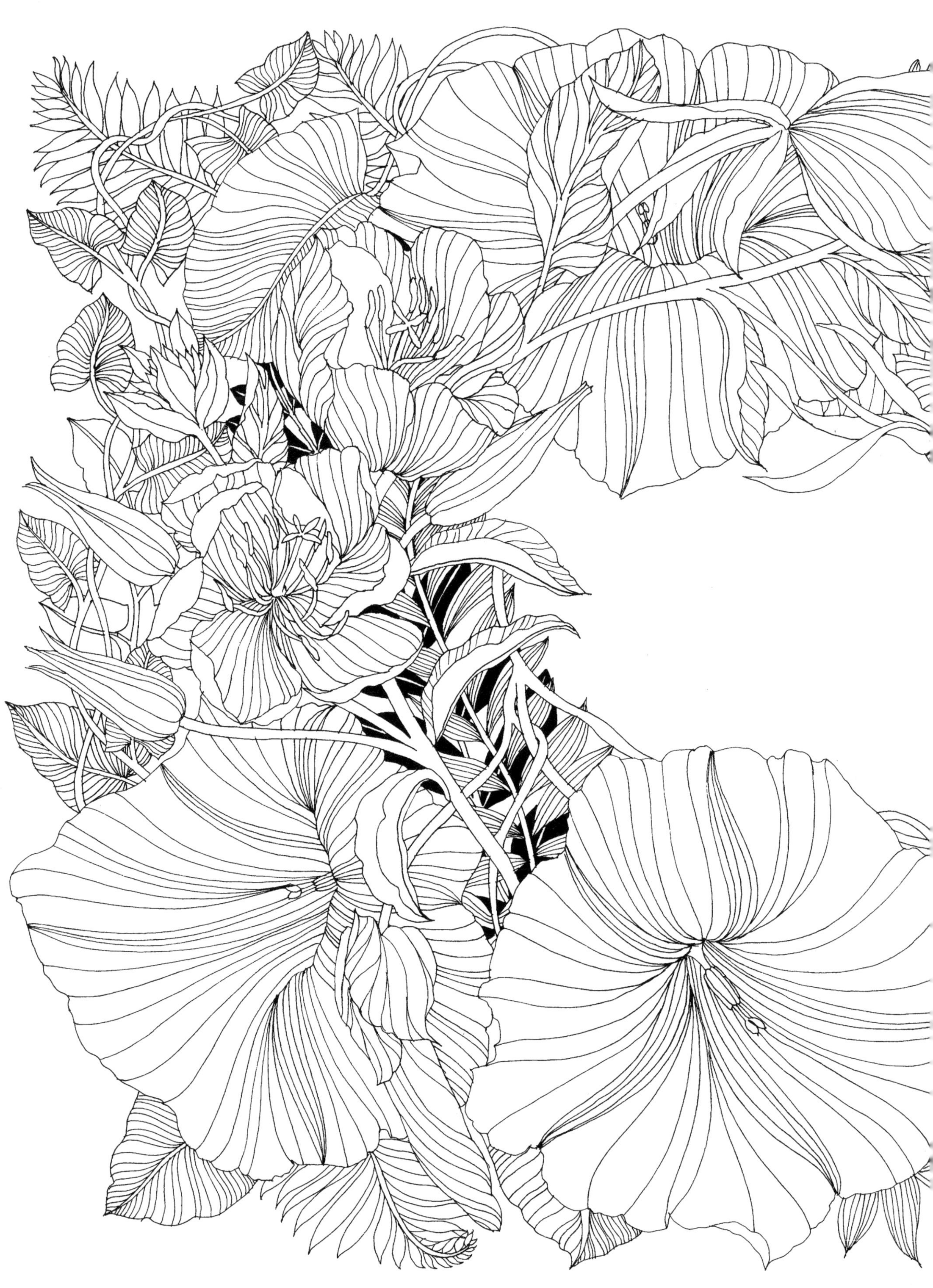

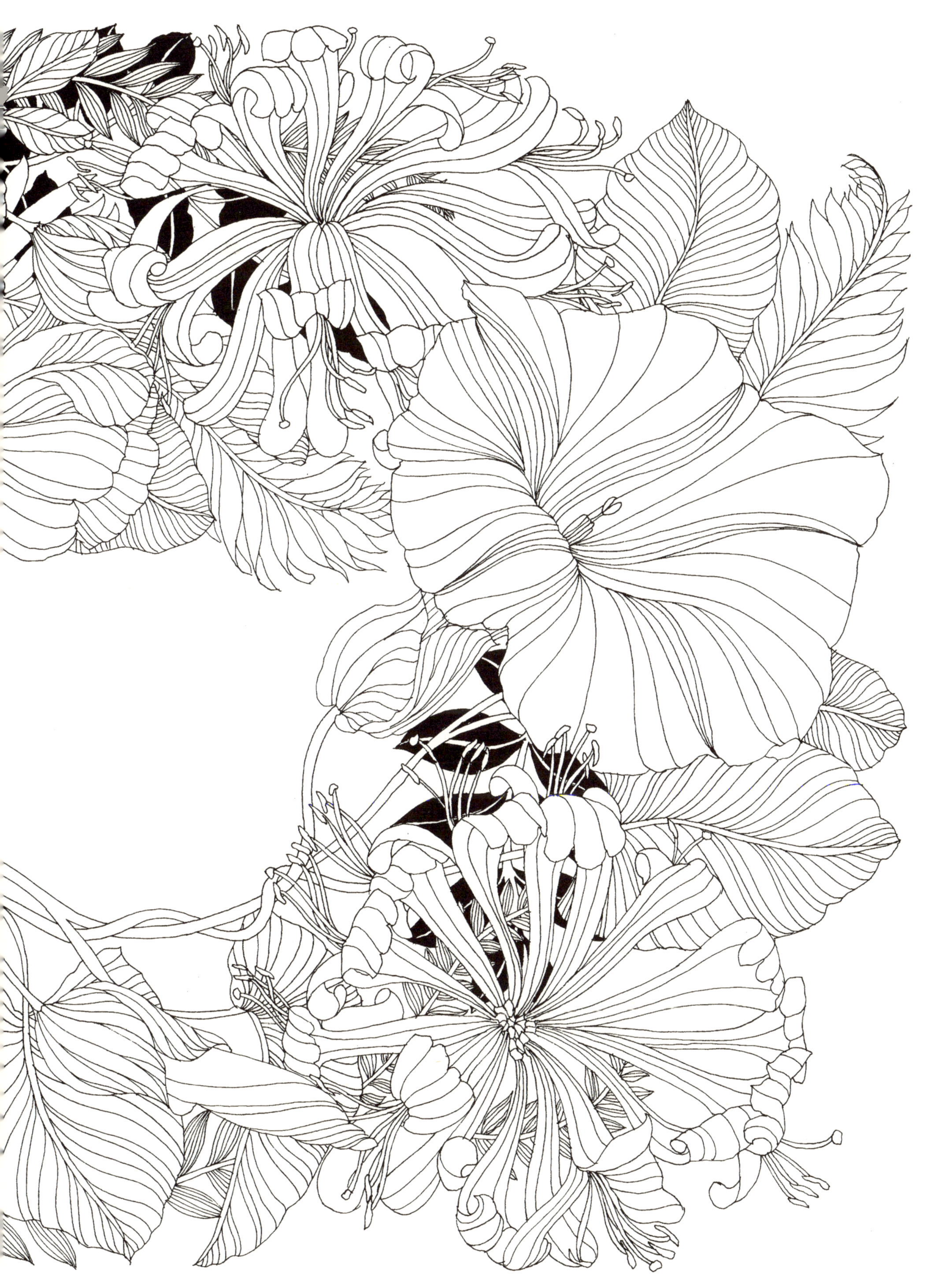

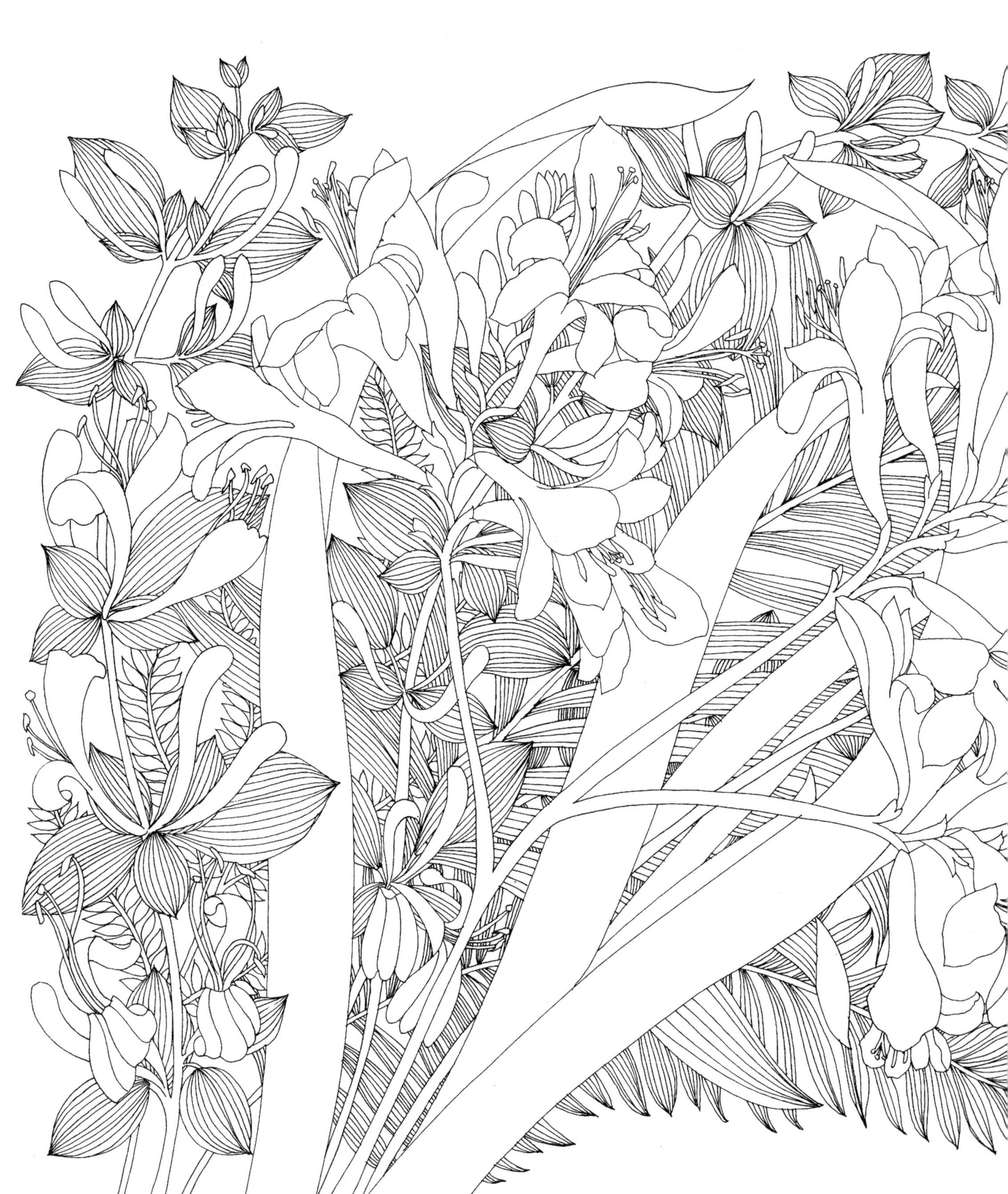

Honeysuckle, Monbretia

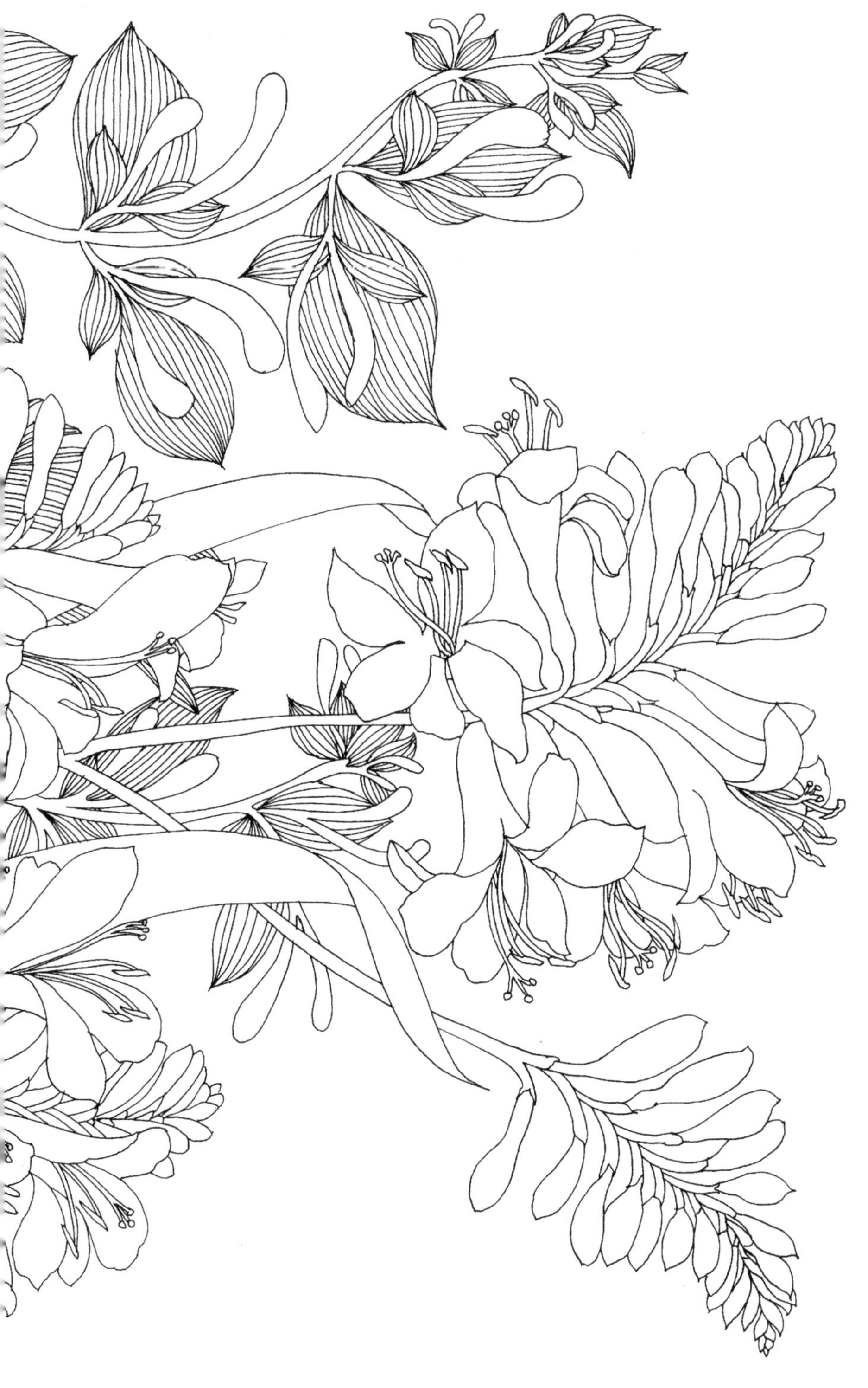

Goosegrass, Poppy

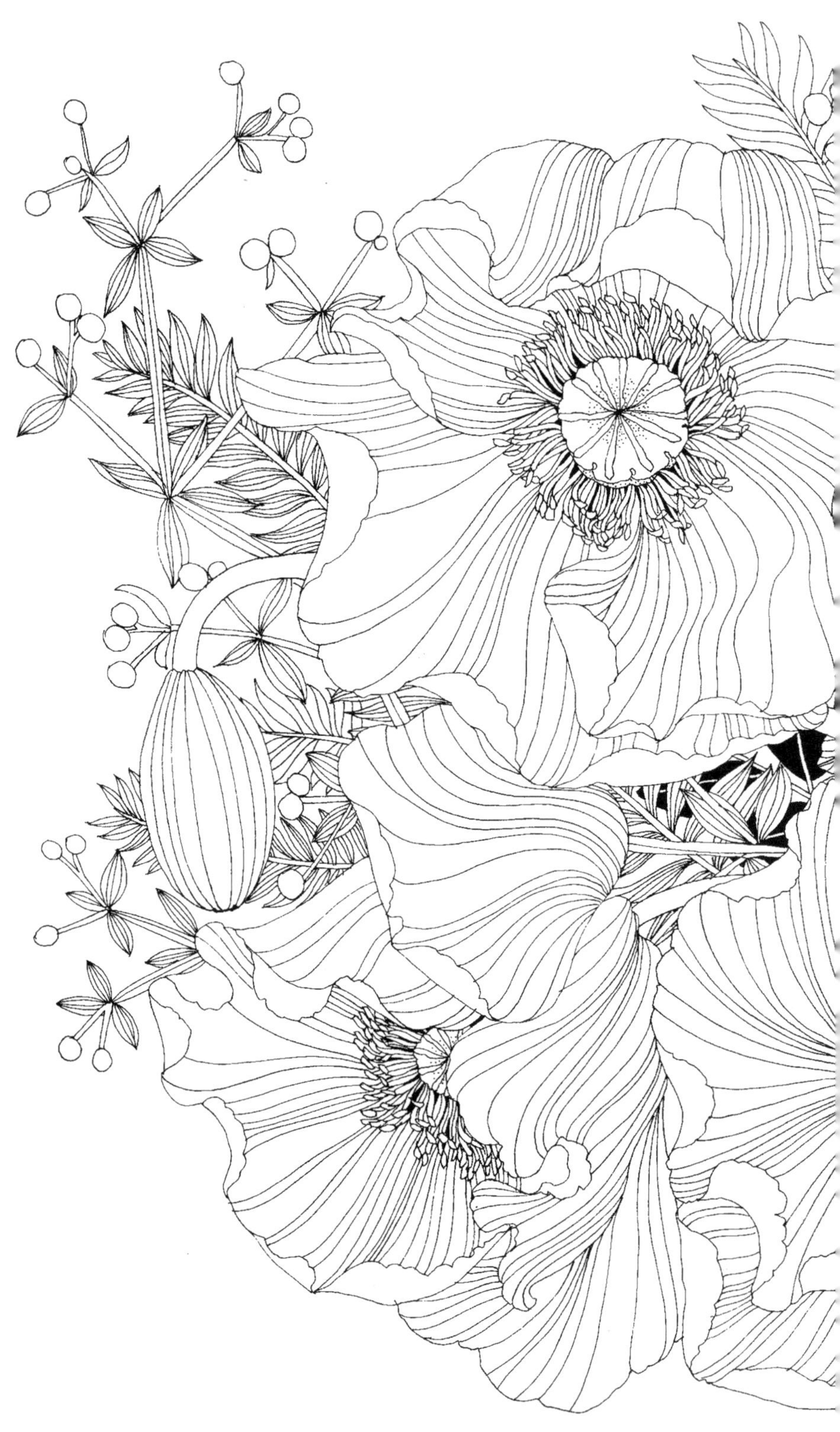

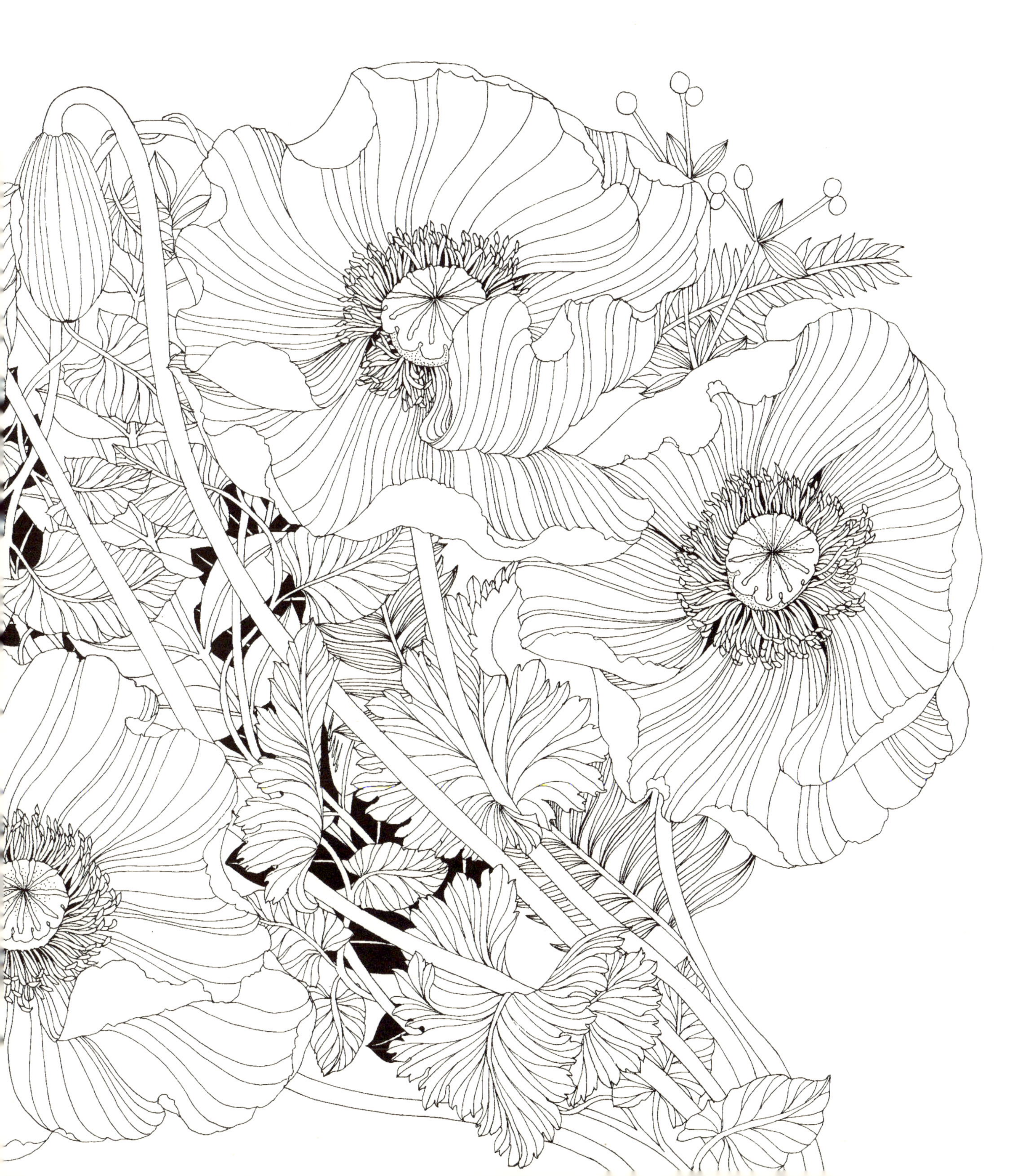

The evening primrose opens anew
Its delicate blossoms to the dew

JOHN CLARE

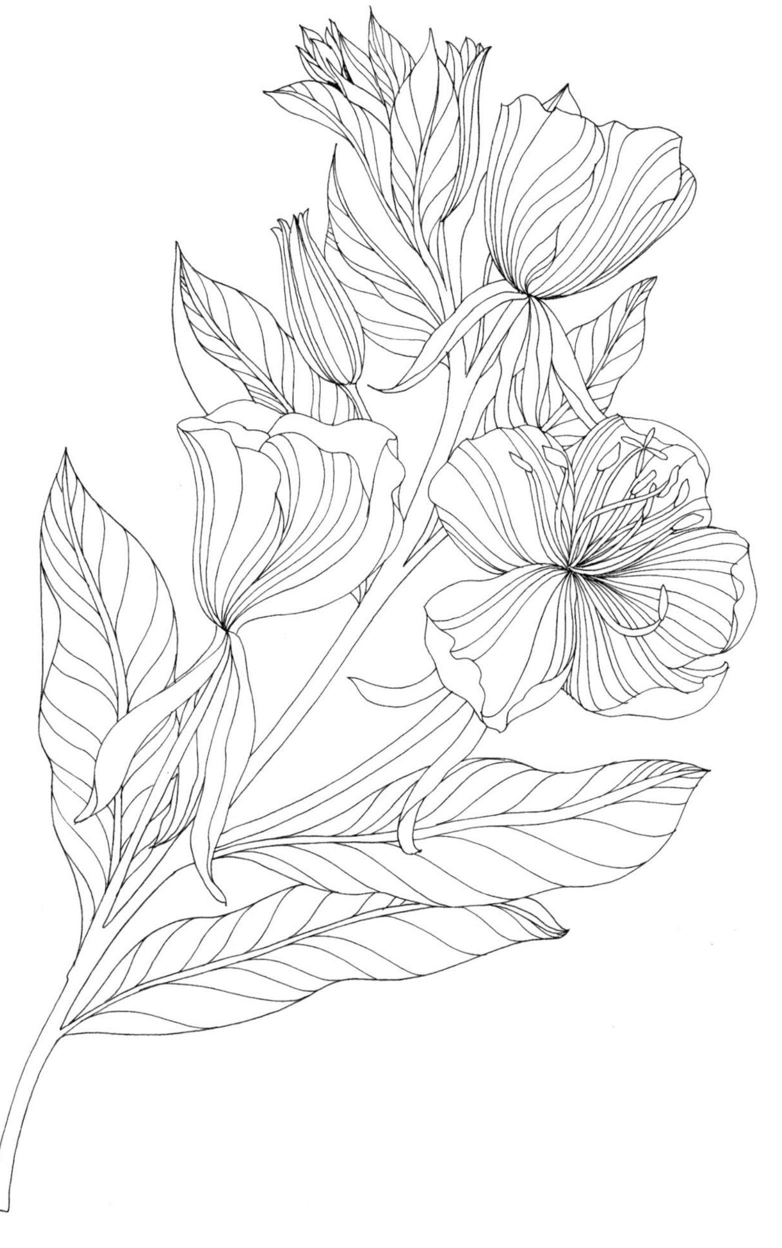

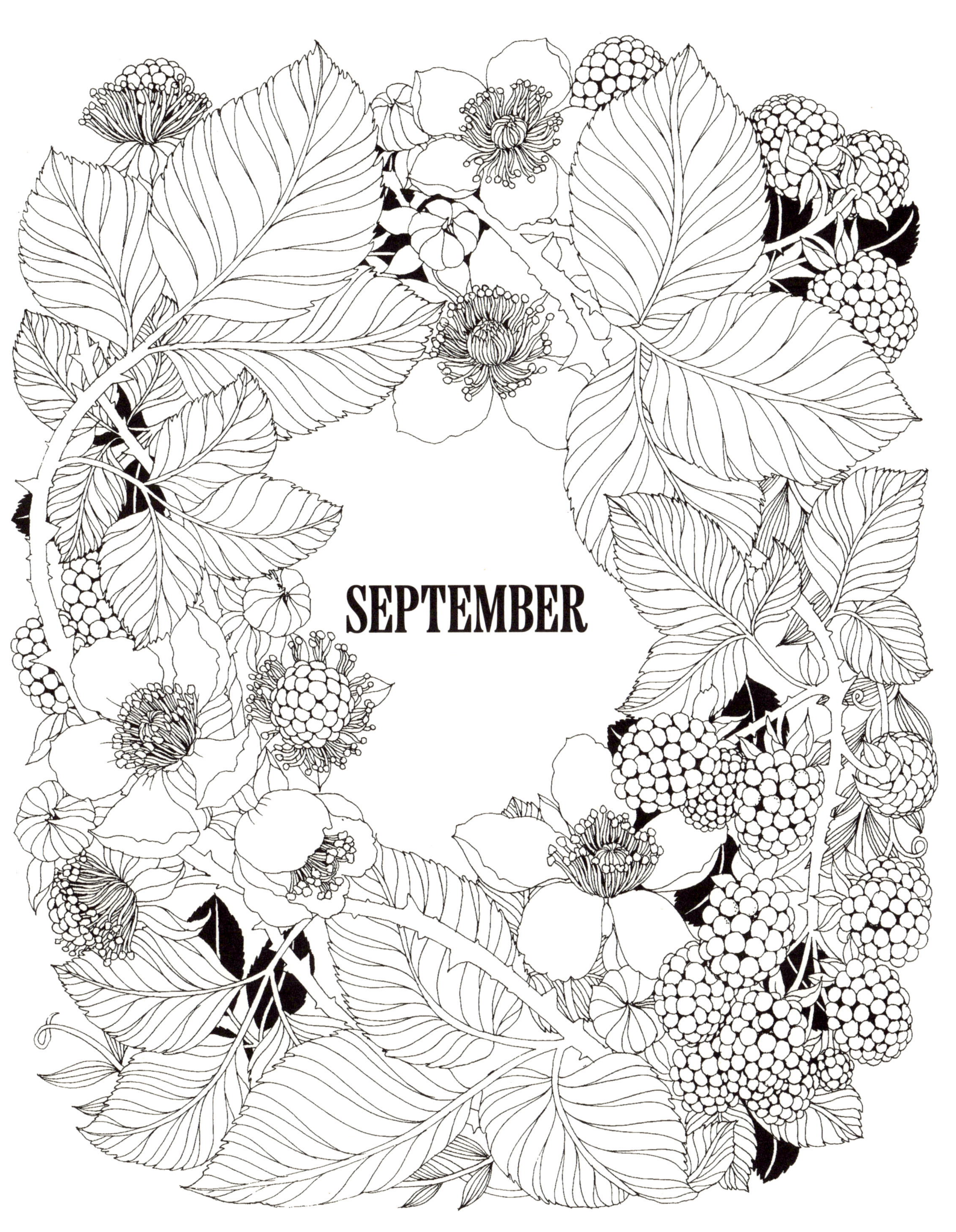
SEPTEMBER

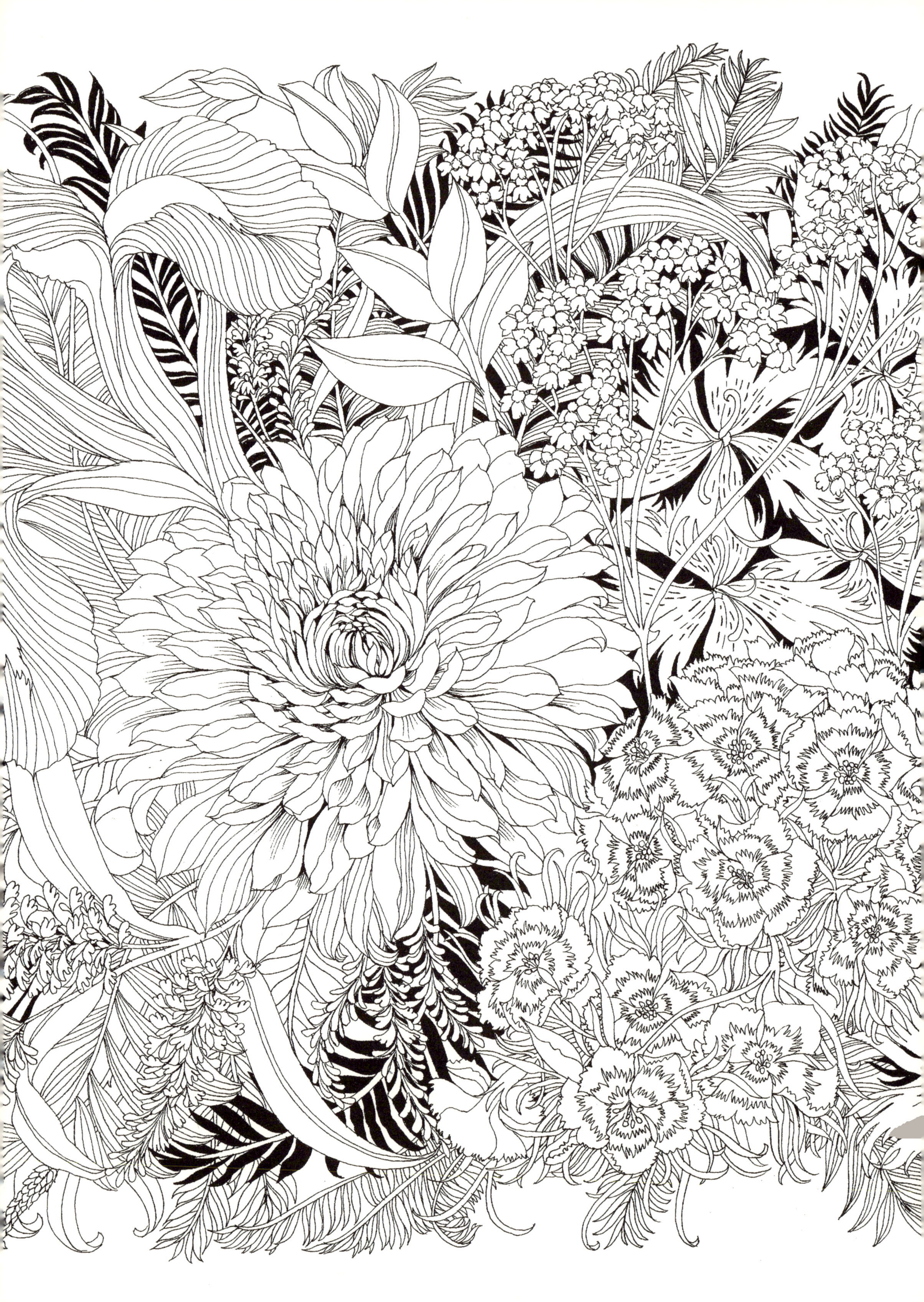

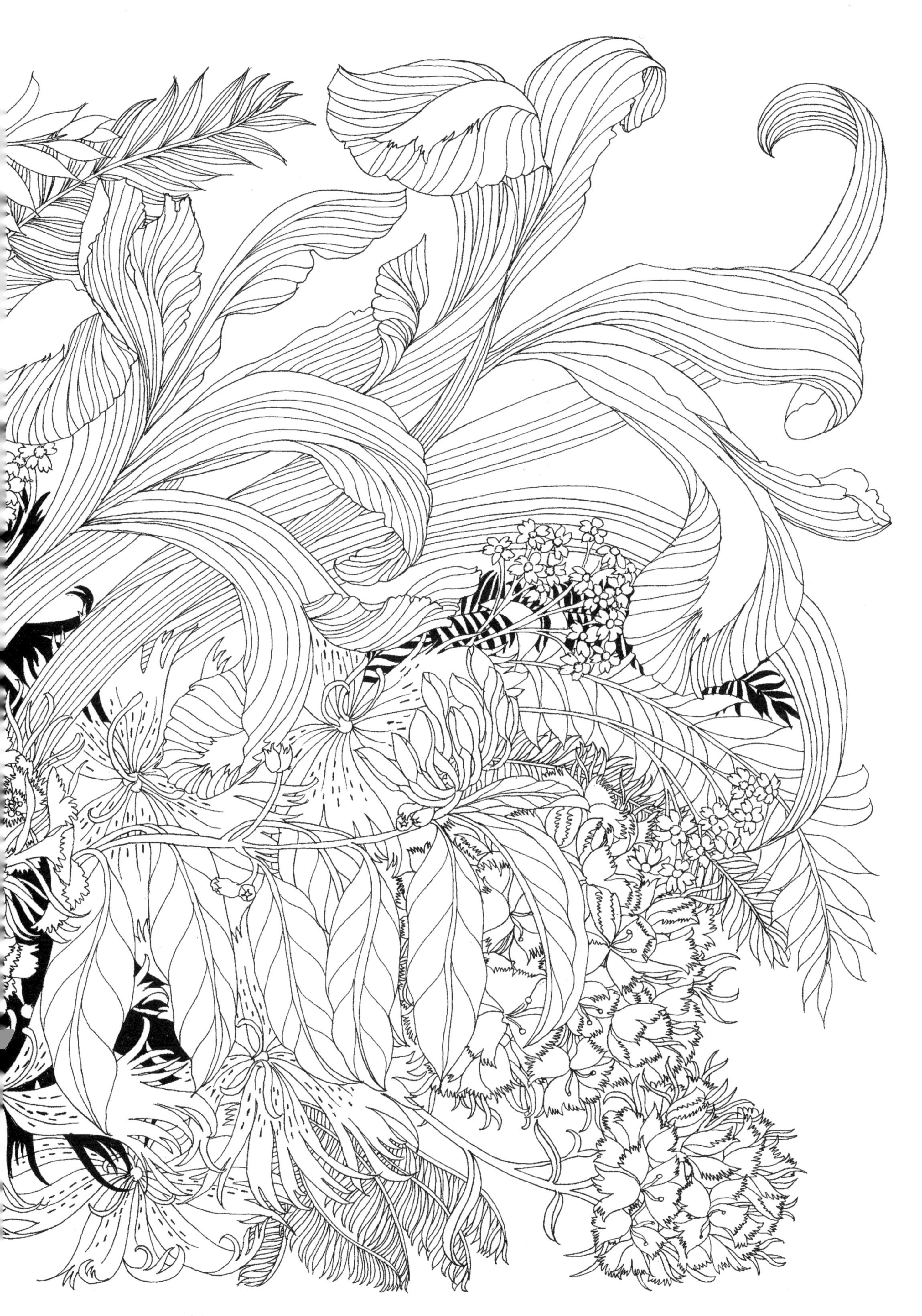

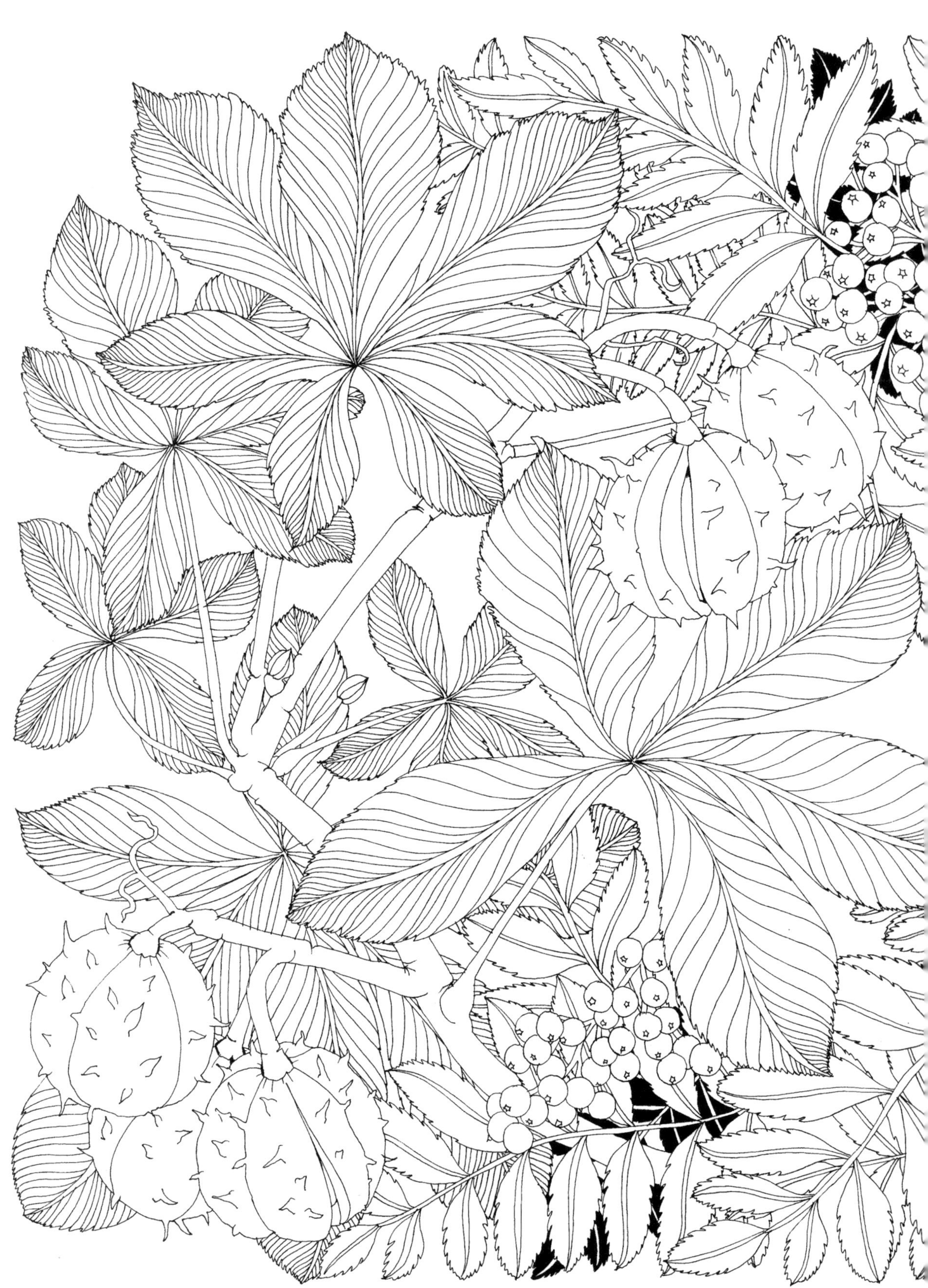

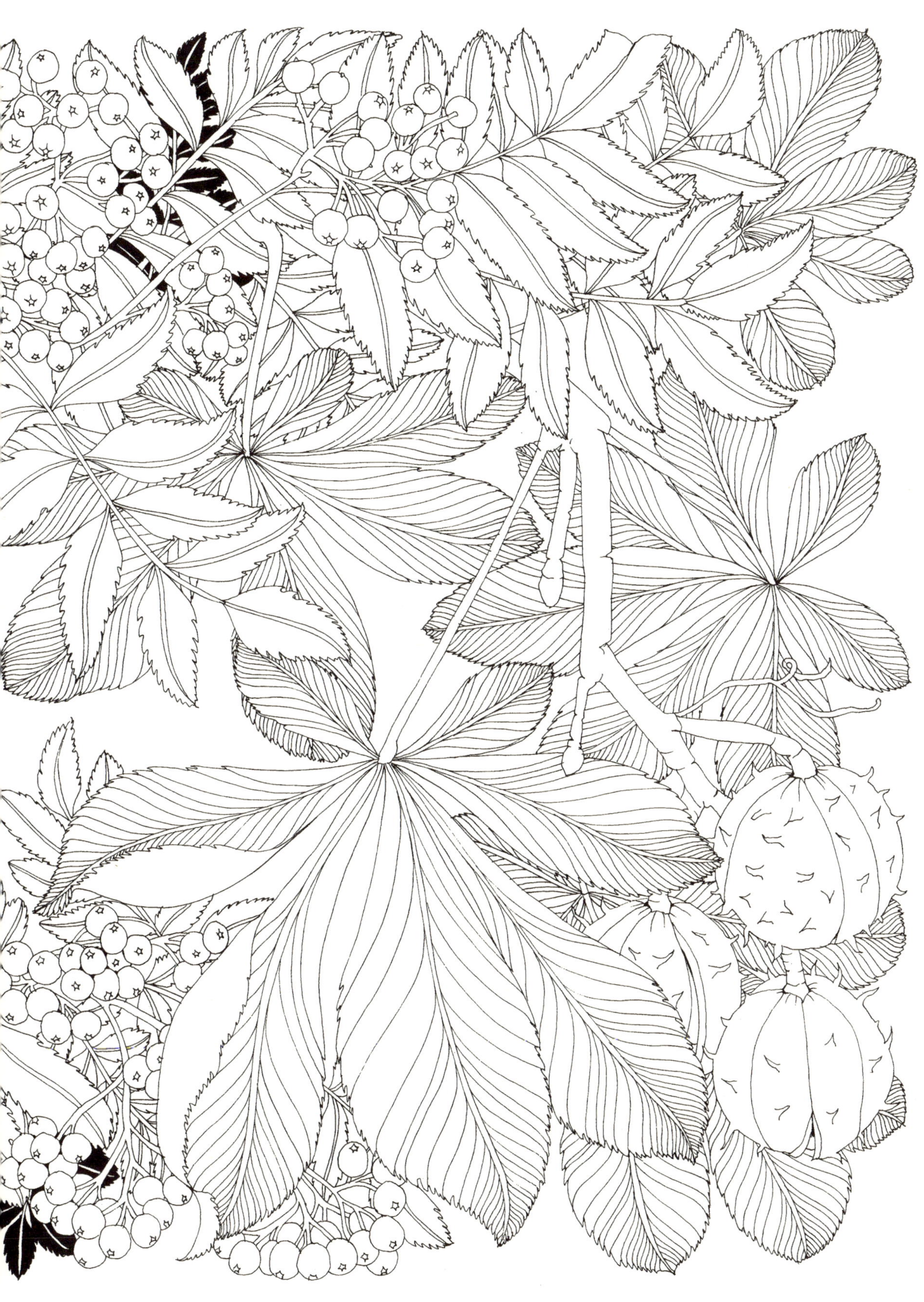

Dahlia, Masterwort, Scabious, Virgin's Bower

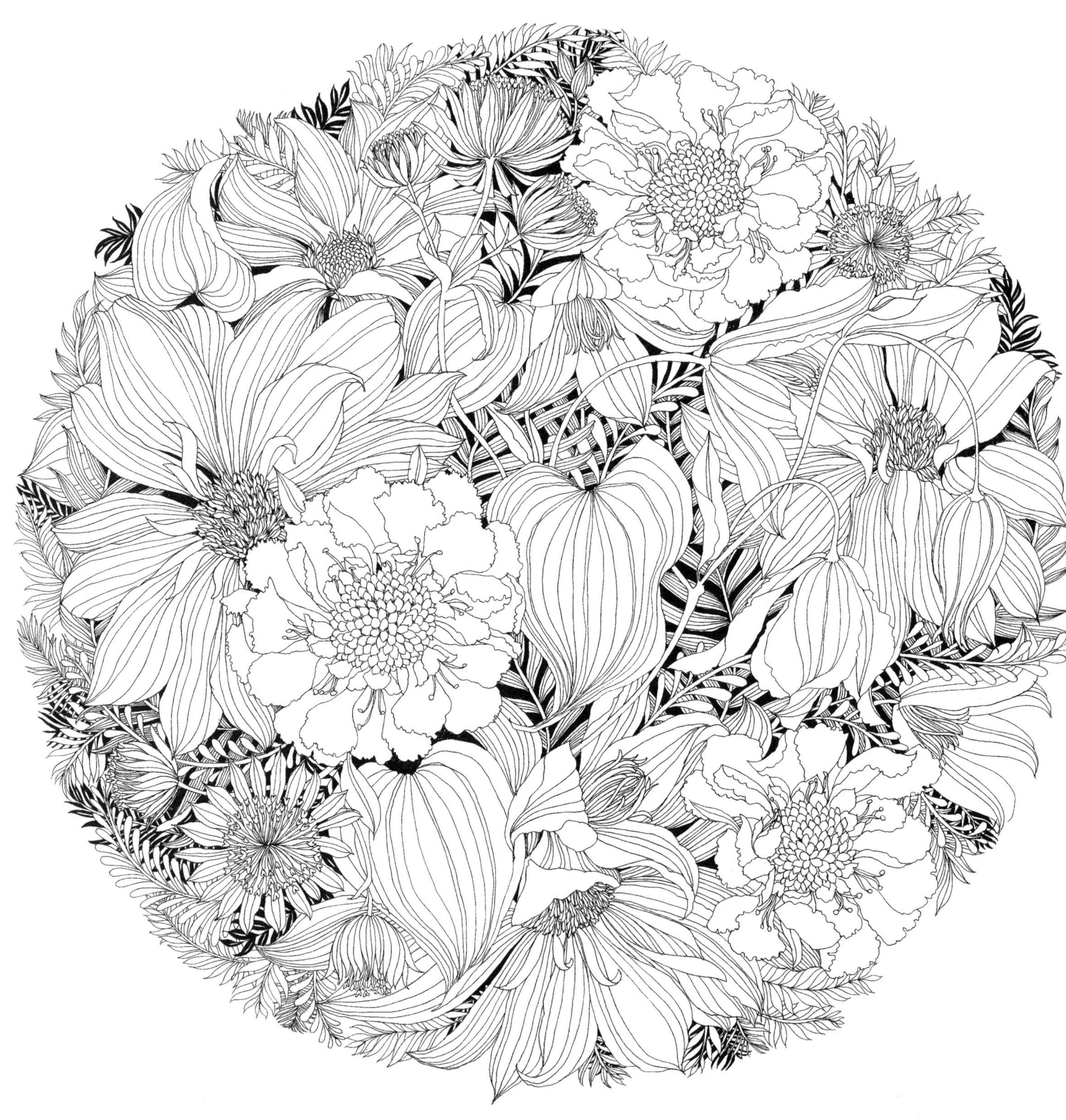

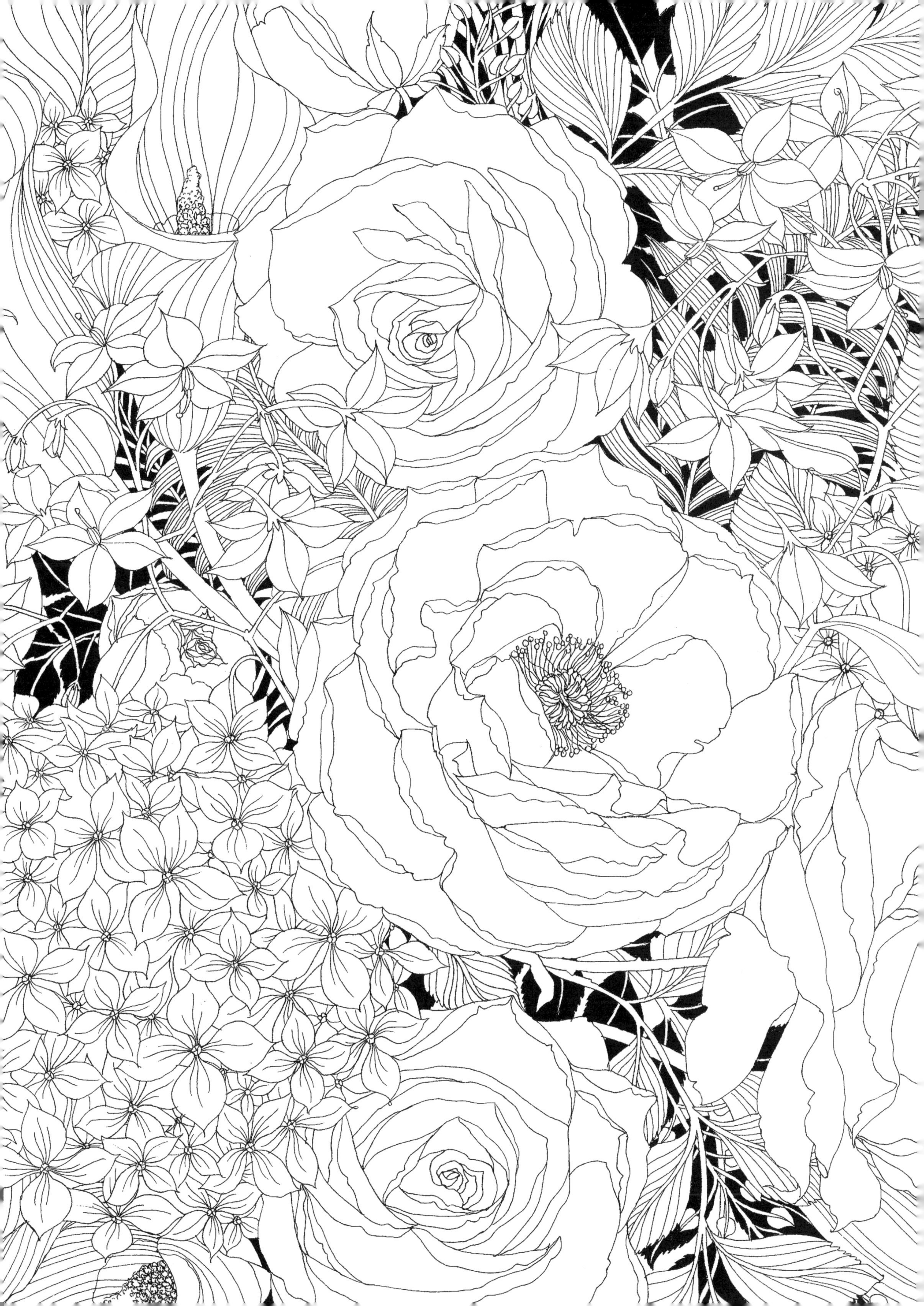

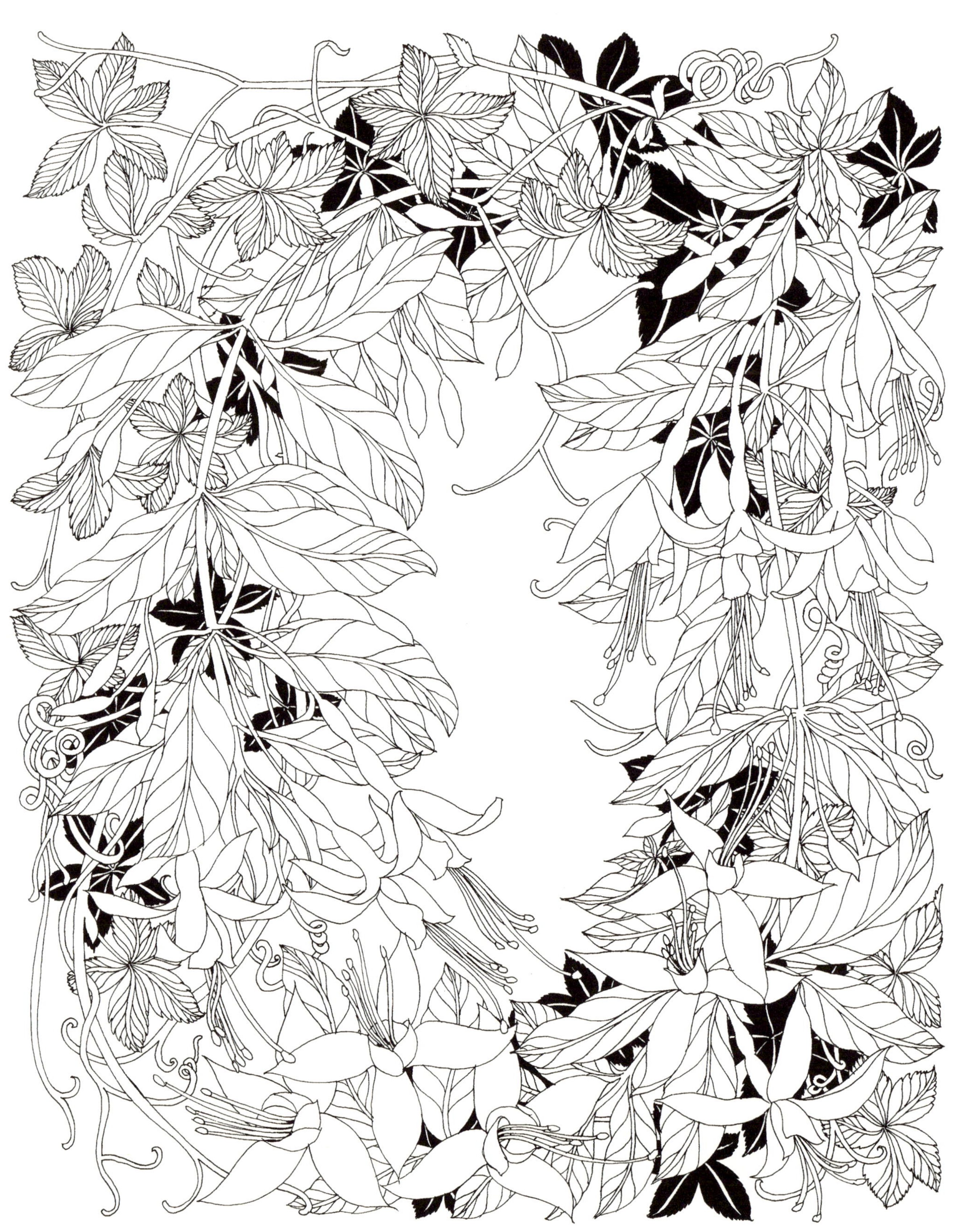

Cornflower, Jasmine, Sweet Pea

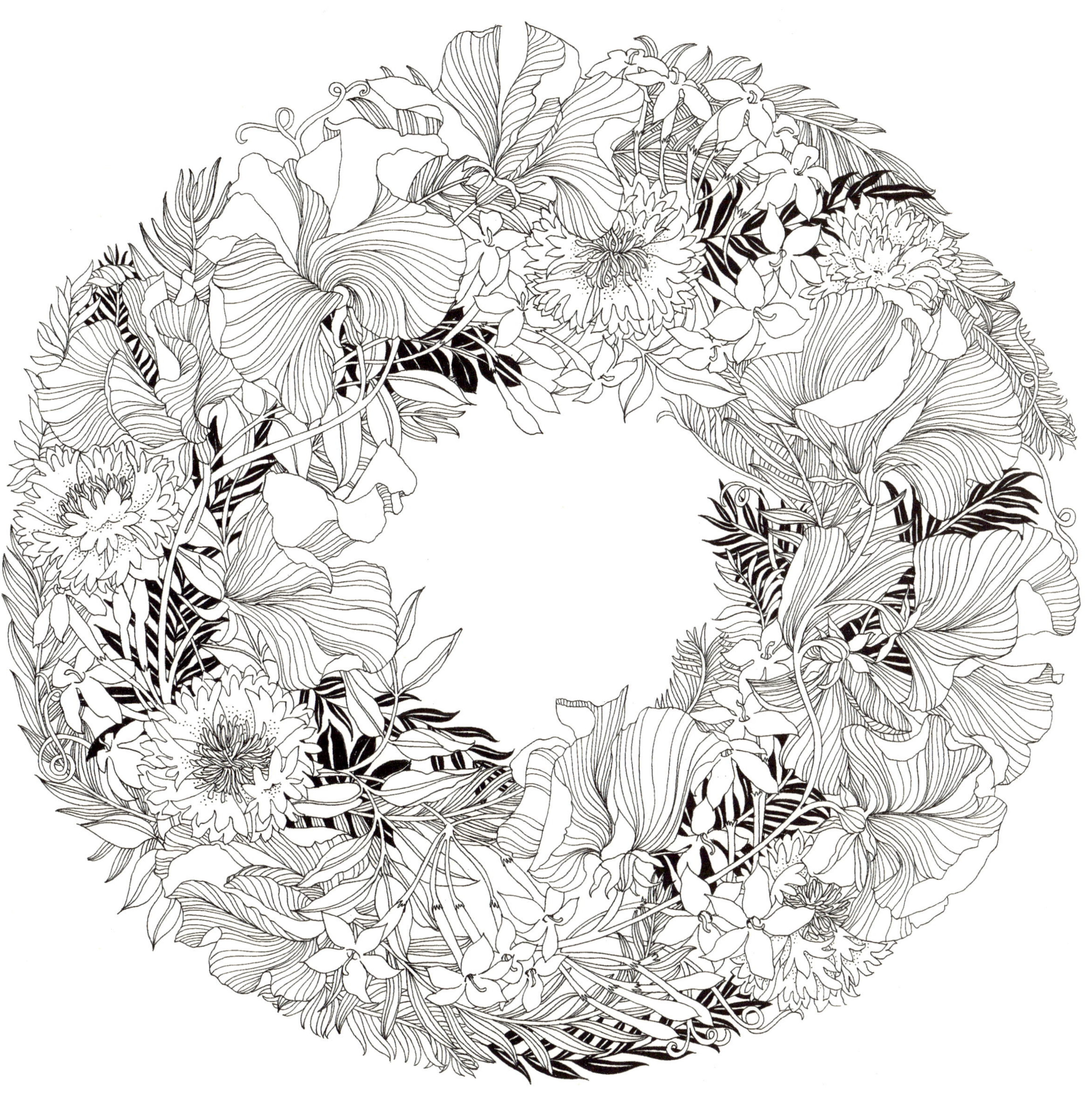

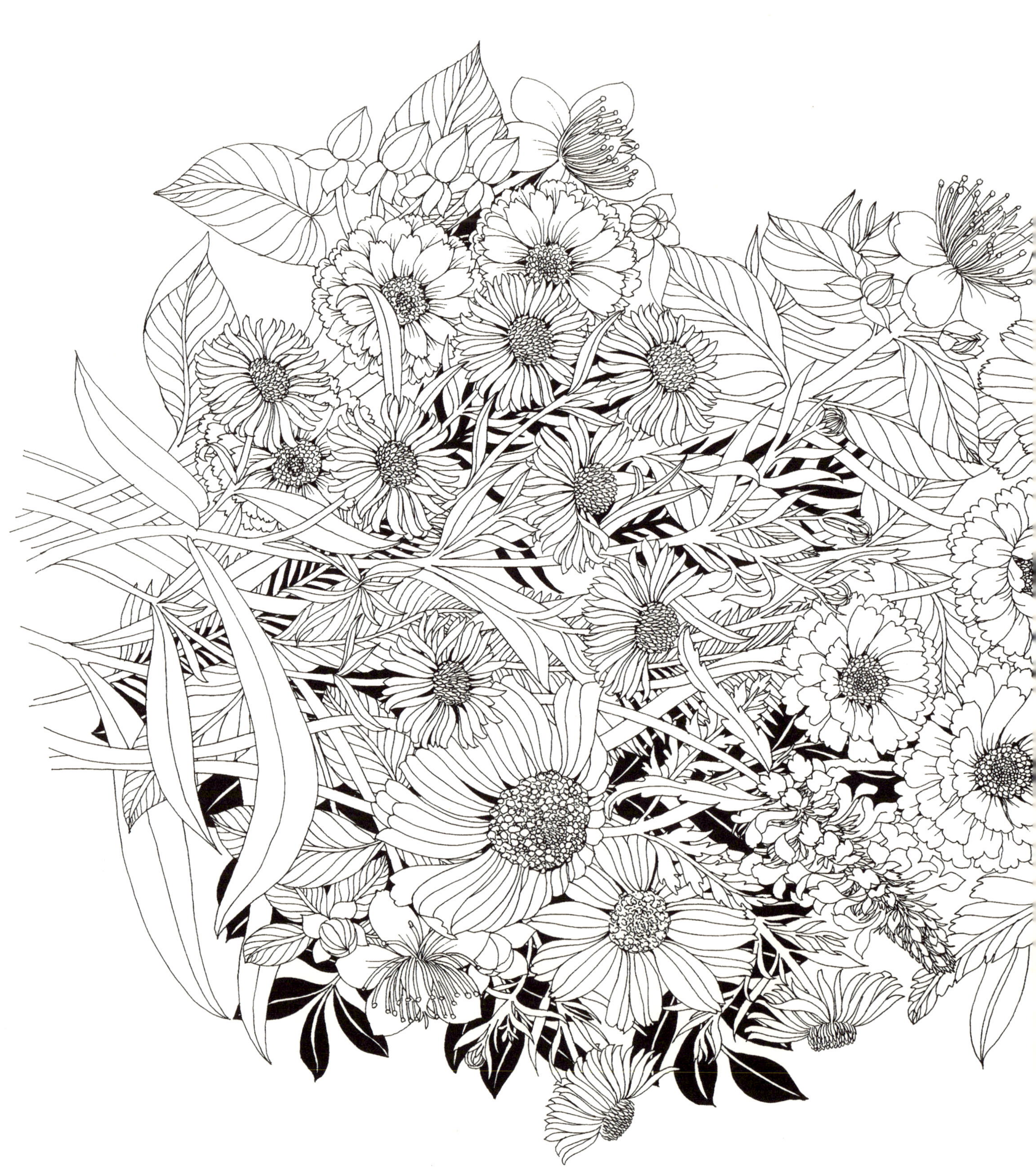

Betony, Corn Marigold, Michaelmas Daisy,
Nettle-Leaved Bellflower,
St John's Wort

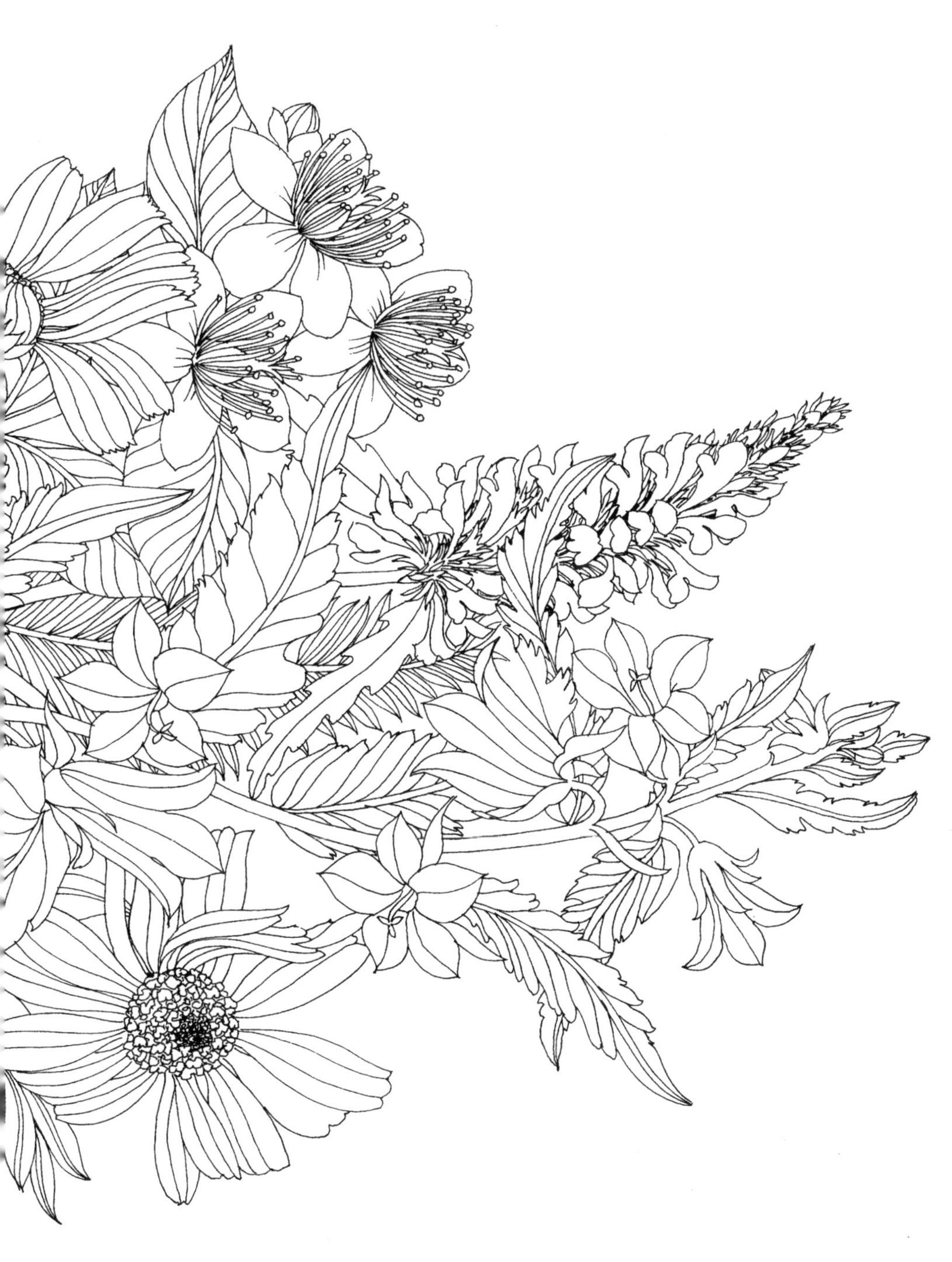

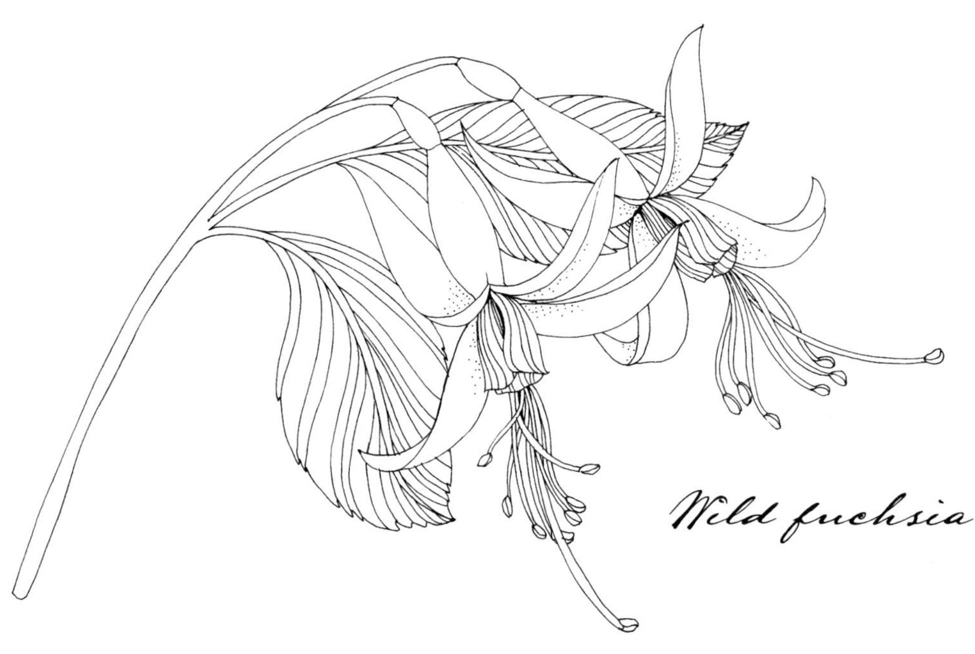
Wild fuchsia

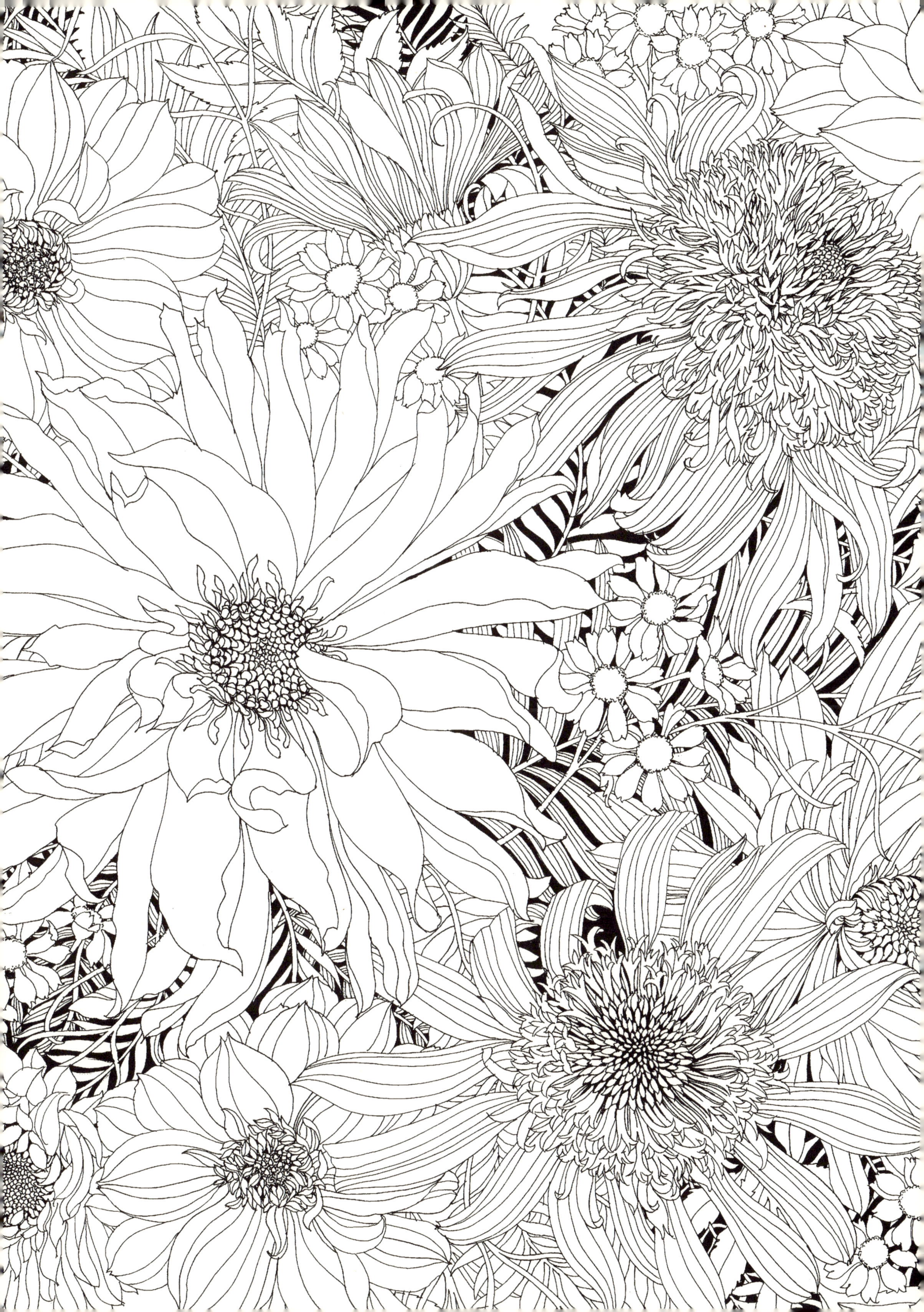

O Rose, though flower of flowers,
thou fragrant wonder

CHRISTINA ROSETTI

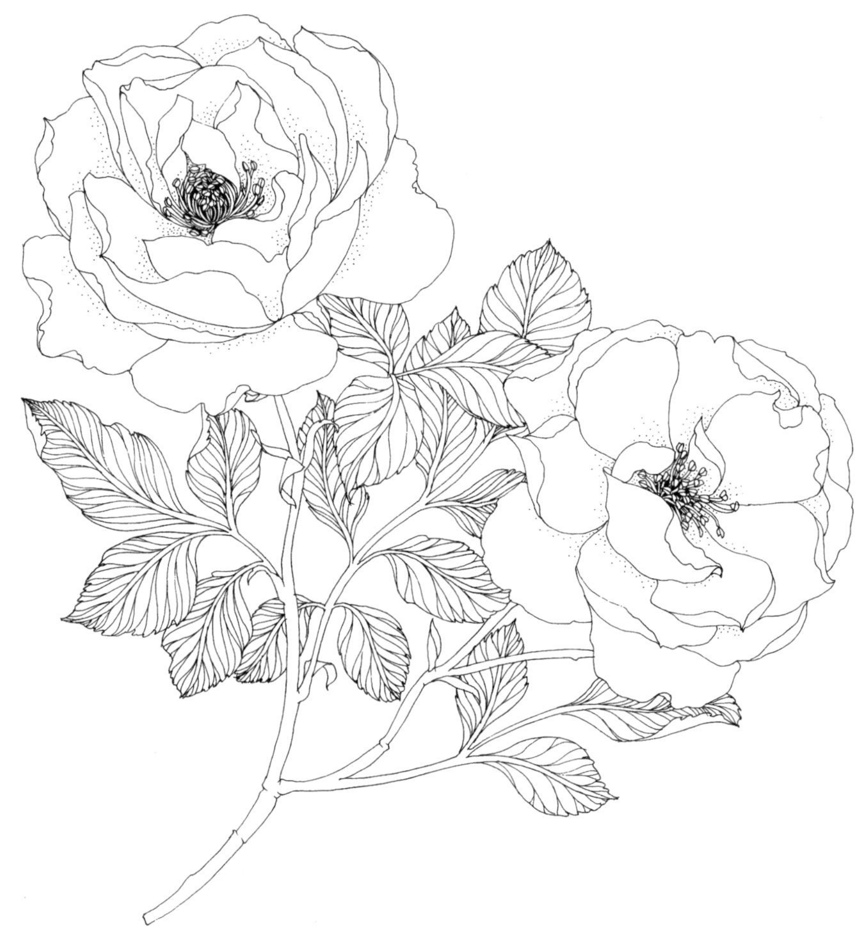

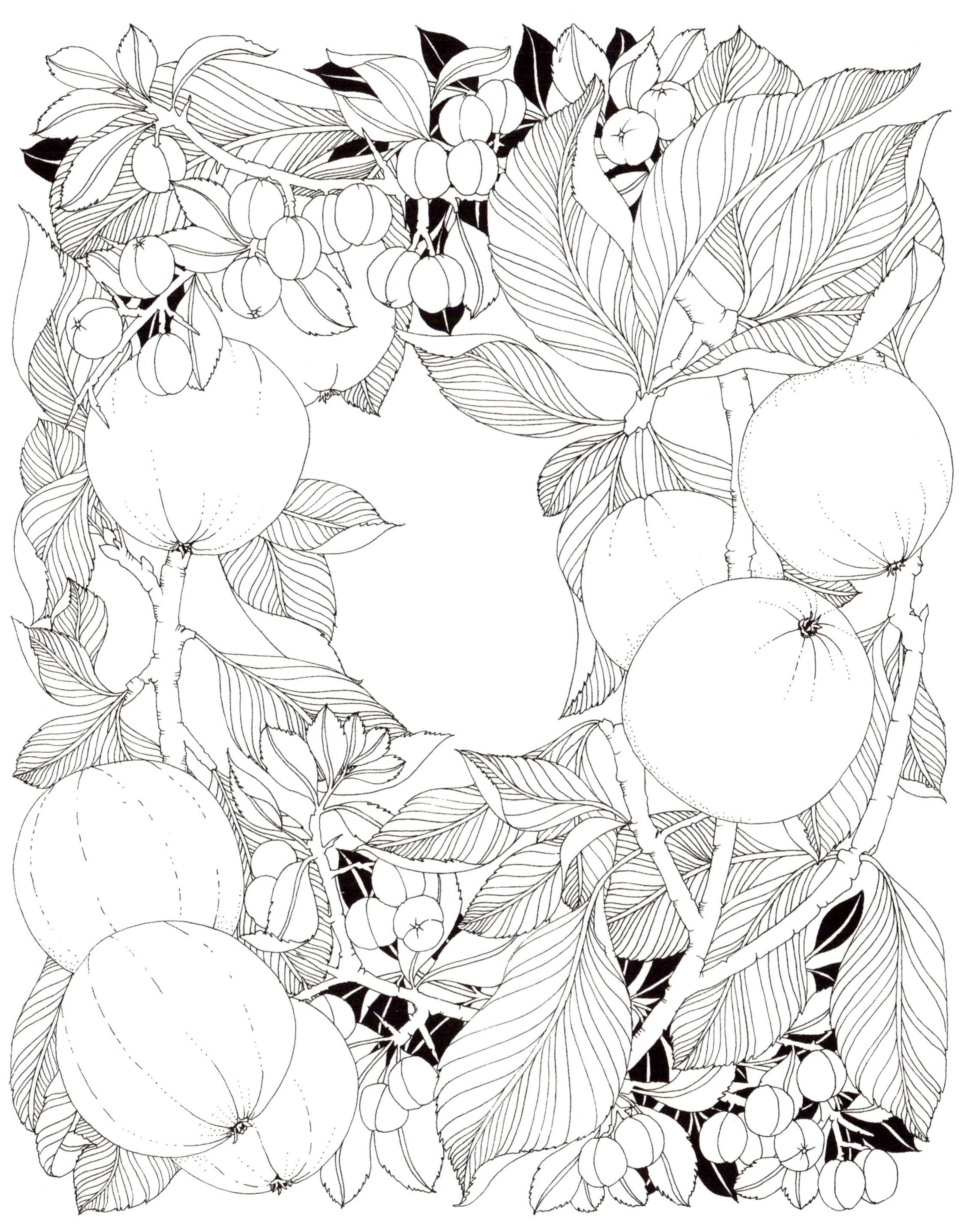

OCTOBER

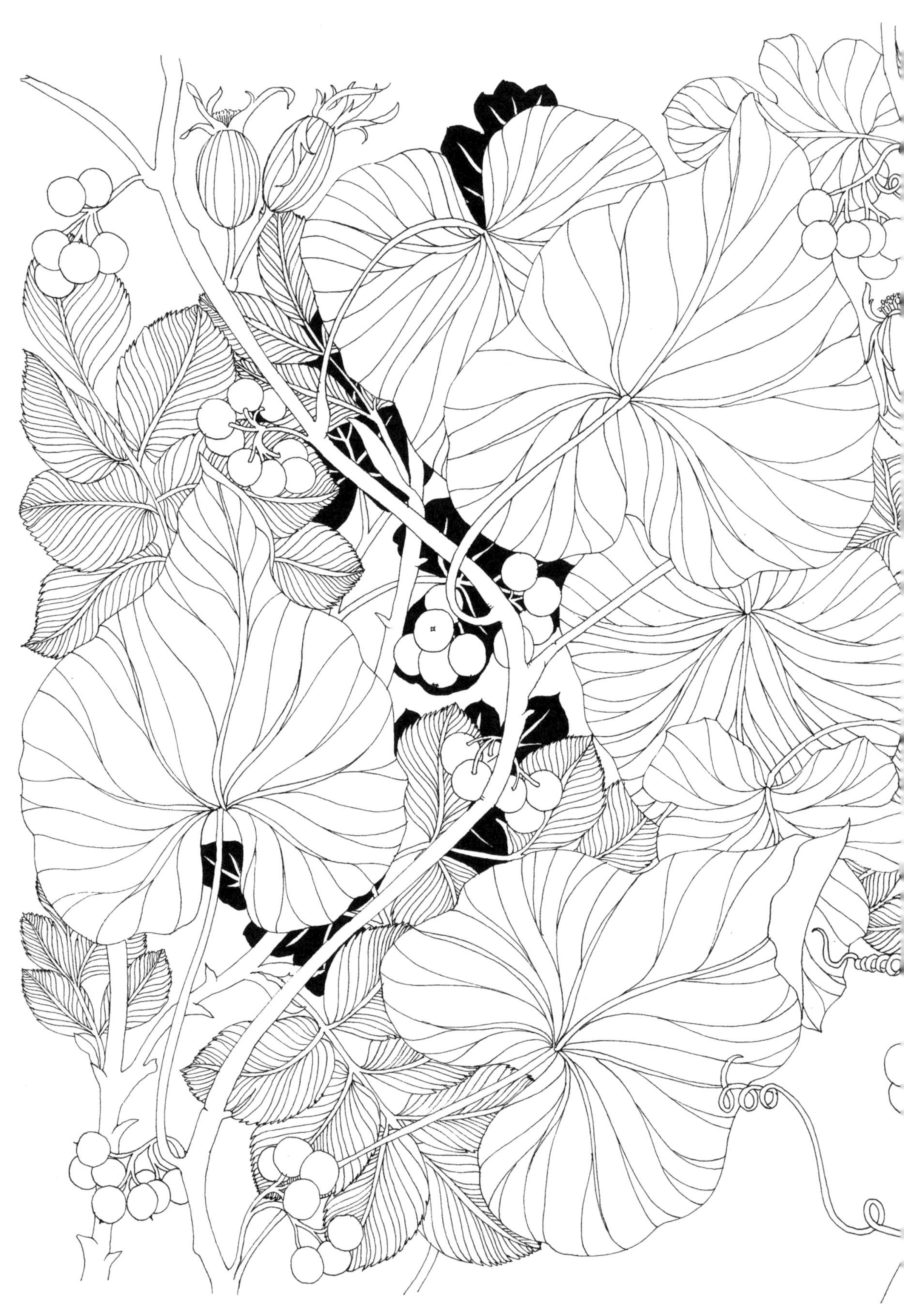

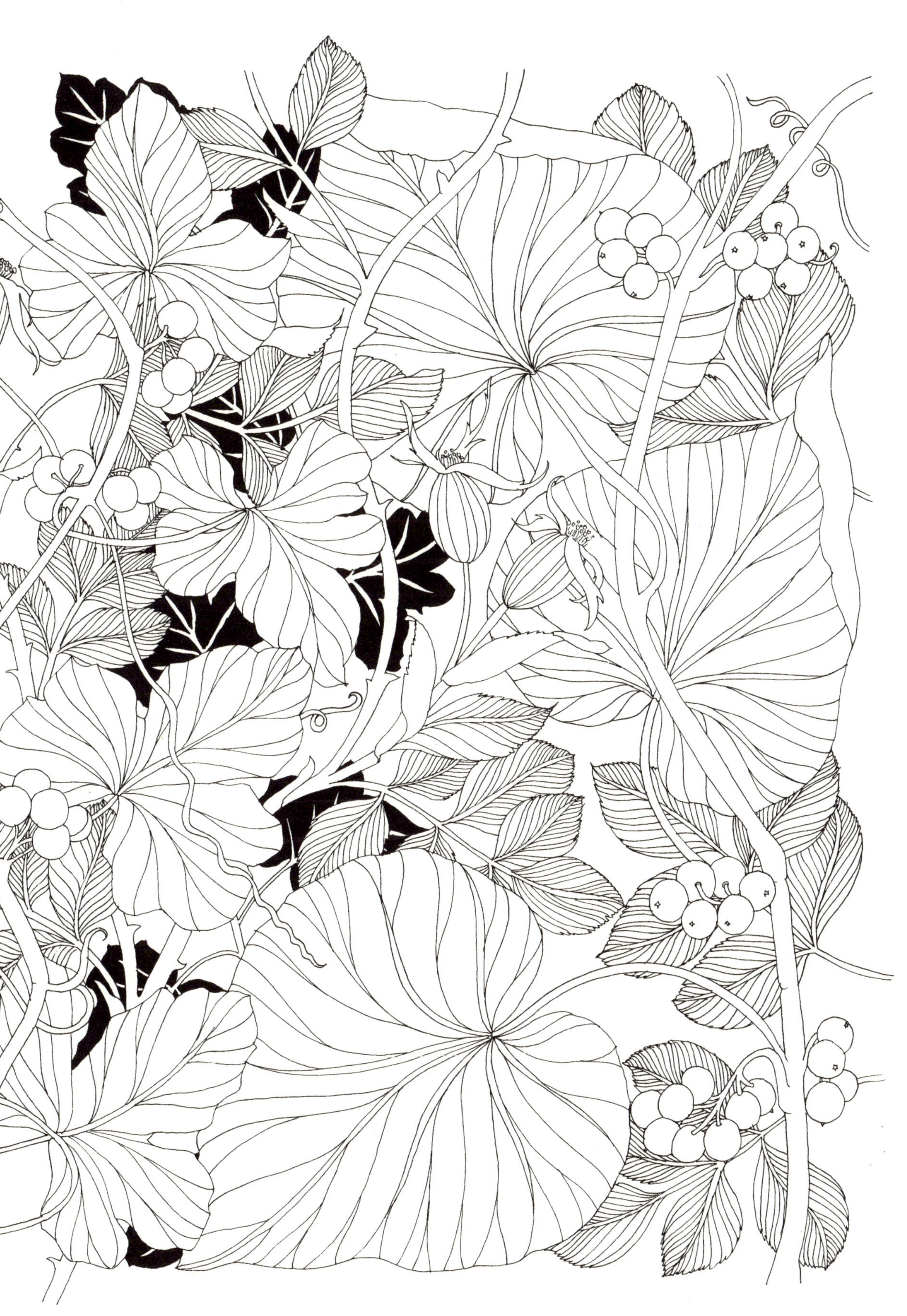

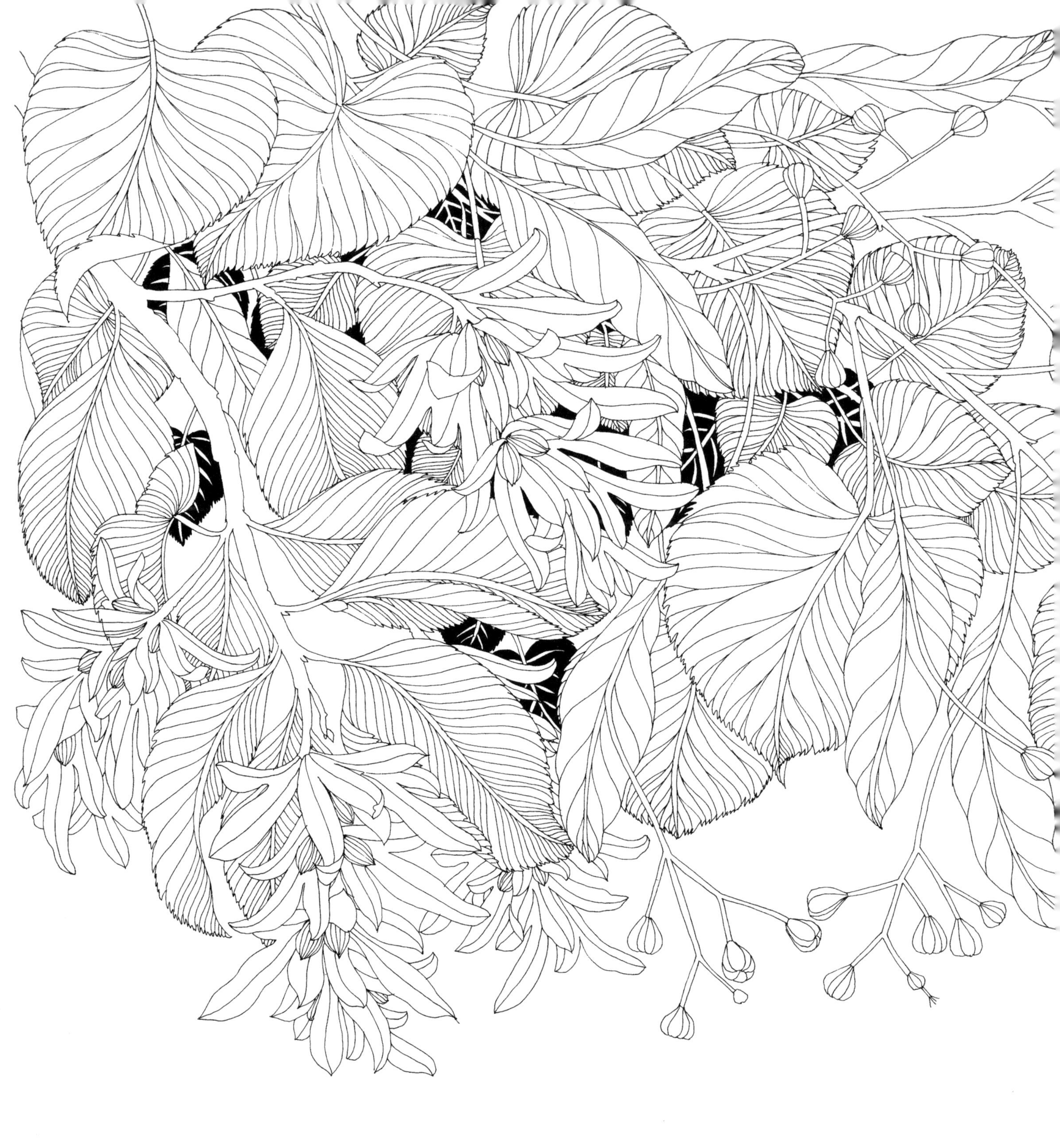

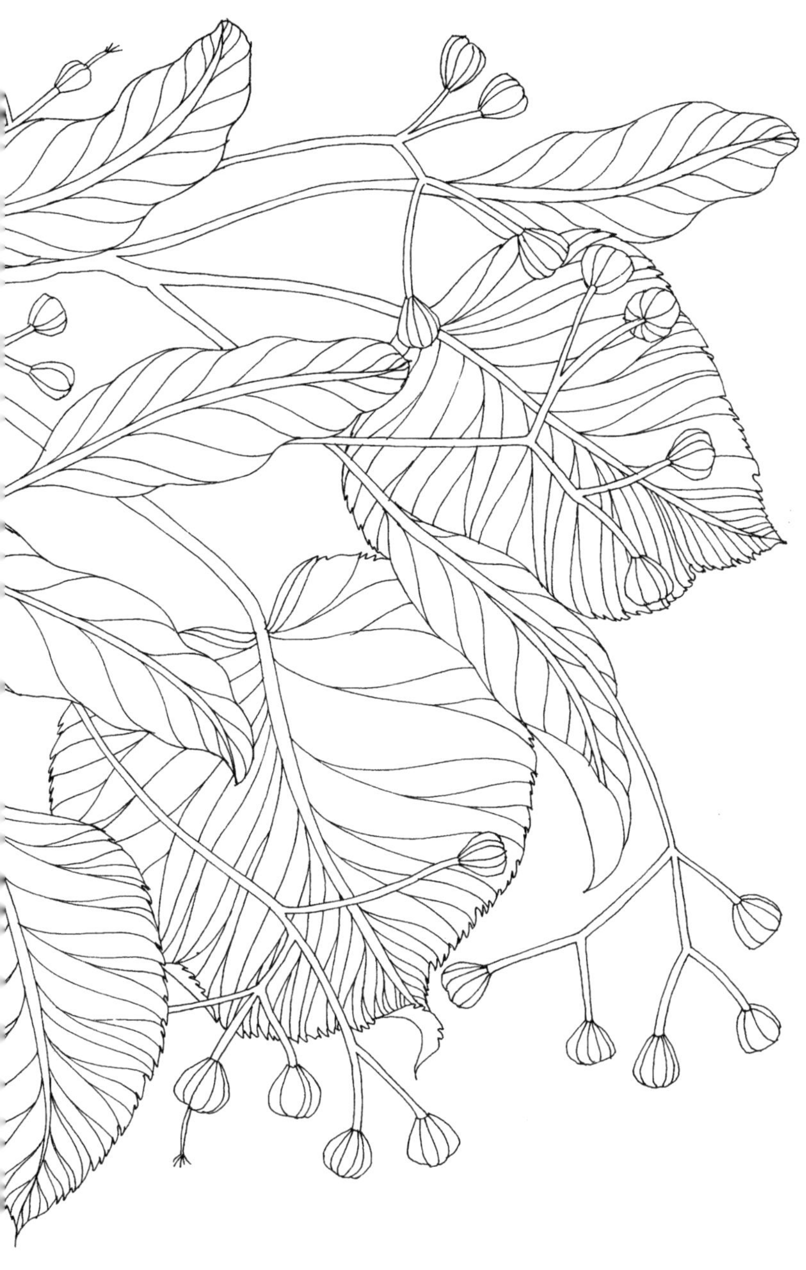

Common Lime, Hornbeam

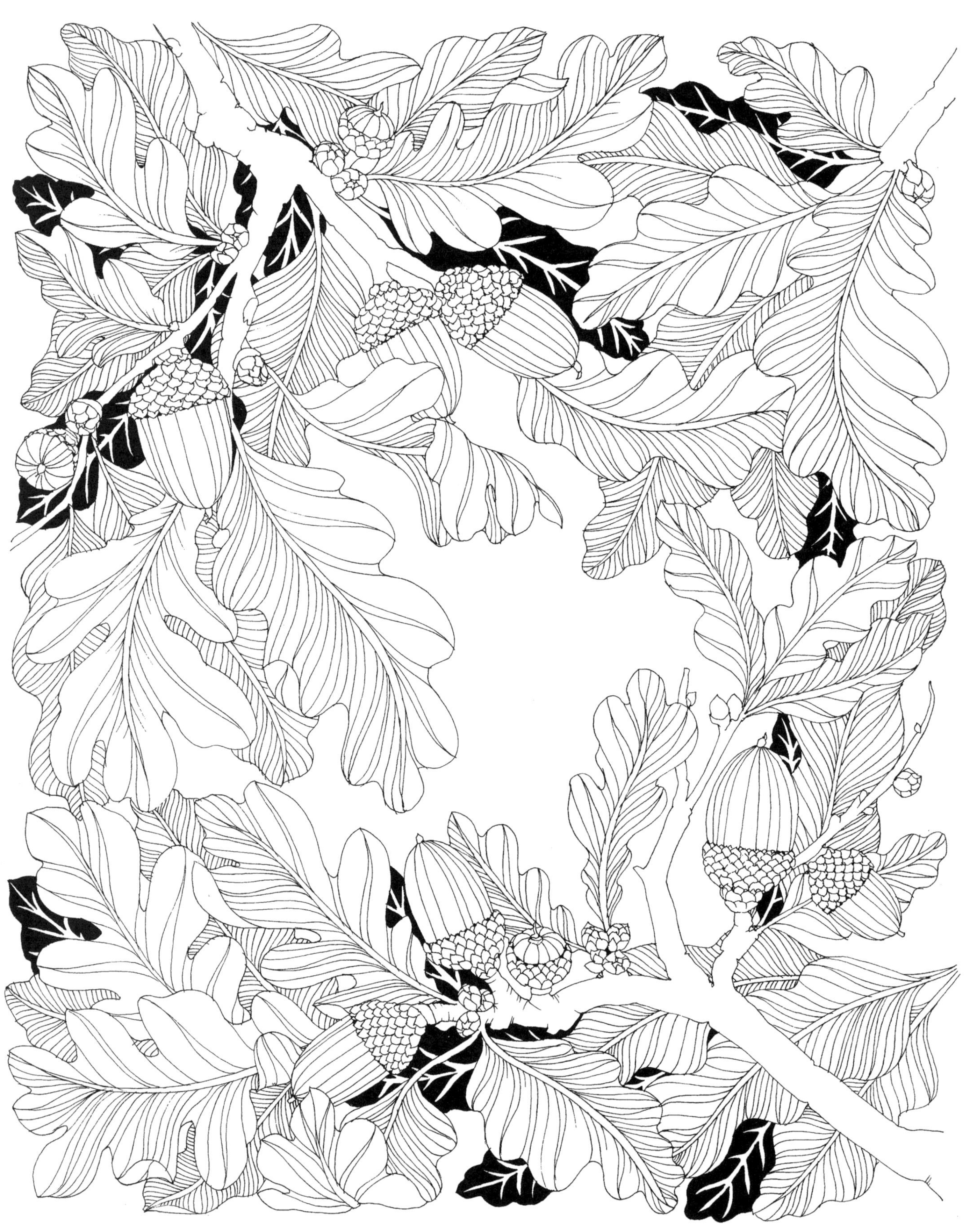

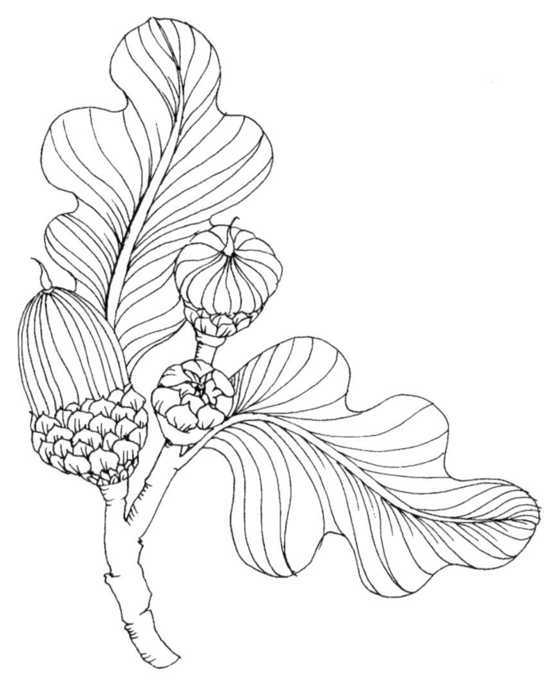

Around me stood the oaks and firs,
Pine – cones and acrons lay on the ground

RALPH WALDO-EMERSON

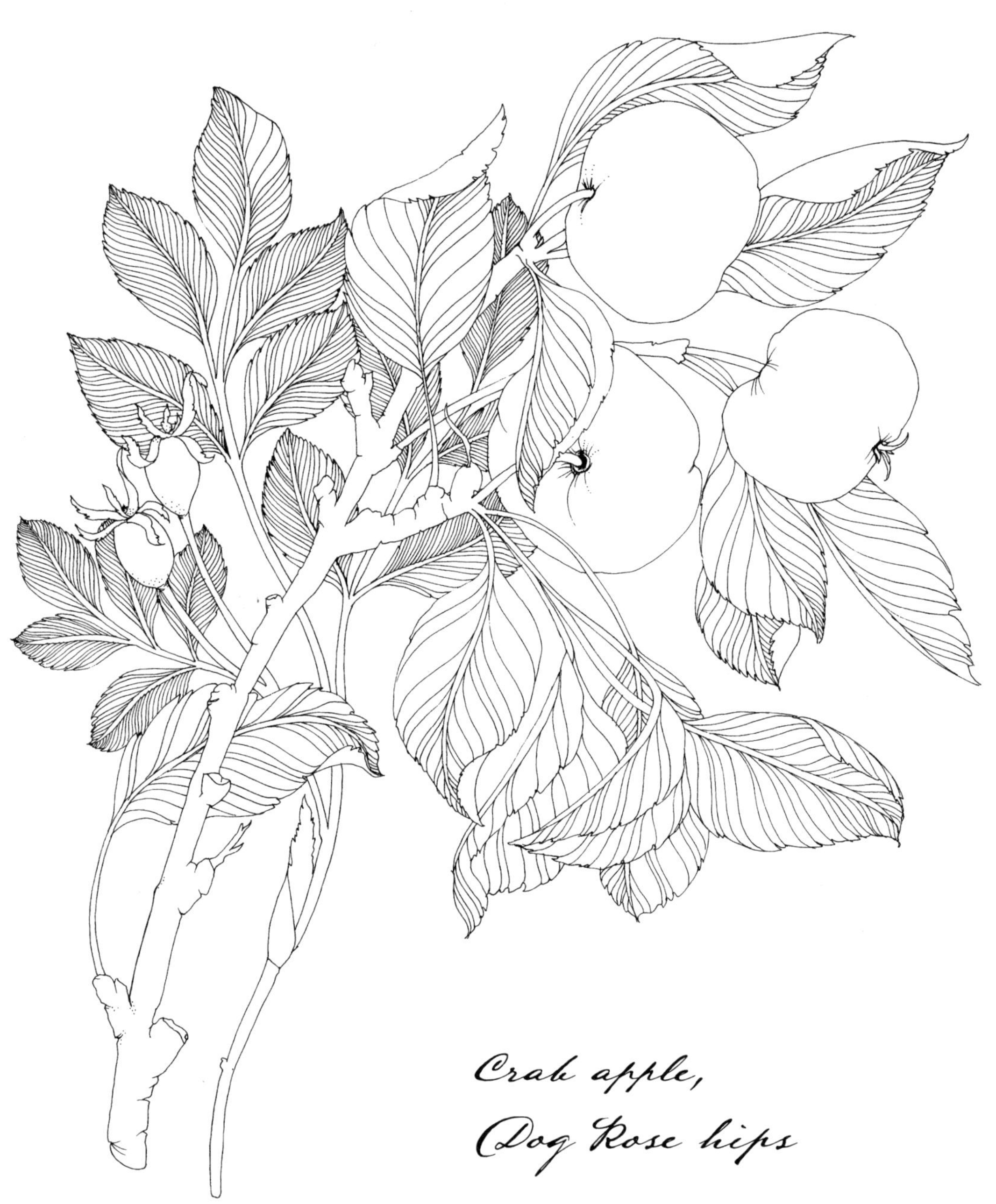
Crab apple,
Dog Rose hips

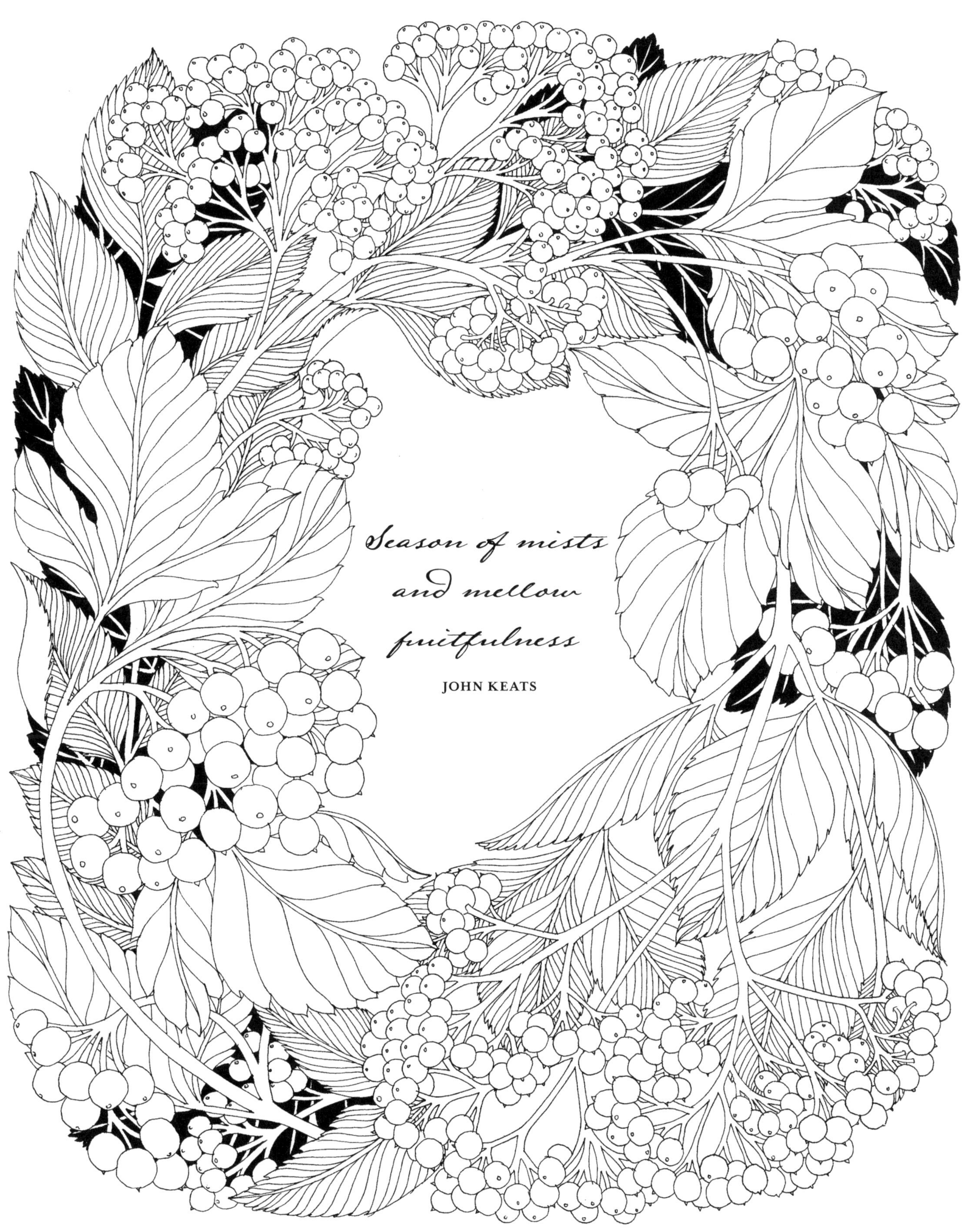

NOVEMBER

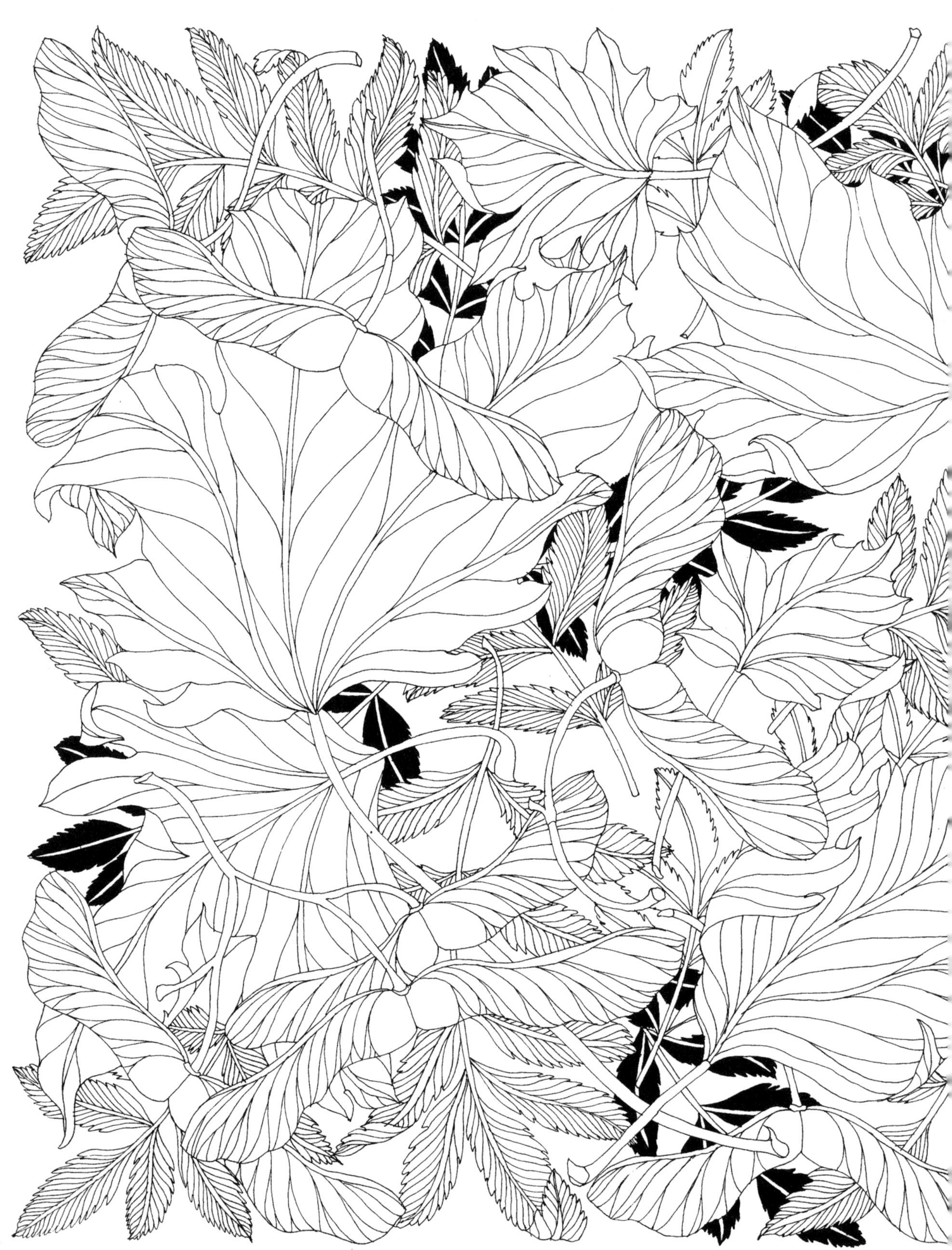

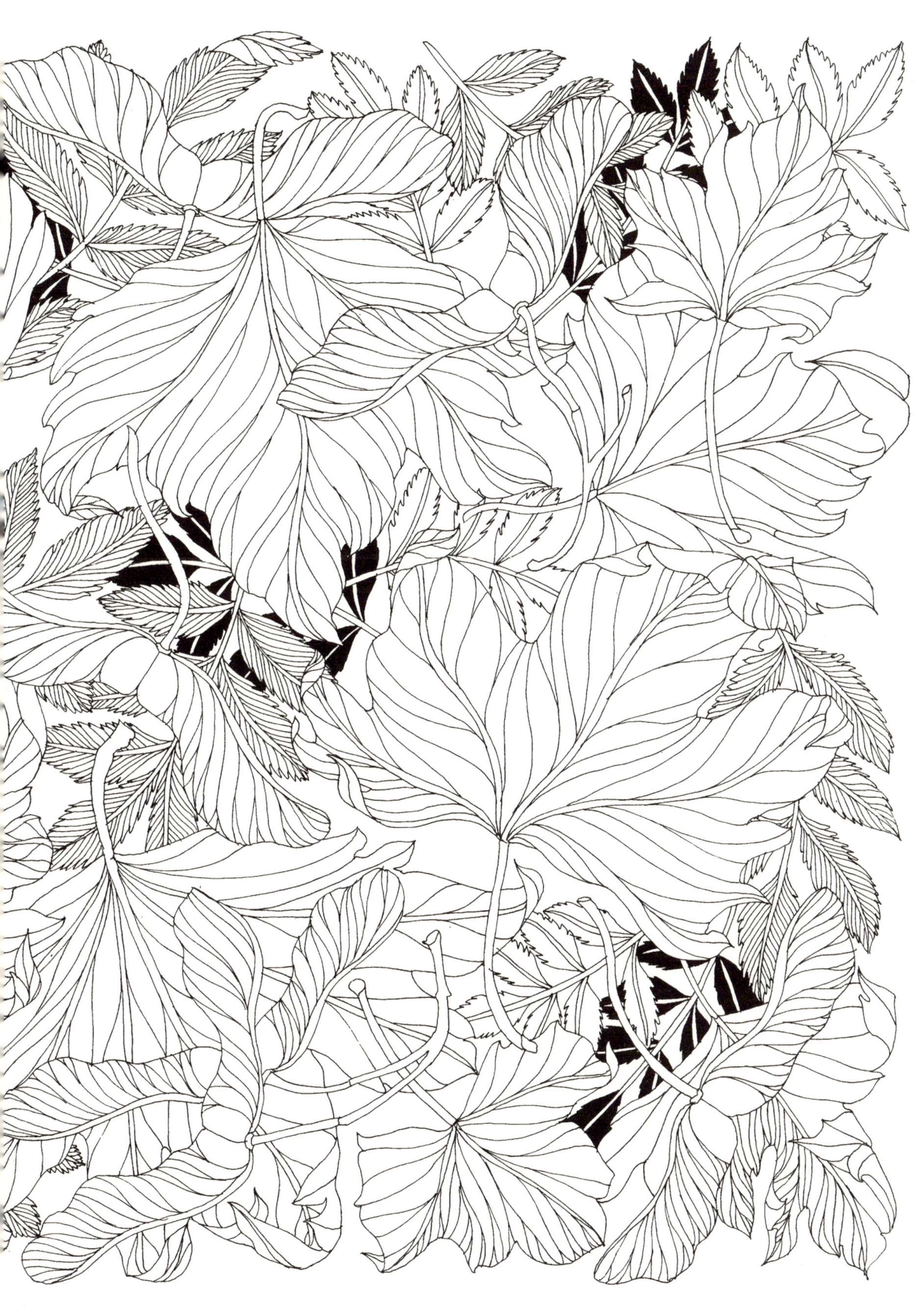

Broad-Leaved Dock, Cow Parsnip

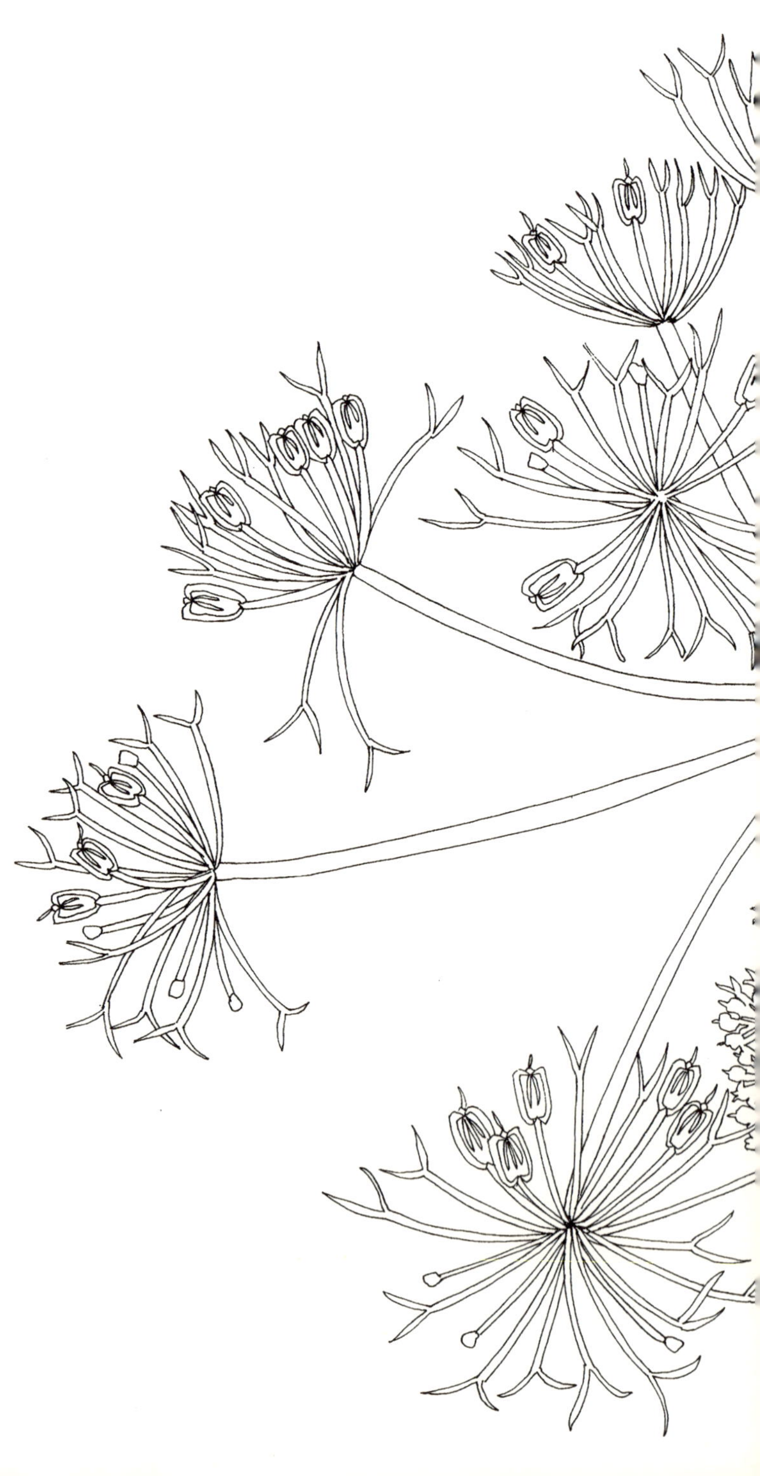

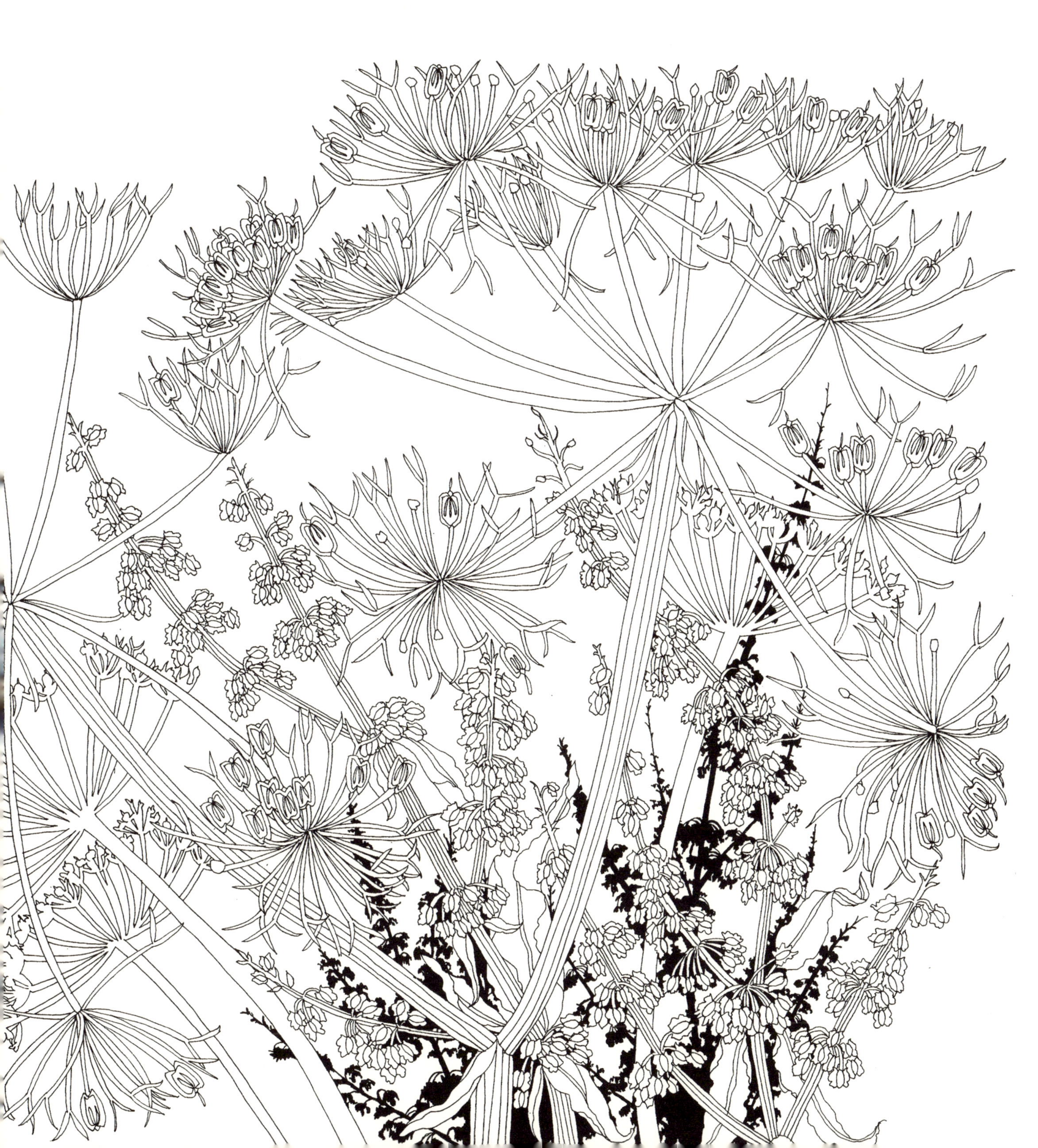

Laurustinus, Rose

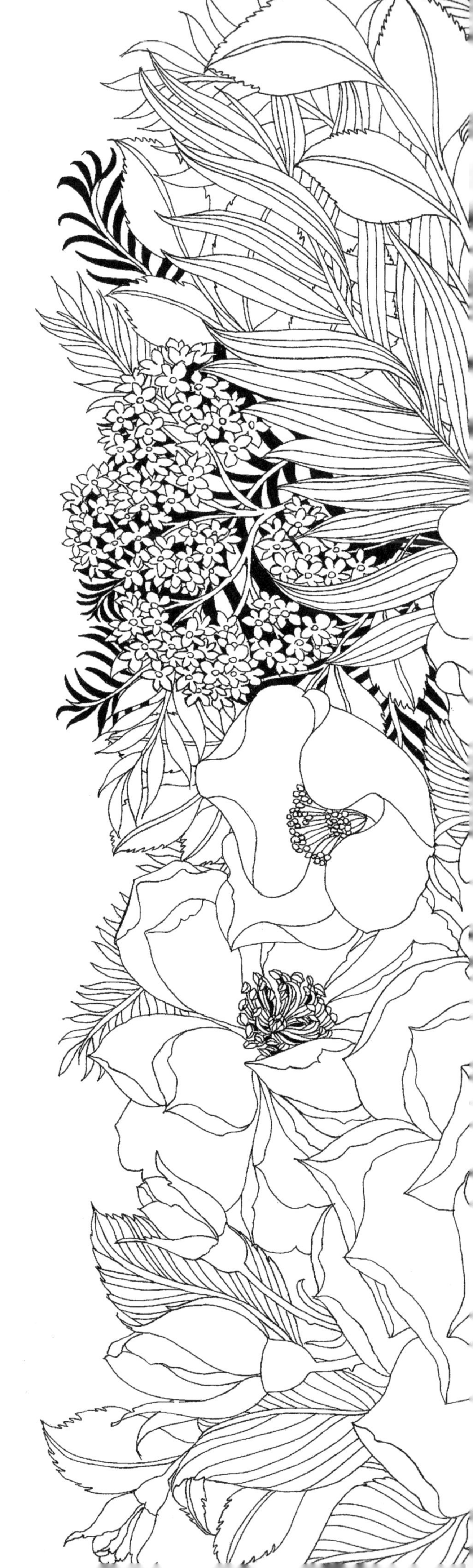

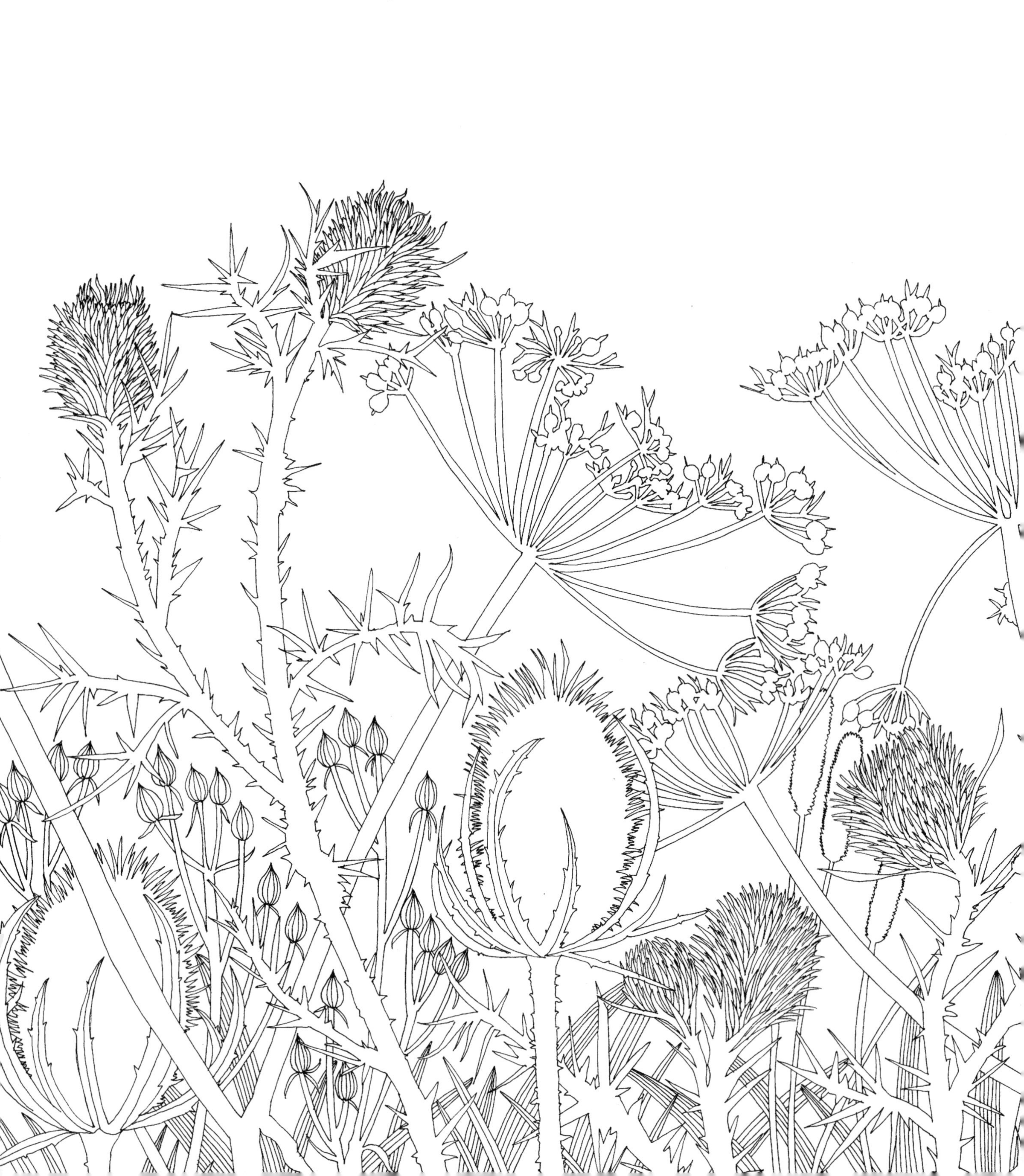

Cow Parsley, Welted Thistle,
Nipplewort, Teasel

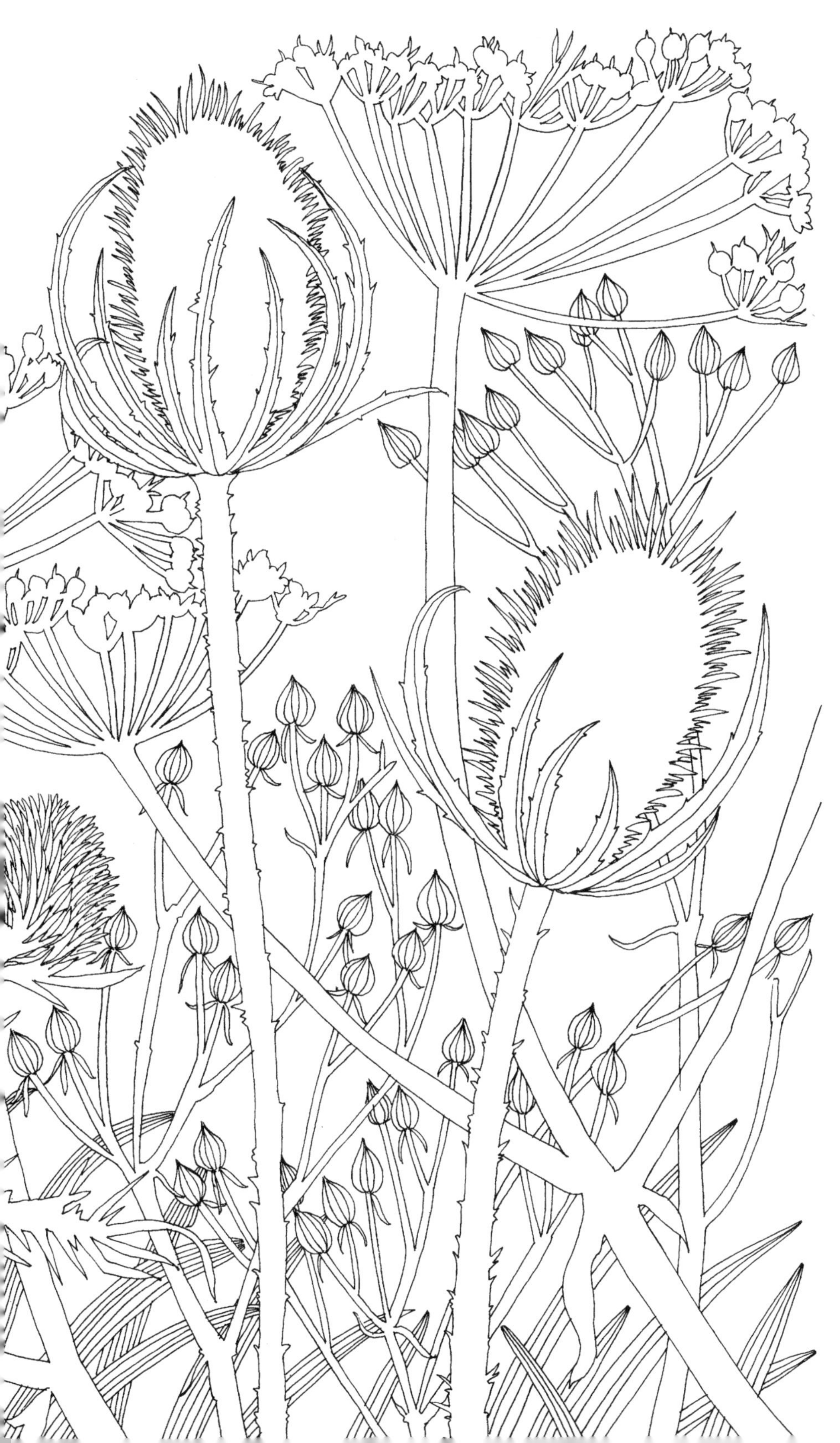

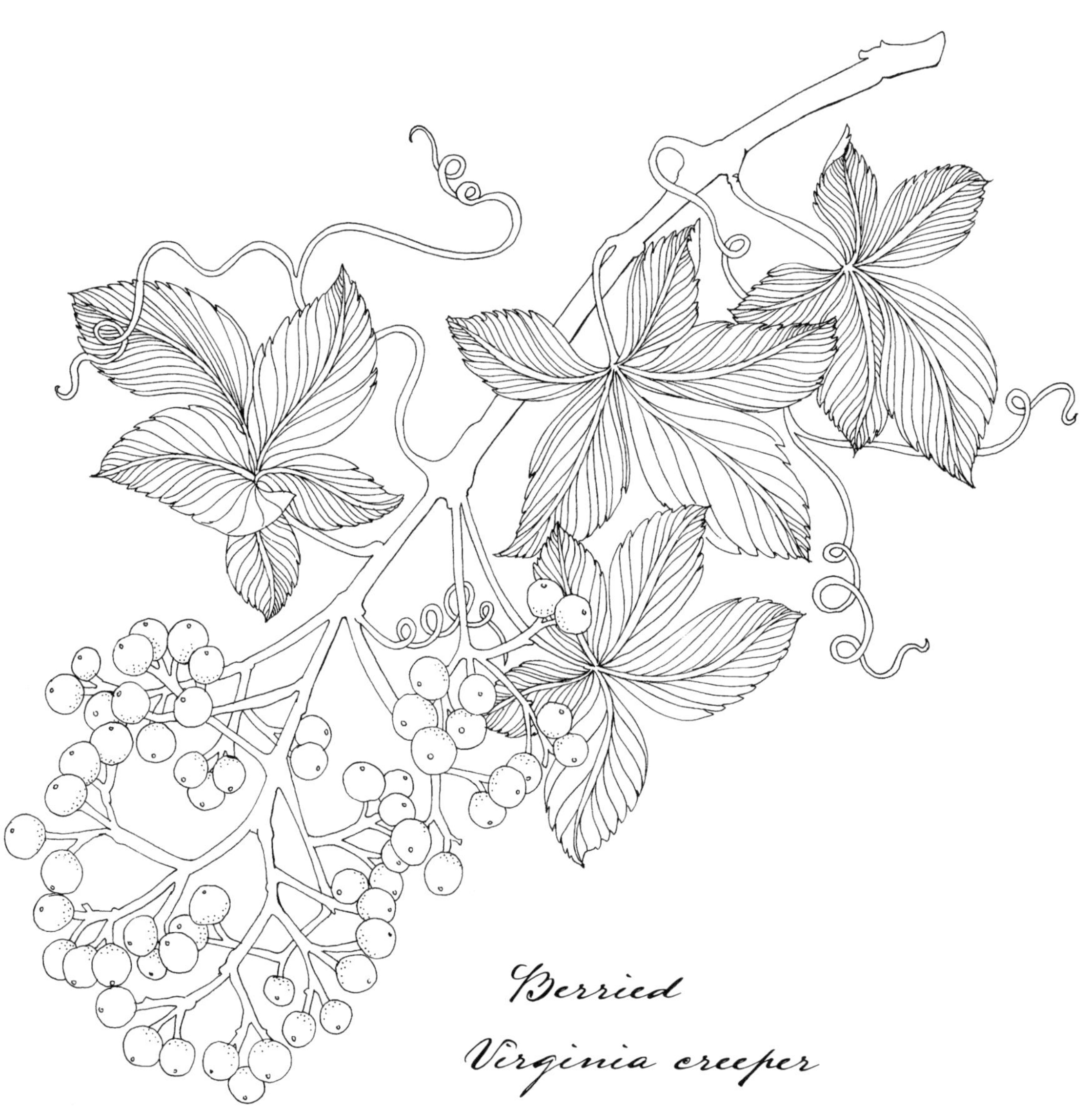
Berried
Virginia creeper

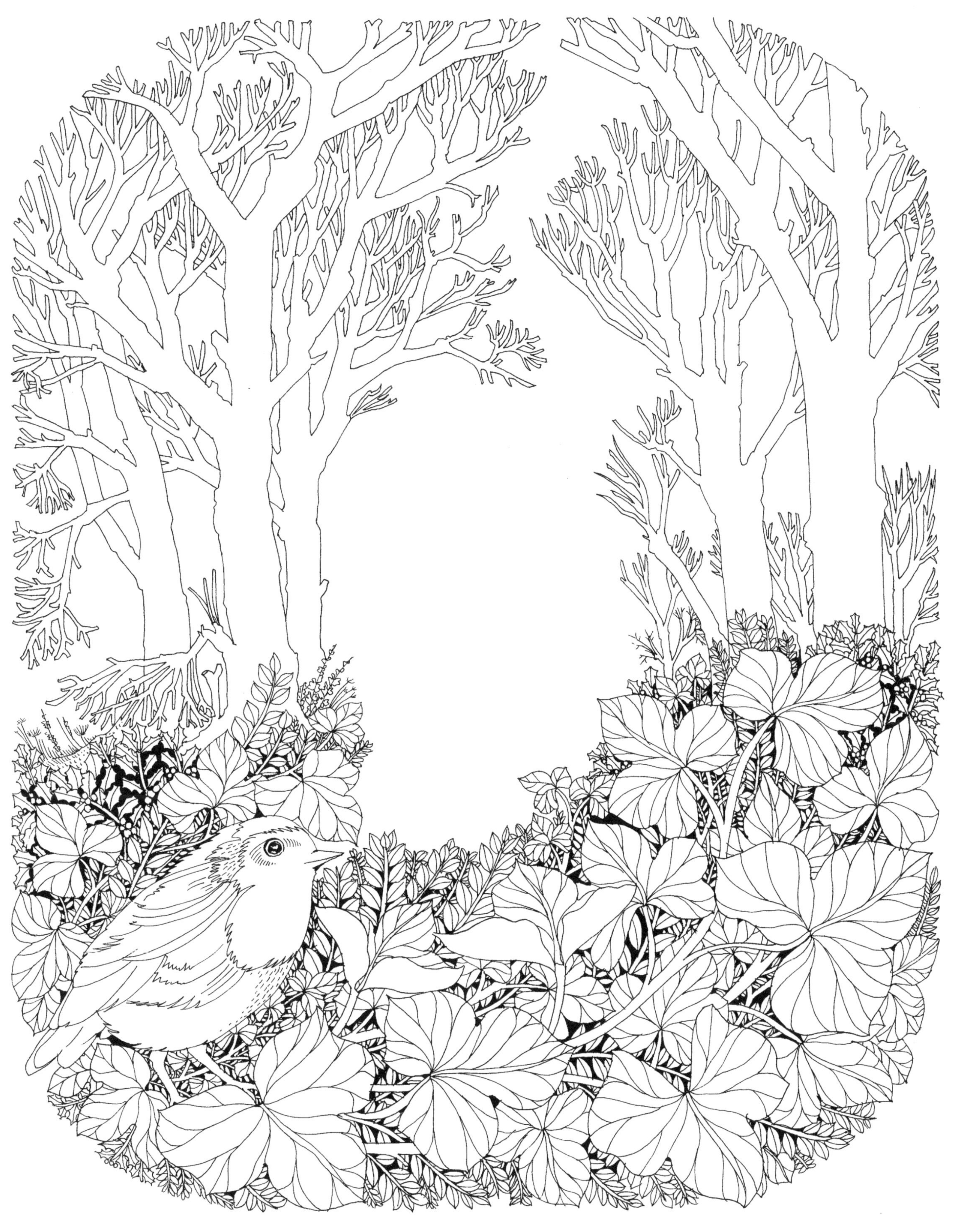

DECEMBER

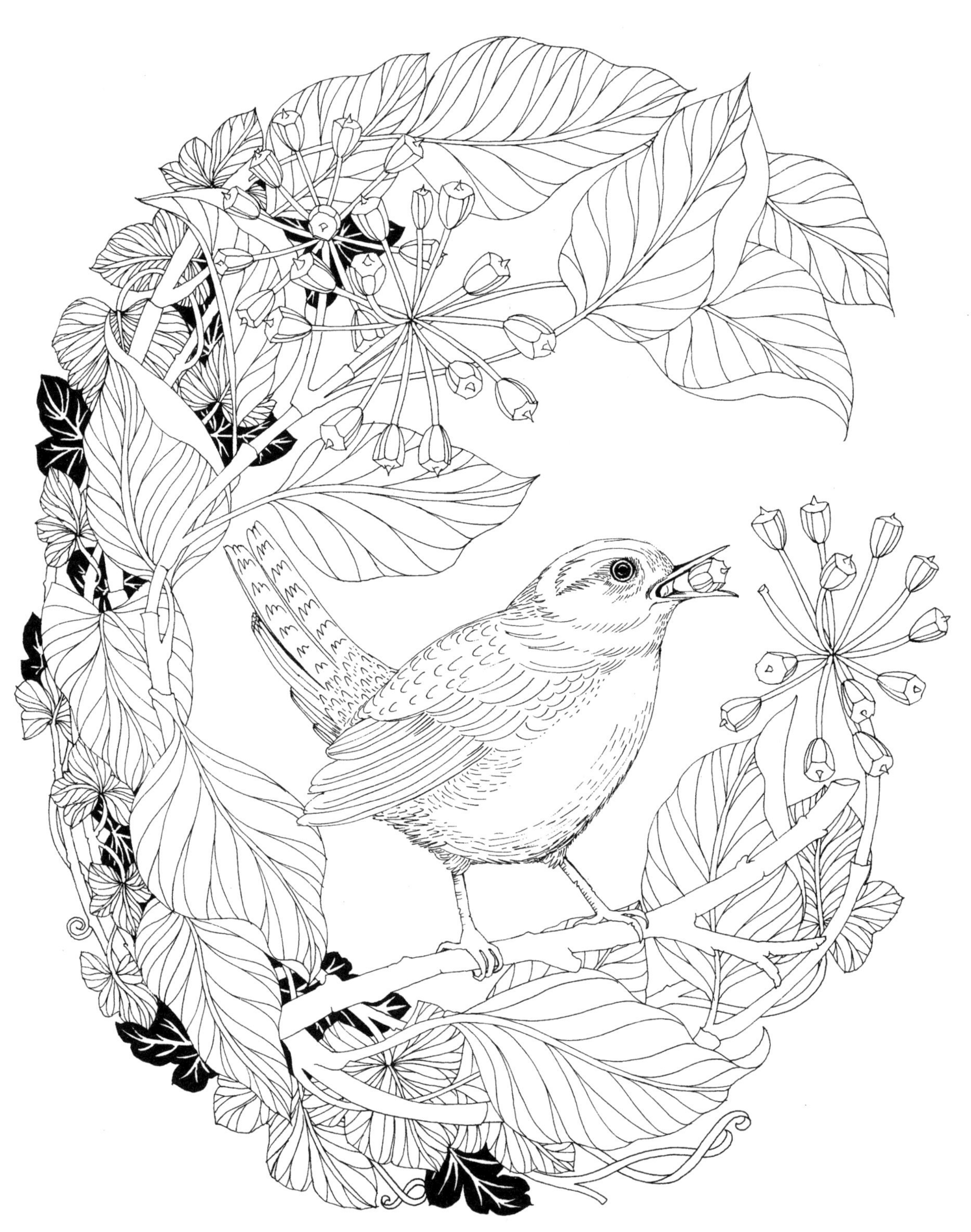

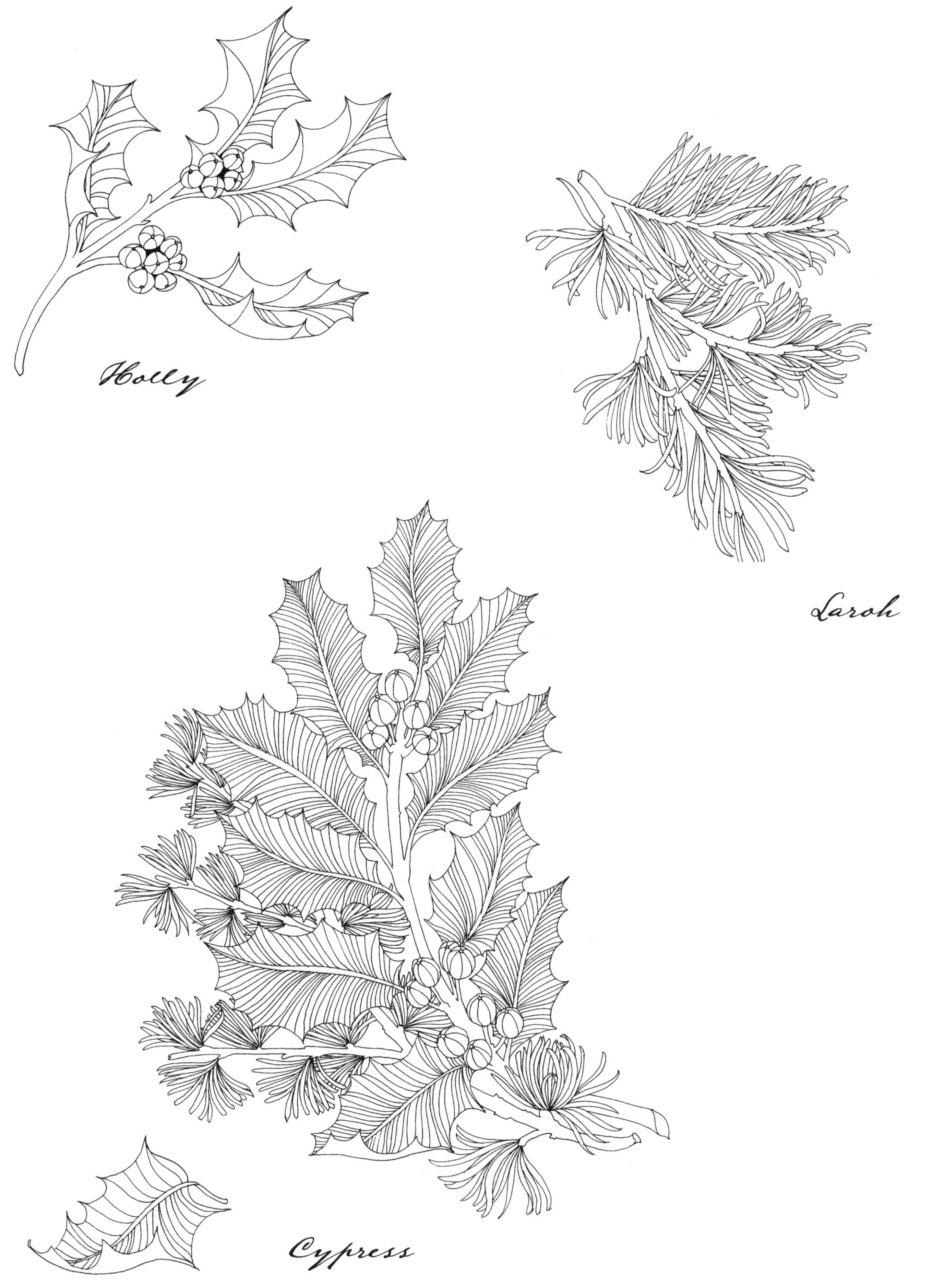
Holly
Larch
Cypress

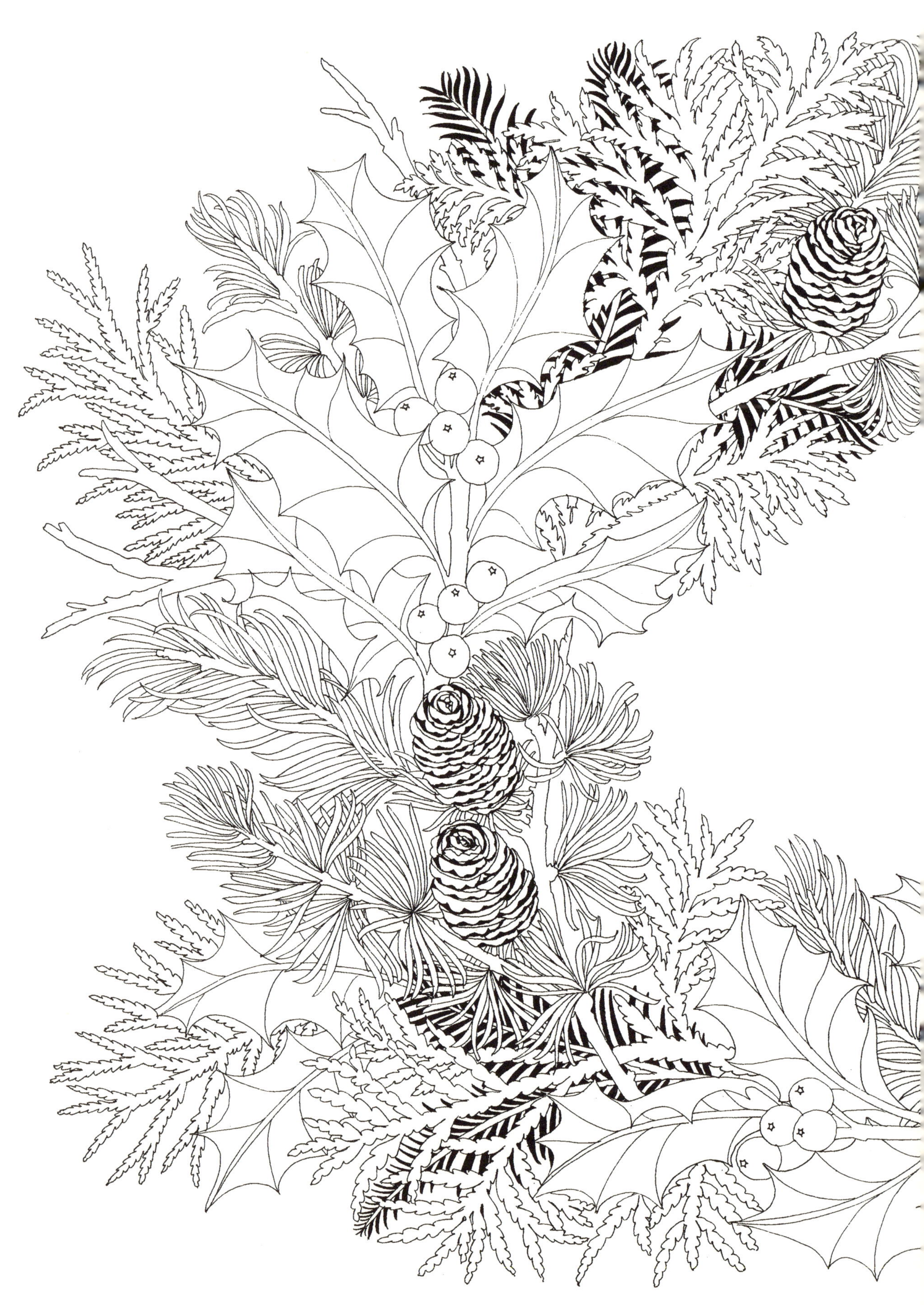

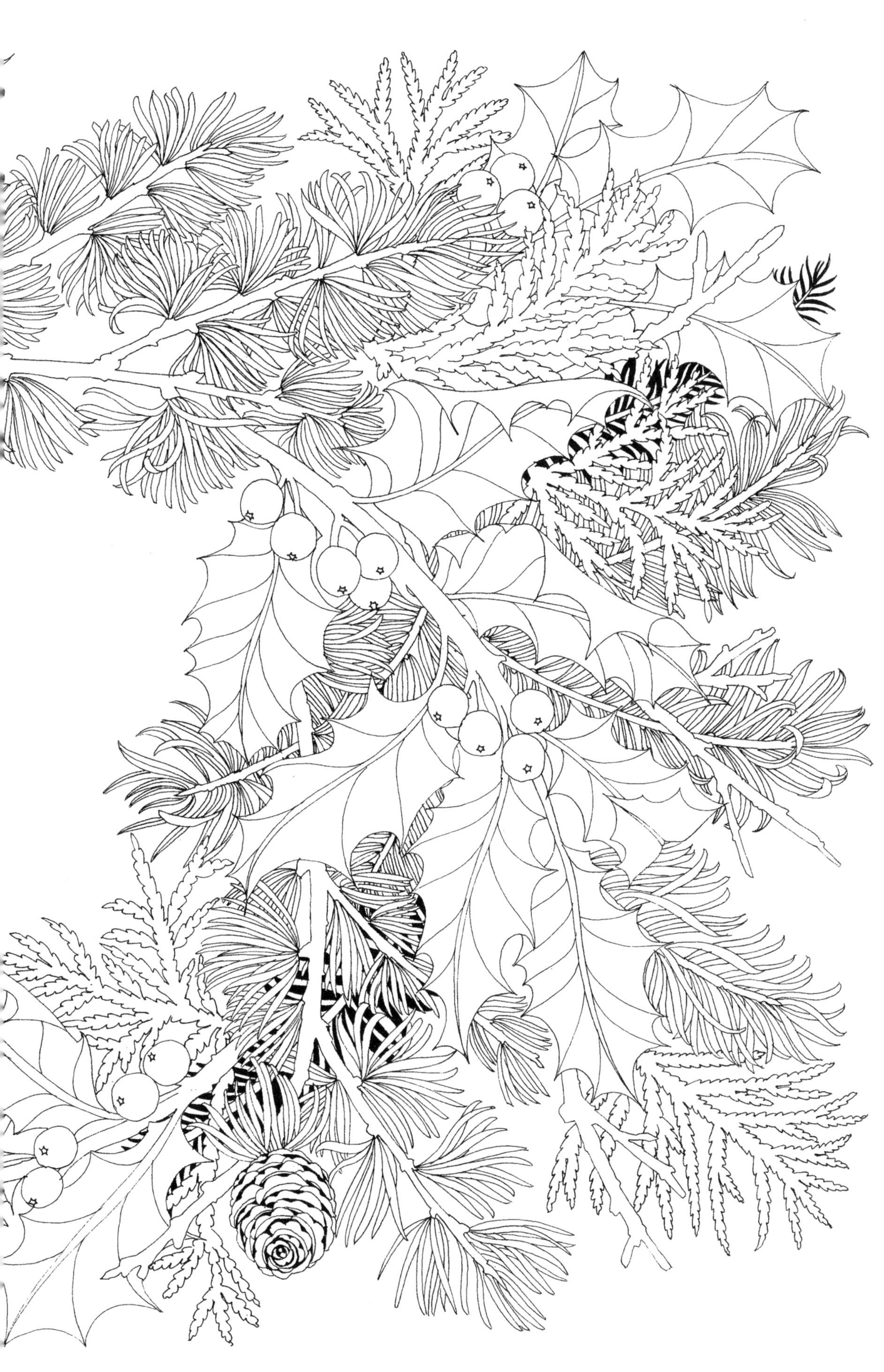

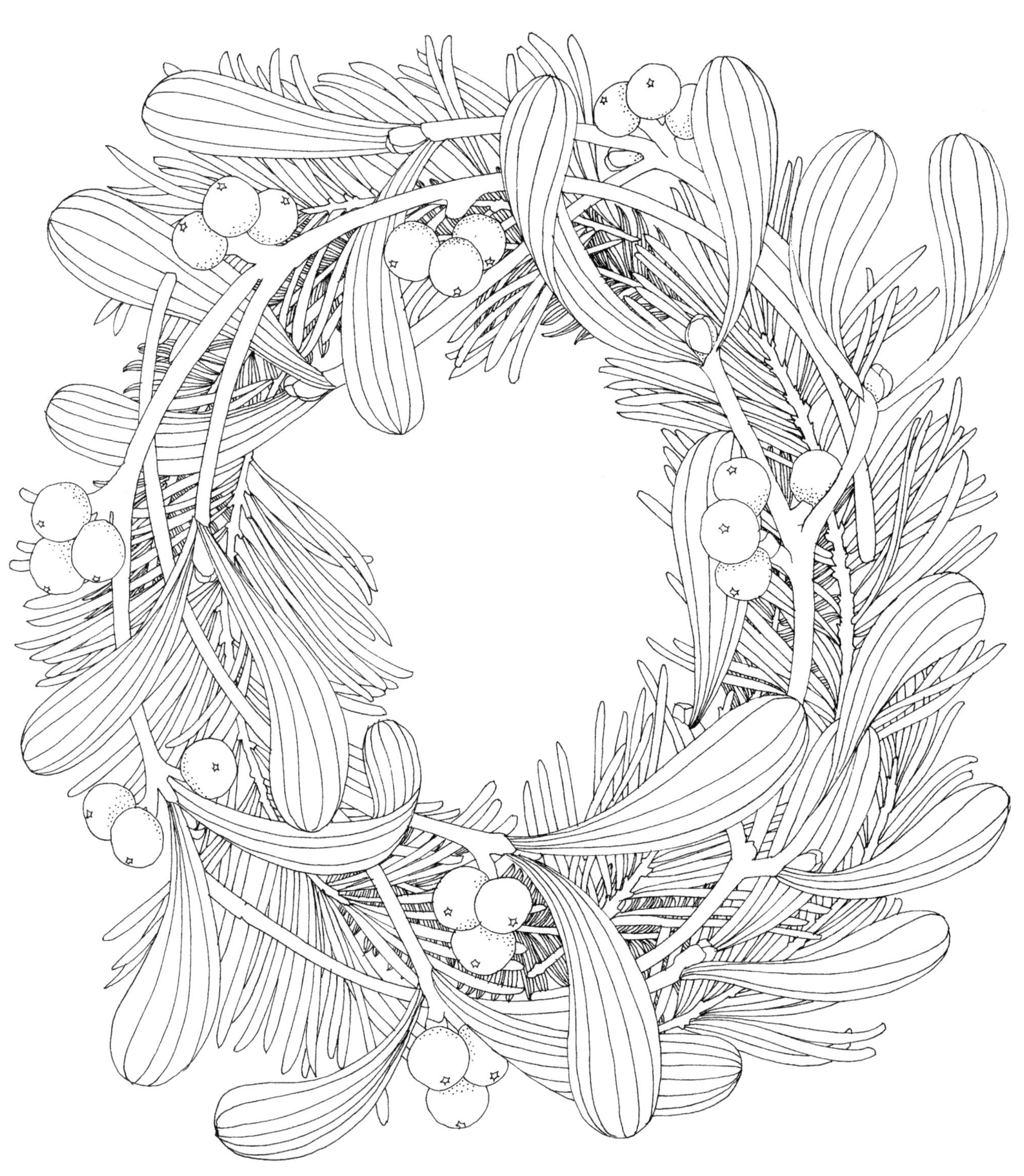

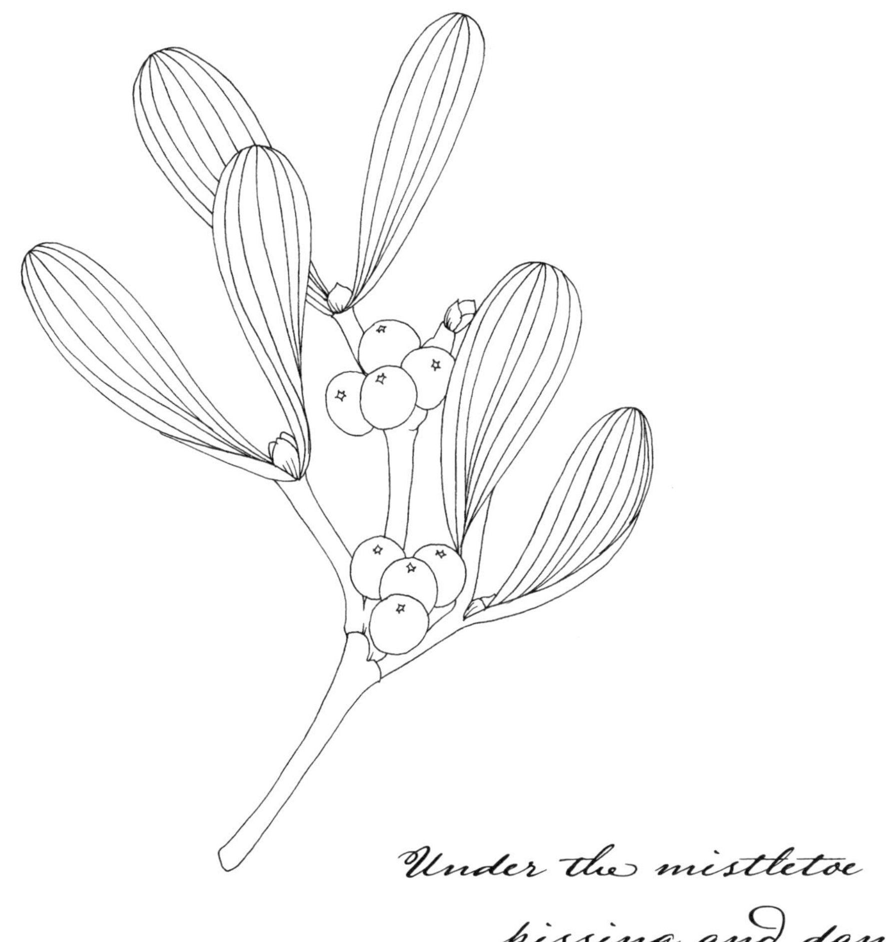

Under the mistletoe

kissing and dancing

MARY ELIZABETH COLERIDGE

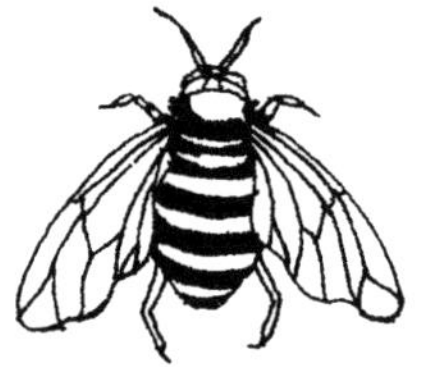

About the Author

....

Leila Duly is a textile print designer and illustrator based in East Sussex. Her work incorporates floral, natural and wildlife scenes developed from pencil sketches and hand-drawn in ink. Leila is inspired by the English countryside, the vibrant flower markets near her home, Victorian etchings and a love of bright vivid color.

Leila has worked as a freelance print designer for the fashion industry since graduating from the University of Brighton in 2000. Her fashion prints sell globally to some of the world's best known fashion brands.

Follow @leiladuly on instagram for color and design inspiration.

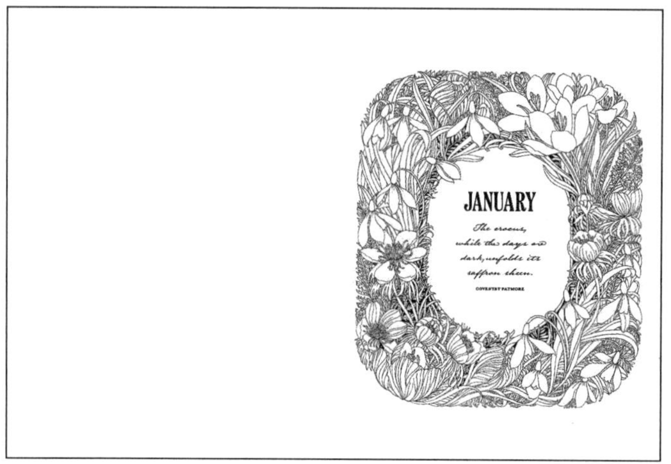

Crocus, Snowdrop, Winter Aconite

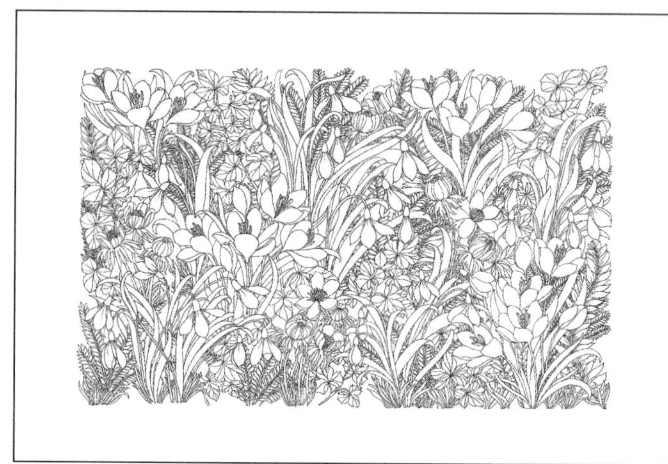

Crocus, Ivy, Snowdrop, Winter Aconite

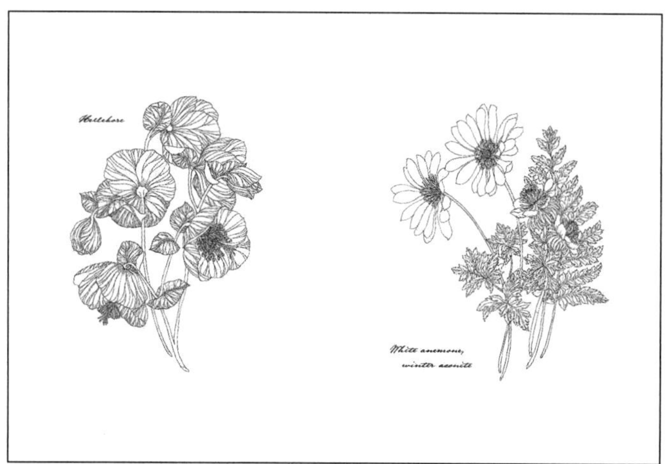

Left: Hellebore
Right: White Anemone, Winter Aconite

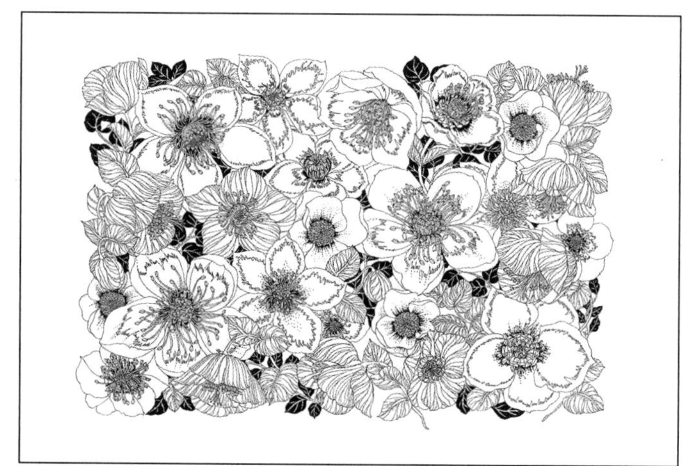

Hellebore

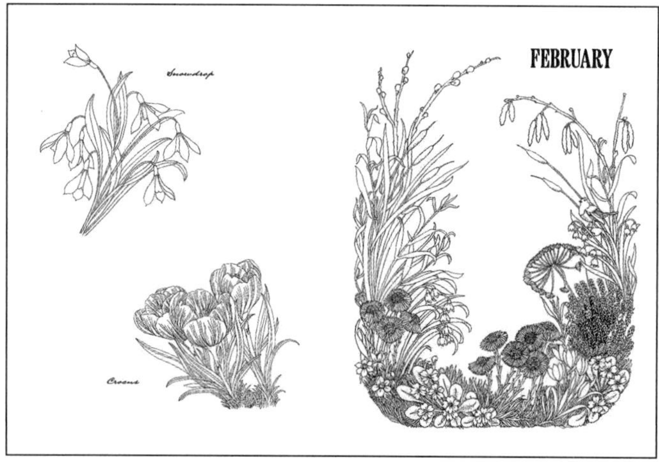

Left: Snowdrop, Crocus Right: Bulrush, Crocus, Coltsfoot, Cow Parsley, Daisy, Hazel Catkins, Primrose, Spring Snowflake, Willow Catkins, Winter Heather, Robin

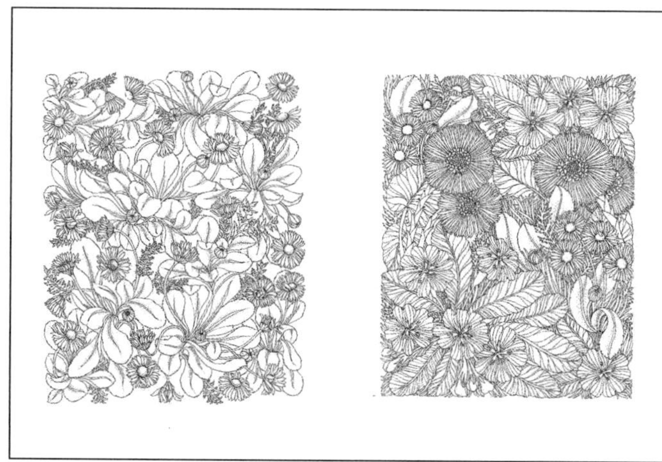

Left: Daisy
Right: Coltsfoot, Daisy, Primrose

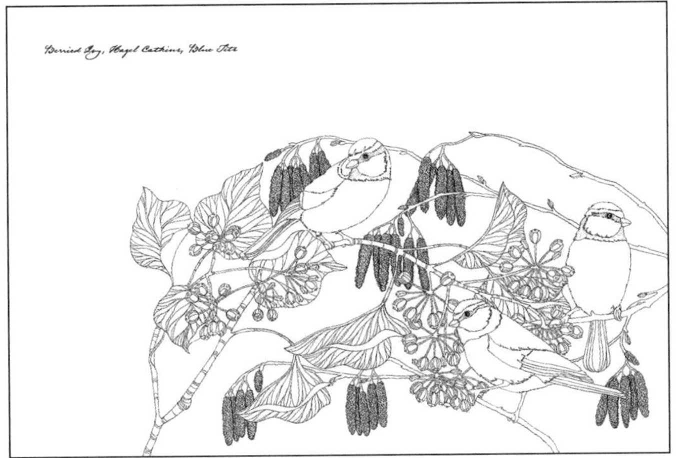

Berried Ivy, Hazel Catkins, Blue Tits

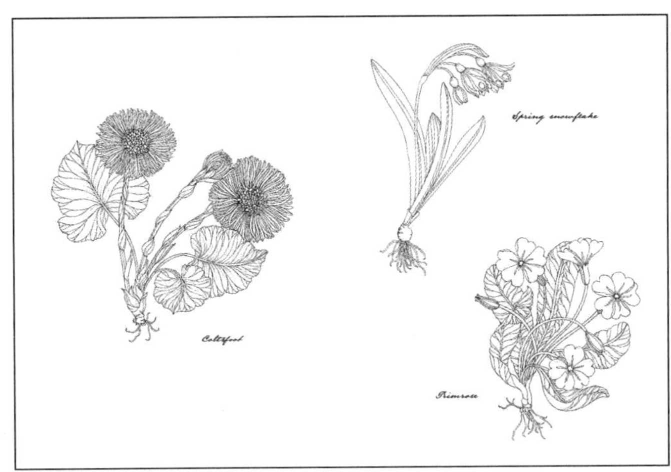

Left: Coltsfoot
Right: Spring Snowflake, Primrose

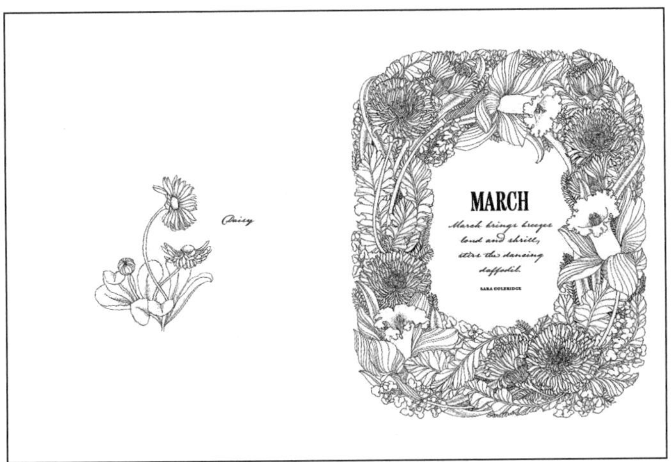

Left: Daisy
Right: Daffodil, Dandelion

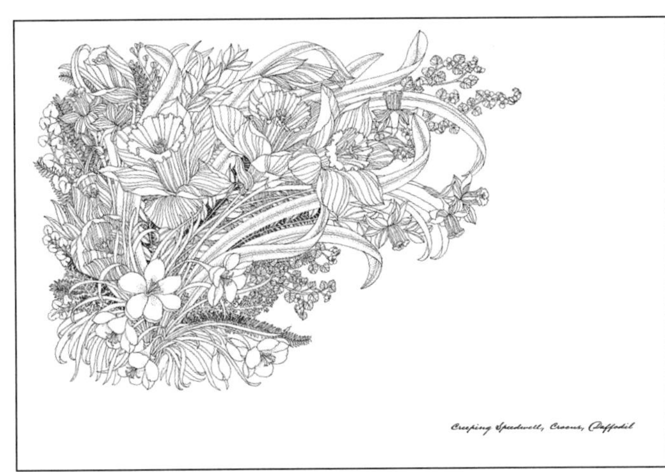

Creeping Speedwell, Crocus, Daffodil

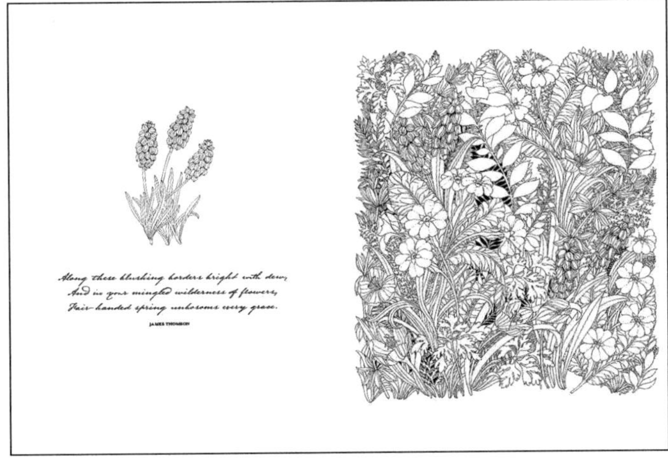

Left: Grape Hyacinth
Right: Crocus, Grape Hyacinth, Primrose

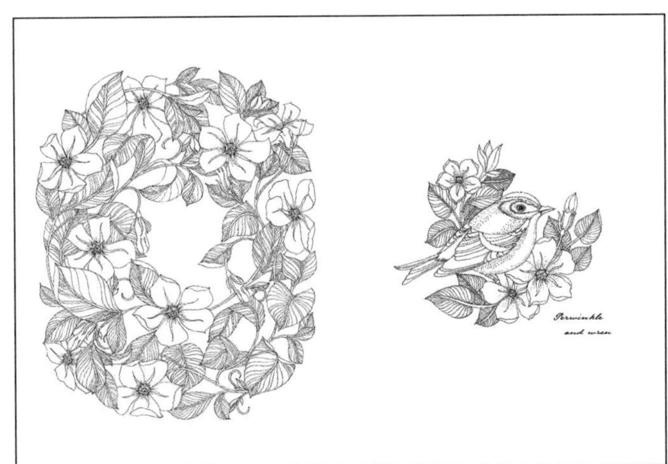

Left: Greater Periwinkle
Right: Greater Periwinkle,
Golden-Crested Wren

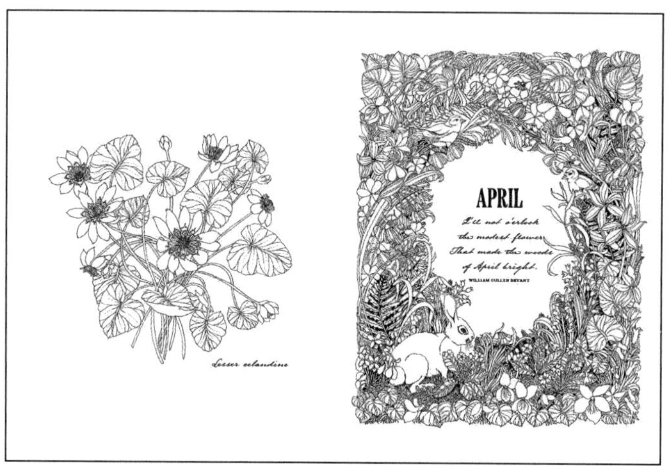

Left: Lesser Celandine Right: Bluebell, Cowslip, Fritillary, Marsh Marigold, Pasque Flower, Primrose, Ramsons, Red Deadnettle, Violet. Wild Strawberry, Wood Sorrel, Chaffinches and Rabbit

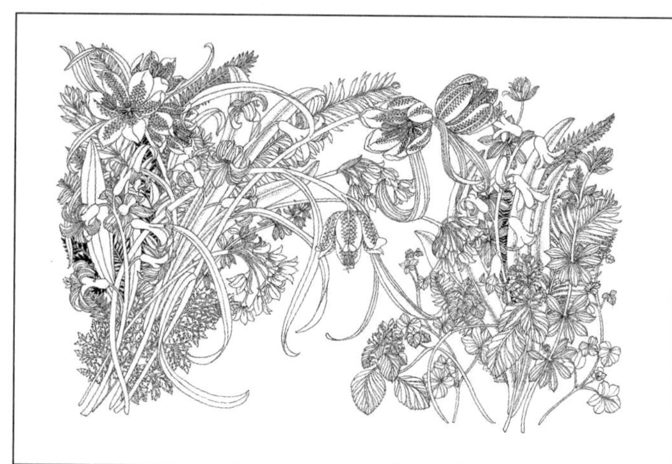

Bluebell, Fritillary, Goosegrass, Red Deadnettle

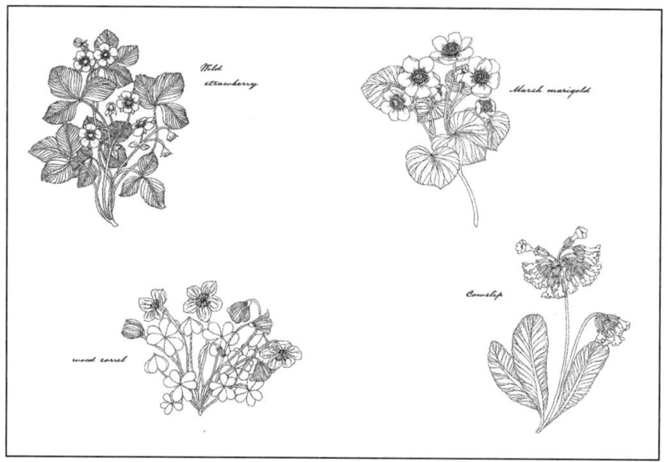

Wild Strawberry, Wood Sorrel, Marsh Marigold, Cowslip

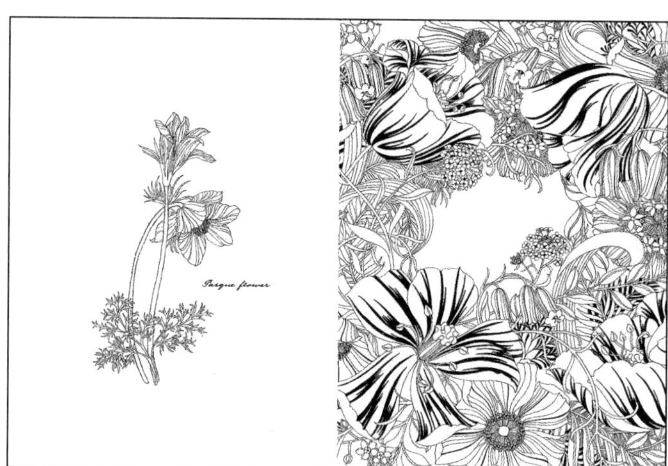

Left: Pasque Flower
Right: Alyssum, Bluebell, Forget-me-not, Tulip, Windflower and Linnia

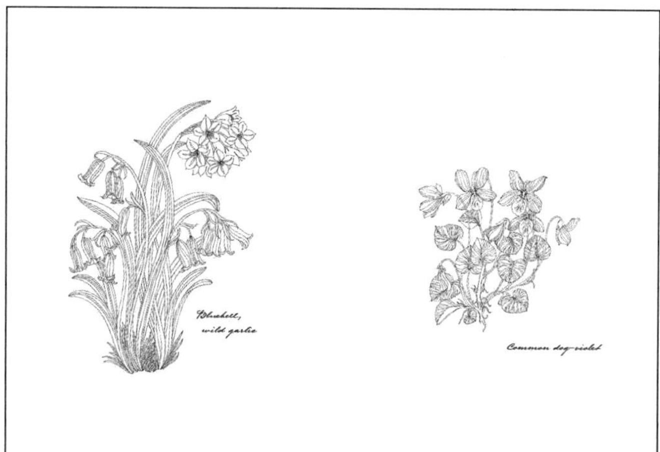

Left: Bluebell, Wild Garlic
Right: Common Dog-Violet

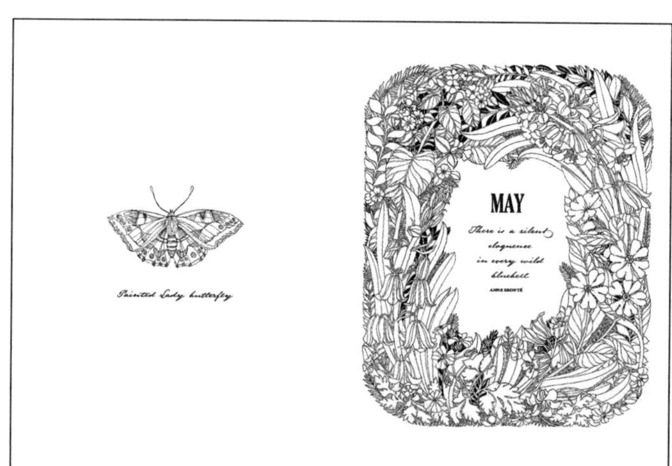

Left: Painted Lady Butterfly
Right: Bluebell, Evergreen Alkanet, Herb Robert, Red Campion

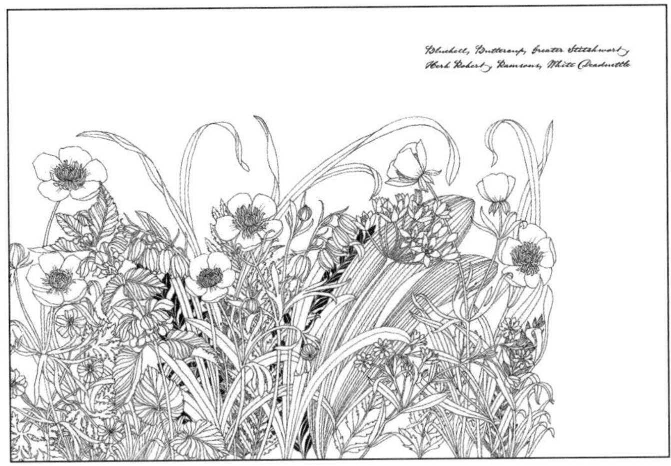

Bluebell, Buttercup, Greater Stitchwort, Herb Robert, Ramsons, White Deadnettle

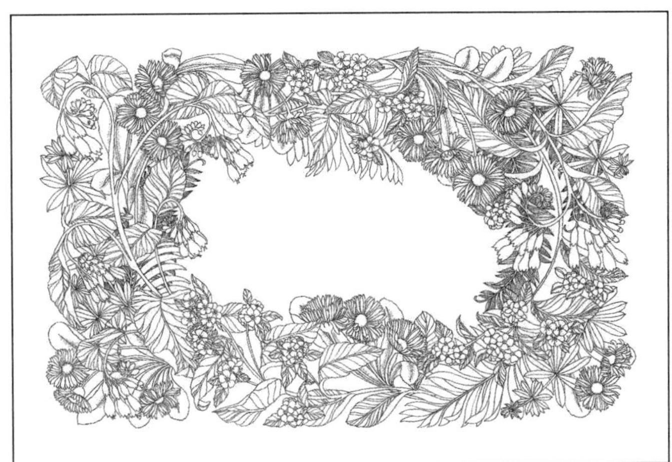

Comfrey, Daisy, Evergreen Alkanet

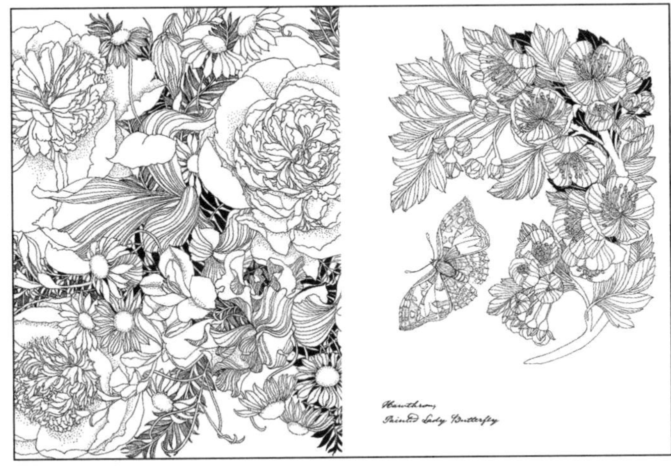

Left: Freesia, Iris, Marguerite Daisy, Peony and Sweet Pea
Right: Hawthorn, Painted Lady Butterfly

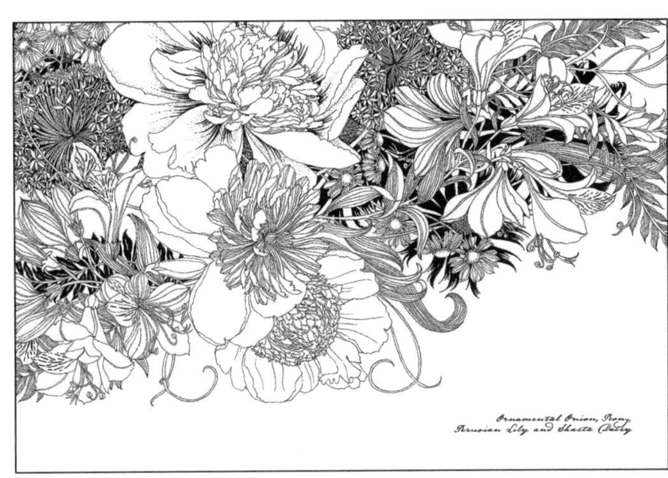

Ornamental Onion, Peony, Peruvian Lily and Shasta Daisy

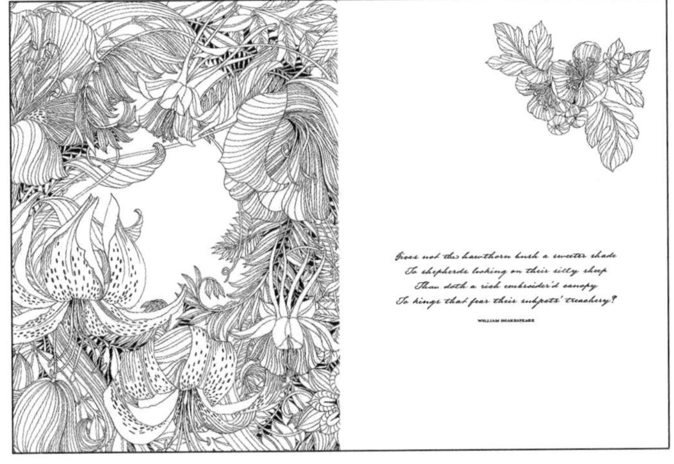

Left: Columbine and Lily
Right: Hawthorne

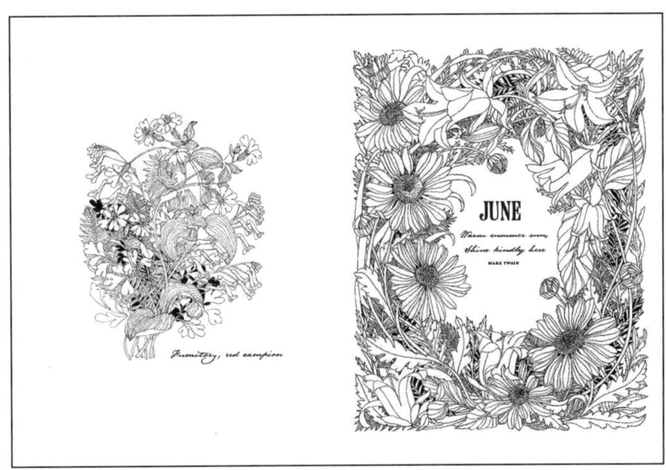

Left: Fumitory, Red Campion
Right: Common Mallow, Field Scabious, Lesser Knapweed, Marguerite Daisy, Nettle-Leaved Bellflower

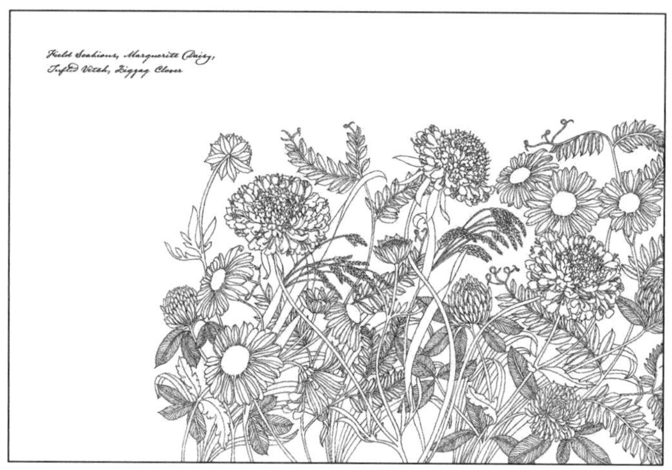

Field Scabious, Marguerite Daisy, Tufted Vetch, Zigzag Clover

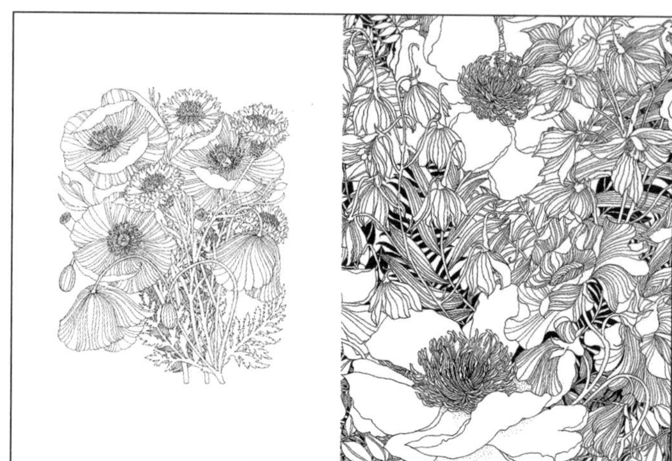

Left: Cornflower, Field Poppy
Right: Delphinium, Peony and Sweet Pea

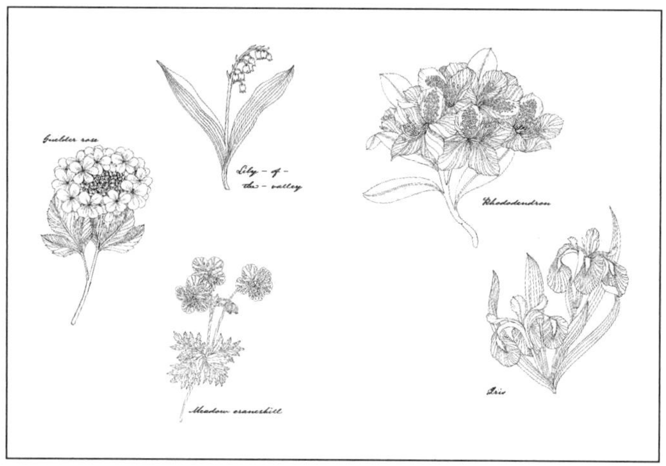

Guelder Rose, Lily-of-the-Valley, Meadow Cranesbill, Rhododendron, Iris

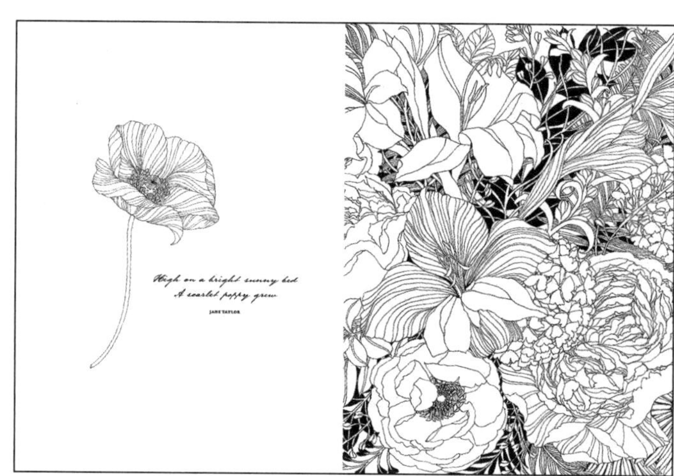

Left: Poppy
Right: Guelder Rose, Michaelmas Daisy, Peony, Sword Lily and Windflower

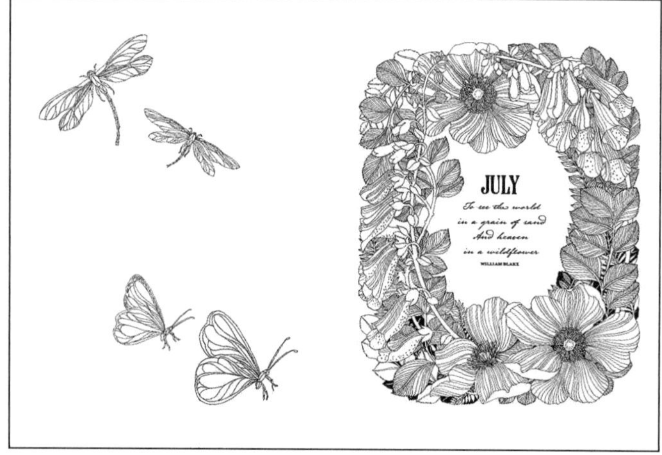

Left: Dragonfly, Butterfly
Right: Dog Rose, Foxglove

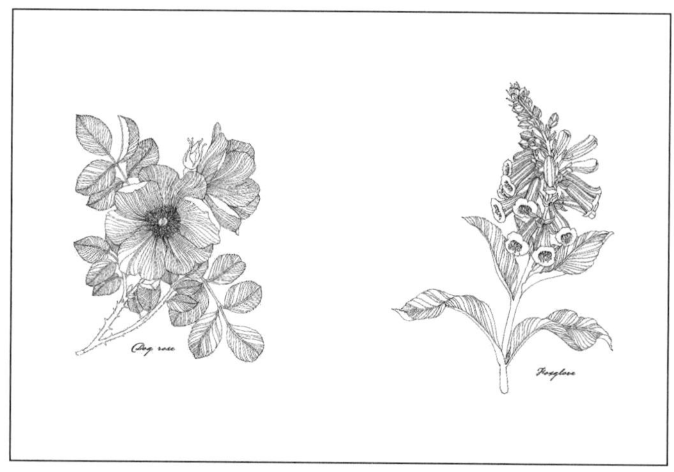

Left: Dog Rose
Right: Foxglove

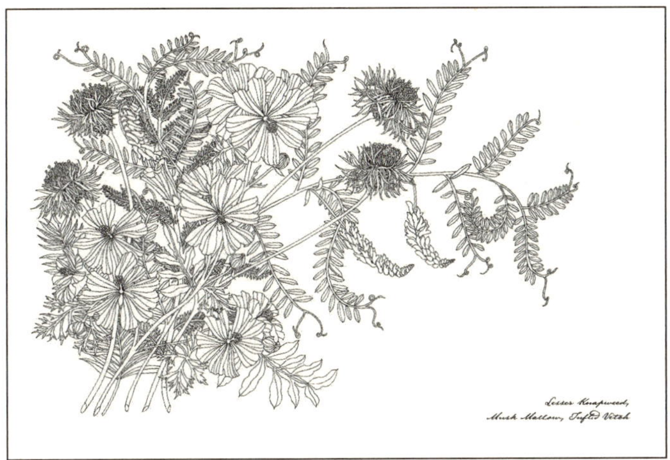

Lesser Knapweed, Musk Mallow, Tufted Vetch

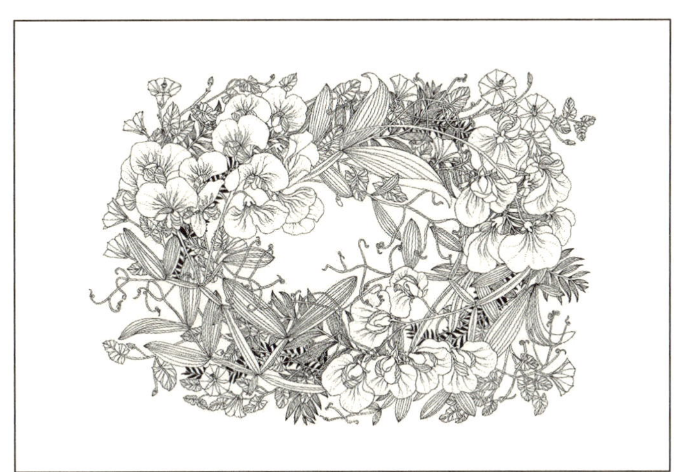

Bindweed, Everlasting Pea

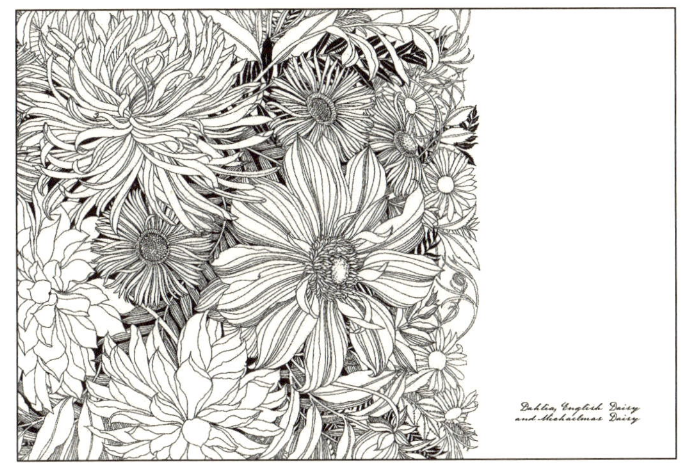

Dahlia, English Daisy and Michaelmas Daisy

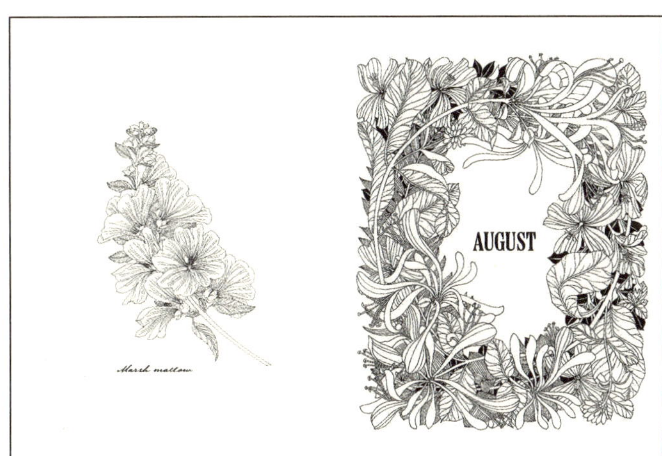

Left: Marsh Mallow
Right: Common Mallow, Honeysuckle

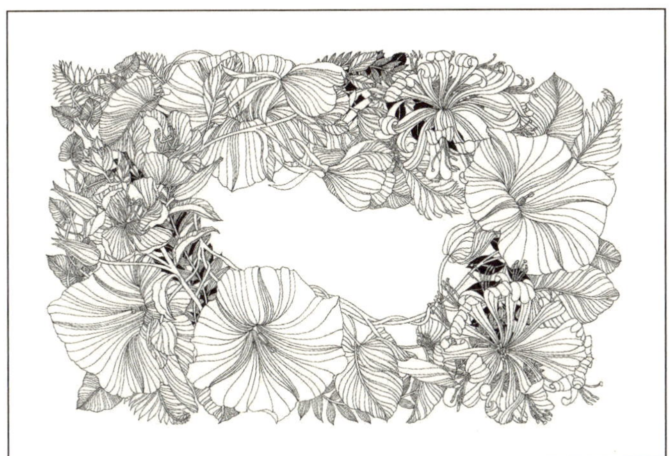

Hedge Bindweed, Honeysuckle, Large-Flowered Evening Primrose

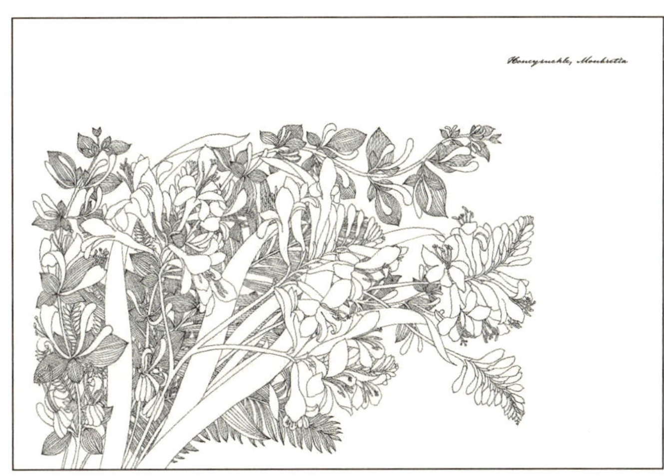

Honeysuckle, Montbretia

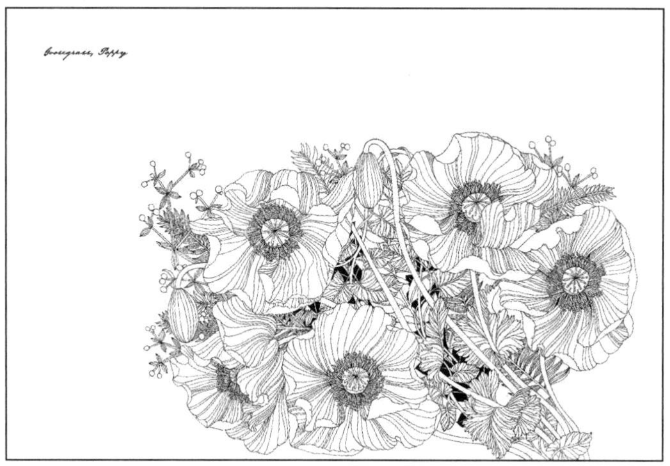

Goosegrass, Poppy

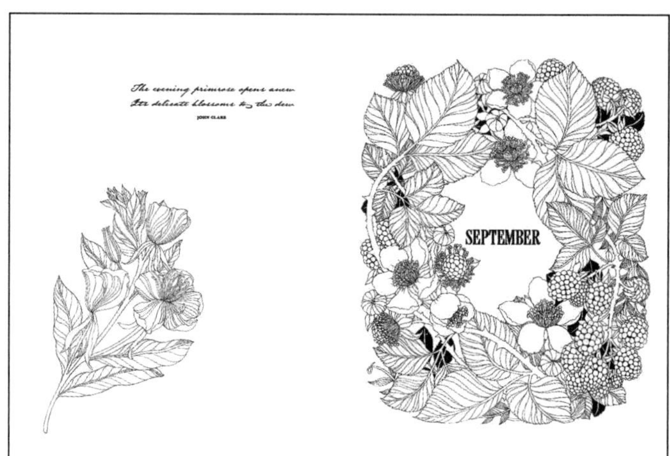

Left: Common Evening Primrose
Right: Blackberry

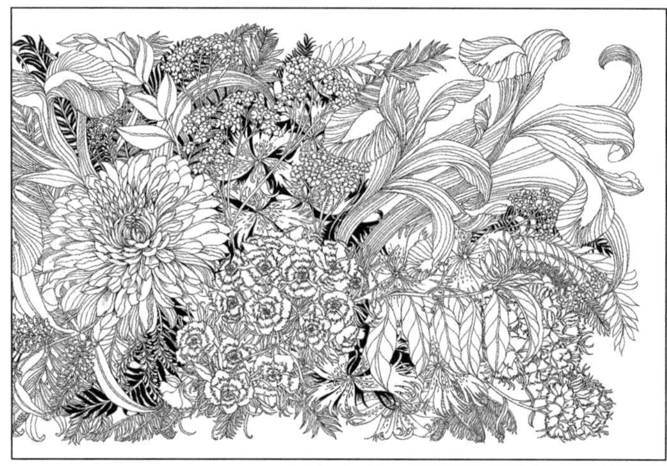

Chrysanthemum, Dianthus, Iris, Honeysuckle, Speedwell, Sweet William, Yarrow

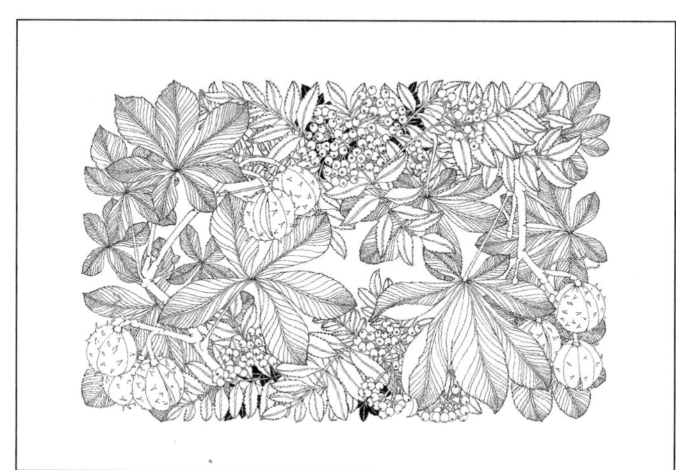

Horse Chestnut, Rowan

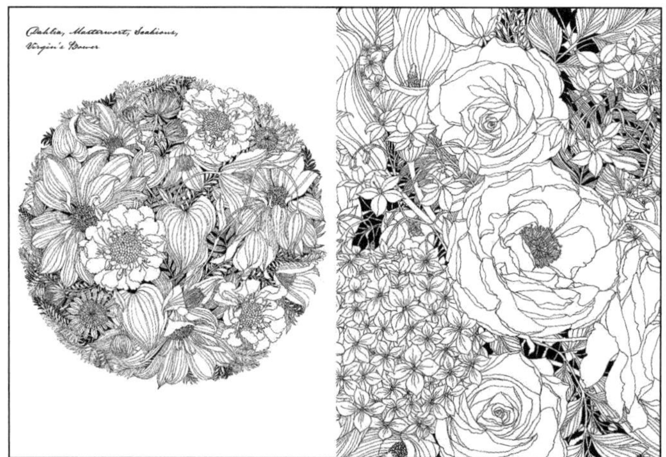

Left: Dahlia, Masterwort, Scabious and Virgin's Bower
Right: Calla Lily, Hydrangea, Potato Vine, Rose

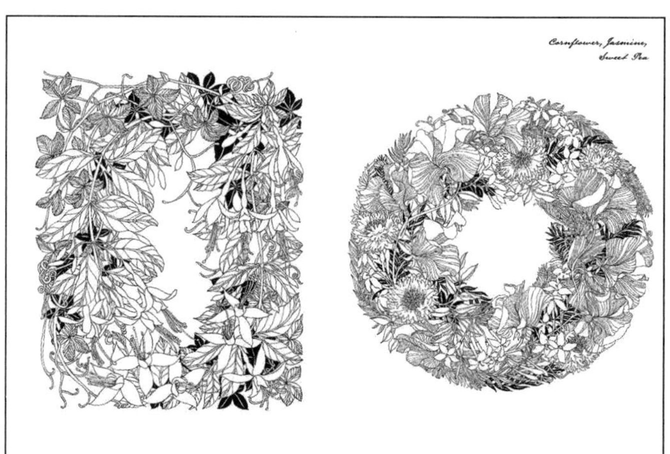

Left: Virginia Creeper, Wild Fuchsia
Right: Cornflower, Jasmine and Sweet Pea

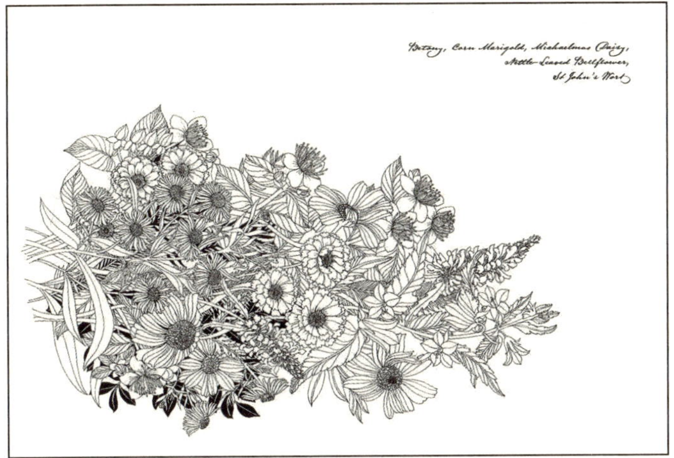

Betony, Corn Marigold, Michaelmas Daisy, Nettle-Leaved Bellflower, St John's Wort

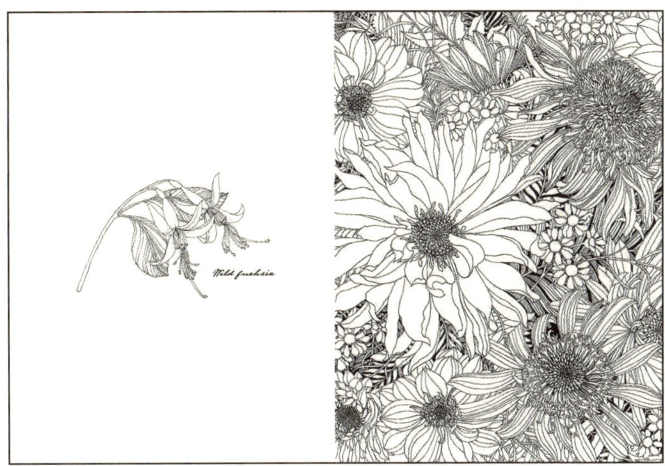

Left: Wild Fuchsia
Right: Chrysanthemum, Cornflower, Dahlia, Feverfew

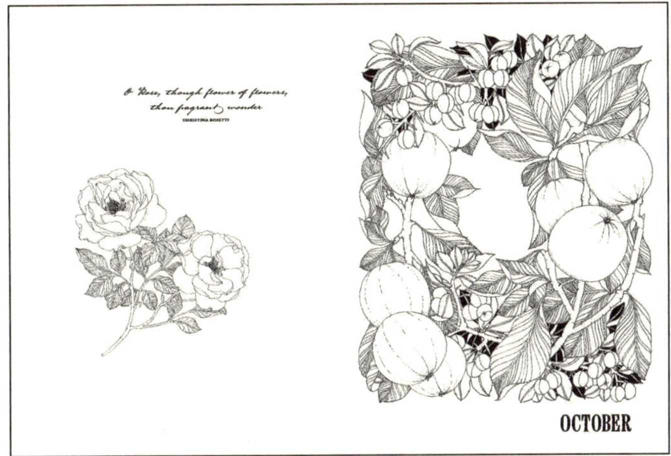

Left: Garden Rose
Right: Crab Apple, Sloe Berries

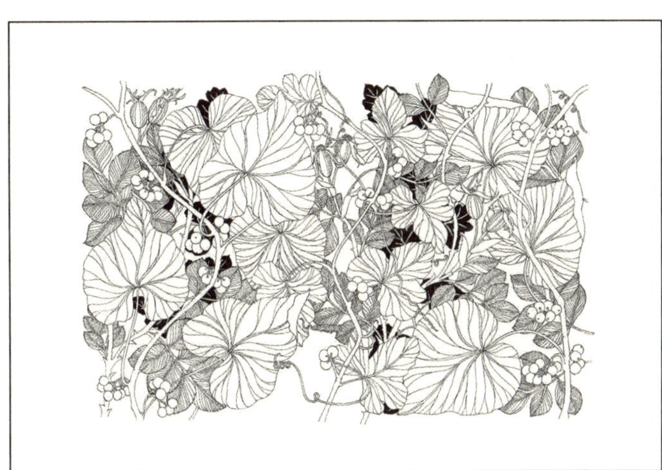

Black Bryony, Dog Rose Hips, White Bryony

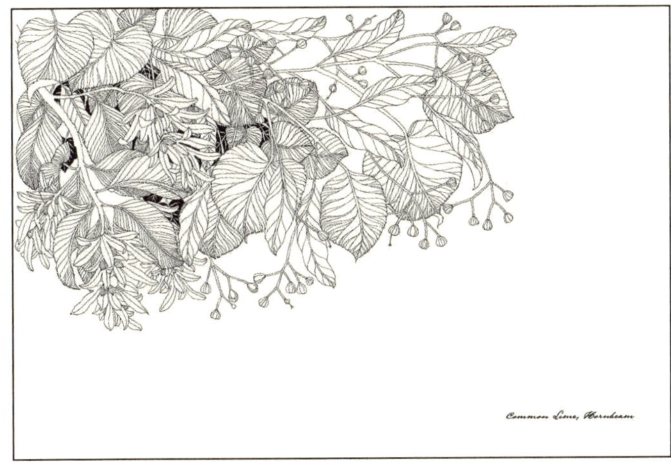

Common Lime, Hornbeam

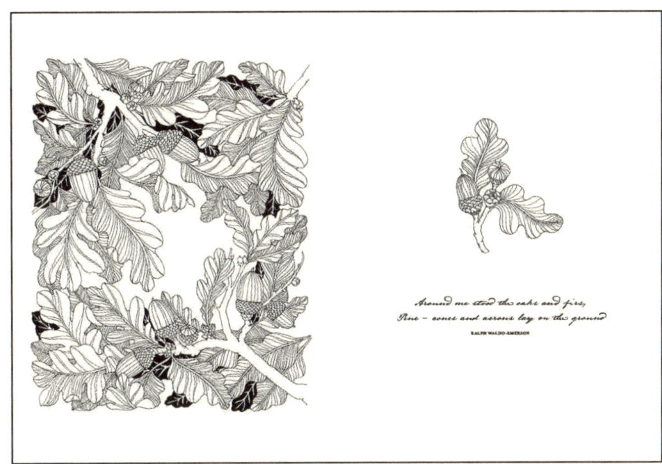

English Oak

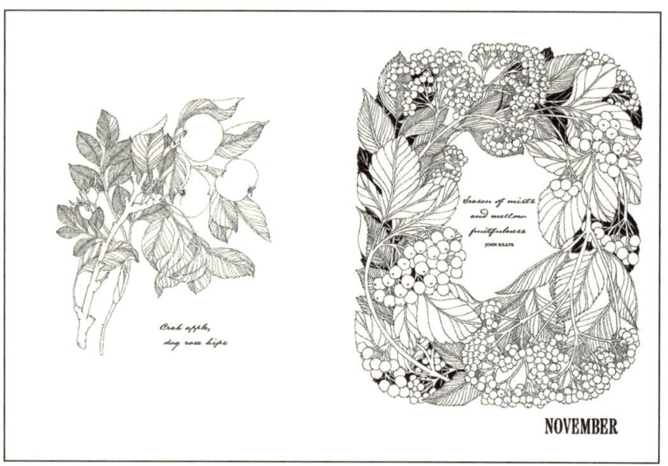

Left: Crab Apple, Dog Rose Hips
Right: Elderberries, Guelder Rose Berries

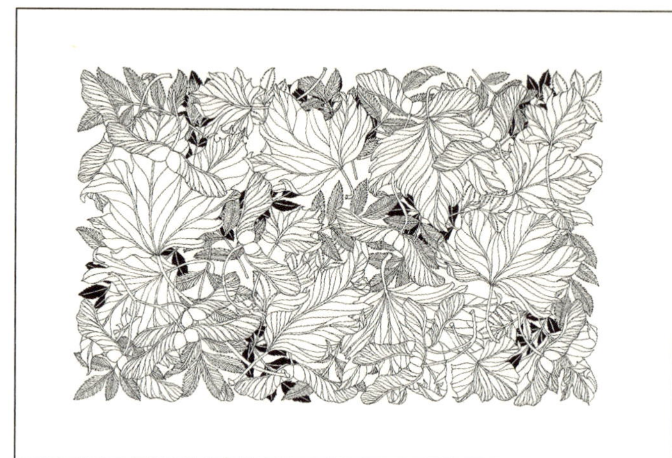

Rowan, Sycamore

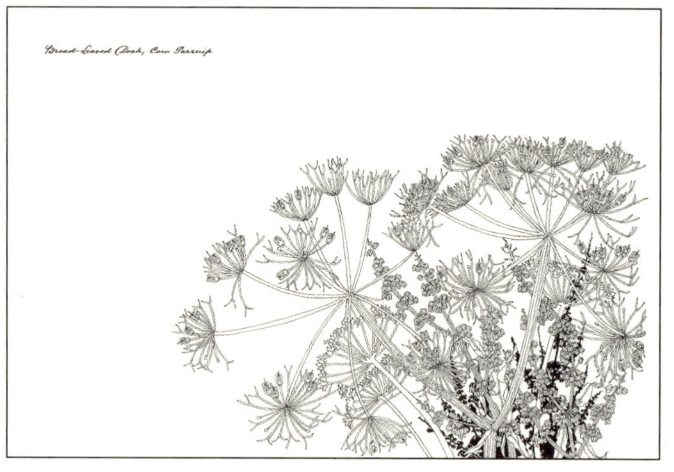

Broad-Leaved Dock, Cow Parsnip

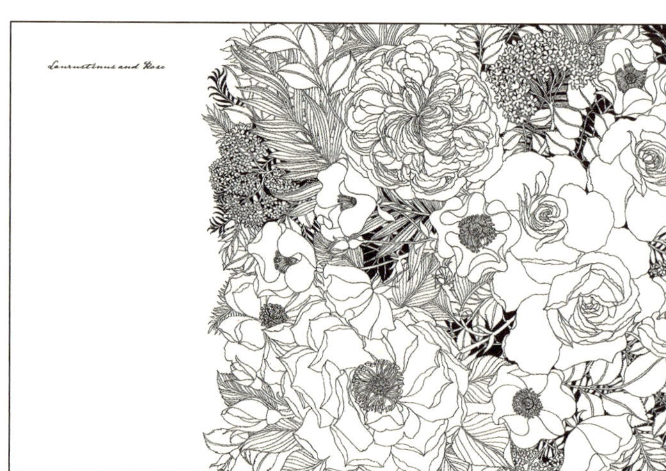

Laurustines, Rose

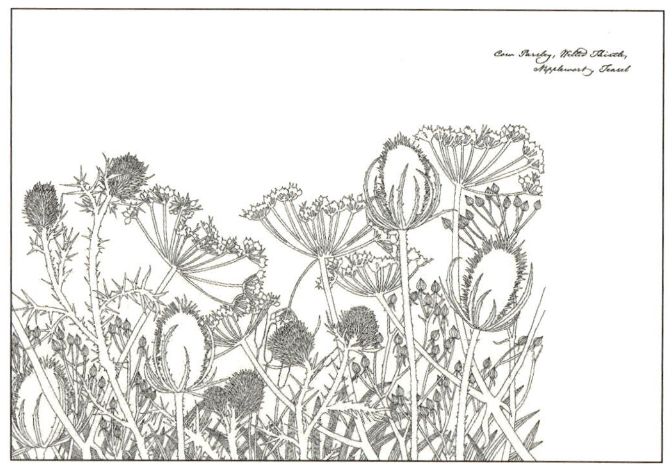

Cow Parsley, Welted Thistle,
Nipplewort, Teasel

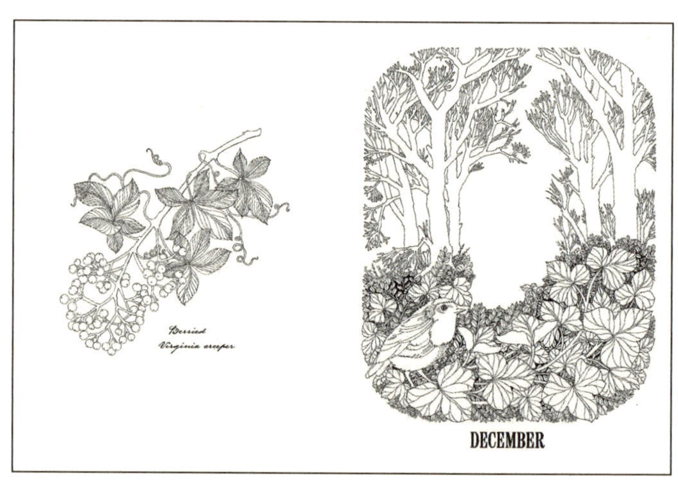

Left: Berried Virginia Creeper
Right: Holly, Ivy, Winter Trees, Robin

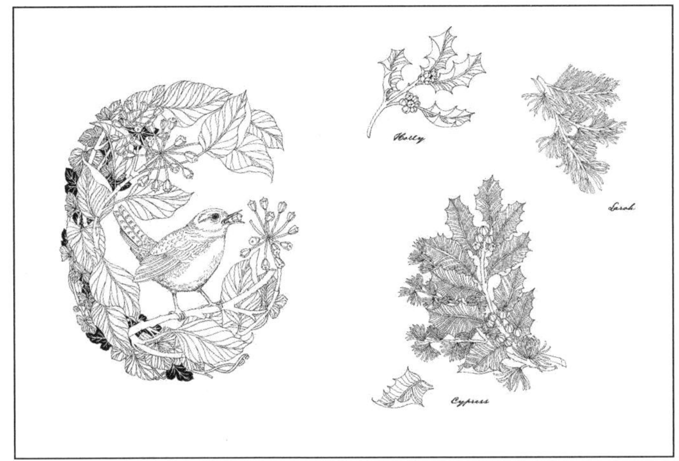

Left: Berried Ivy, Wren
Right: Holly, Larch, Cypress

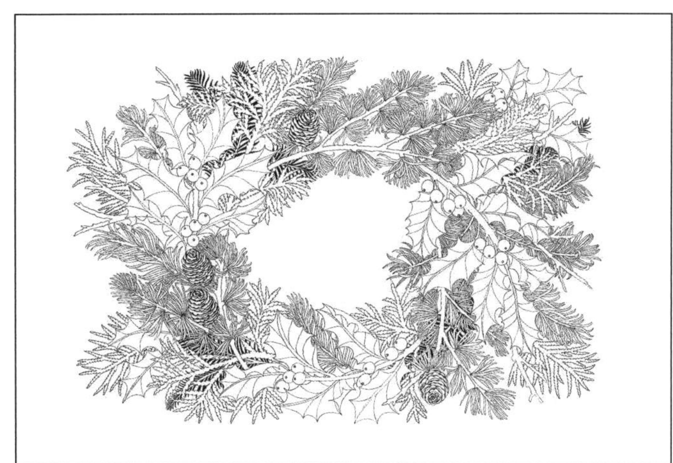

Holly, Larch, Cypress

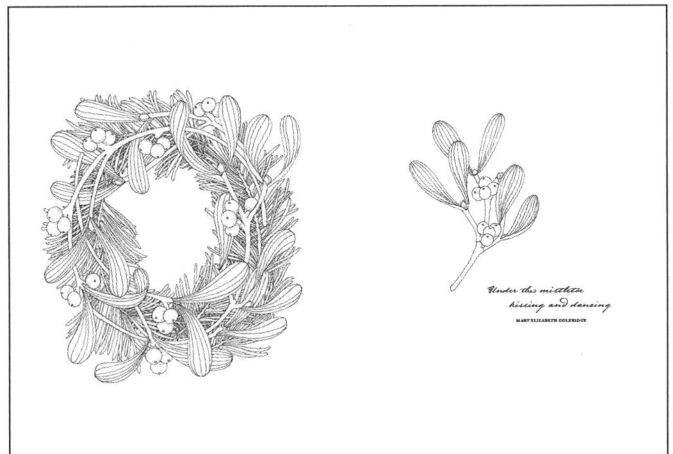

Mistletoe, Pine

Notes

Sketches

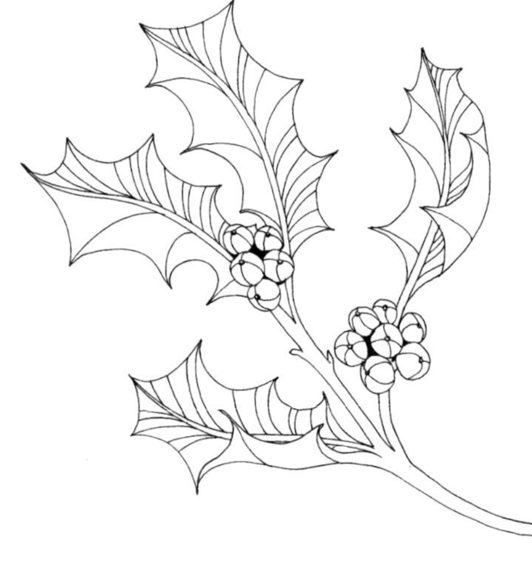

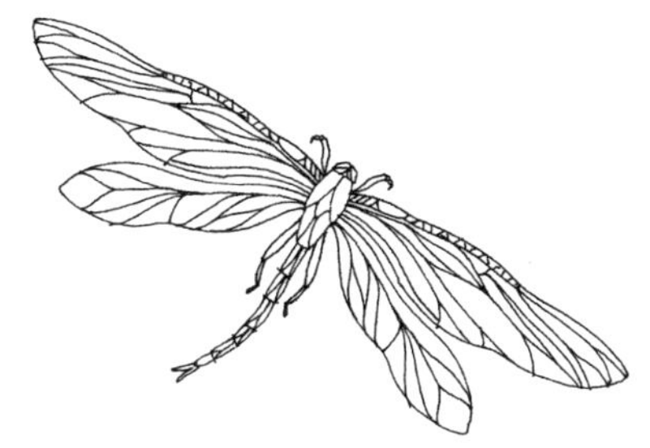

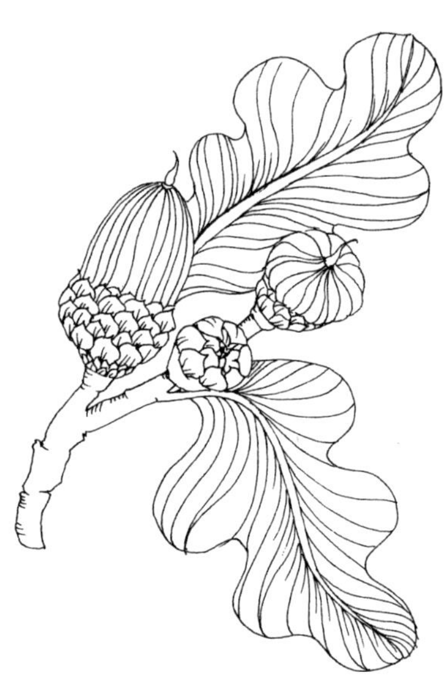

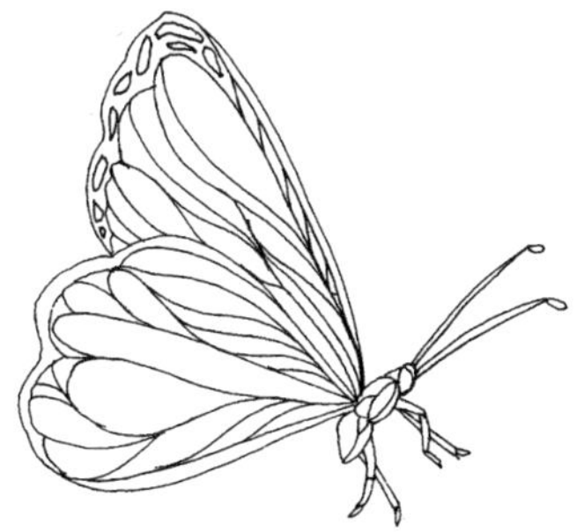

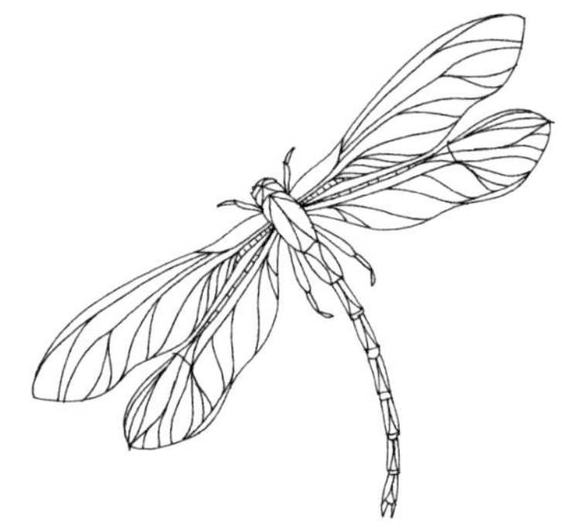

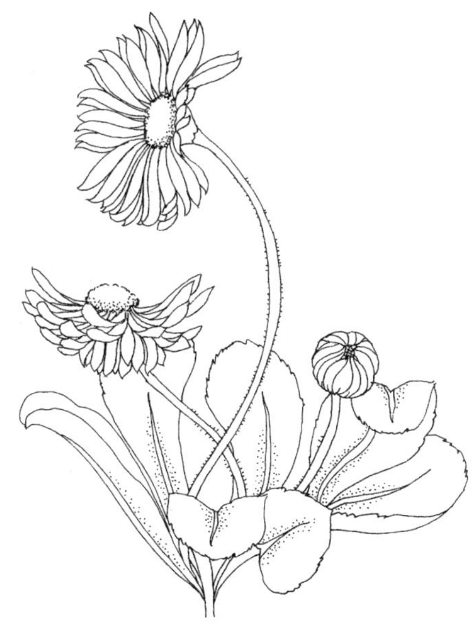

First published in Great Britain in 2024 by Laurence King
an imprint of The Orion Publishing Group Ltd
Carmelite House, 50 Victoria Embankment
London EC4Y 0DZ

An Hachette UK Company

10 9 8 7 6 5 4 3 2 1

A CIP catalogue record for this book is
available from the British Library.

ISBN 978 1 39962 203 5

Design by Dan Jackson

Origination by F1 Colour Ltd, UK
Printed in China by C&C Offset Printing Co. Ltd

www.laurenceking.com
www.orionbooks.co.uk